Good Practices and Innovative Experiences in the South: Volume 3

Citizen Initiatives in Social Services, Popular Education and Human Rights

Edited by
Martin Khor and Lim Li Lin

Zed Books
London & New York

Third World Network
Penang, Malaysia

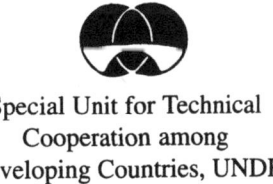
Special Unit for Technical
Cooperation among
Developing Countries, UNDP

Good Practices and Innovative Experiences in the South: Volume 3
Citizen Initiatives in Social Services, Popular Education and Human Rights
was first published in the United Kingdom by
Zed Books Ltd., 7 Cynthia Street,
London N1 9JF, UK
and Room 400, 175 Fifth Avenue,
New York, NY 10010, USA
in 2001.

Distributed exclusively in the United States on behalf of Zed Books by
Palgrave,
a division of St Martin's Press, LLC,
175 Fifth Avenue,
New York, NY 10010, USA.

Published originally by
The Special Unit for Technical Cooperation among Developing Countries,
United Nations Development Programme,
304 East 45th Street (12th Floor),
New York, NY 10017, USA
and
Third World Network,
228 Macalister Road,
10400 Penang, Malaysia.

Copyright © UNDP and TWN, 2001

Printed by Jutaprint,
2 Solok Sungai Pinang 3,
11600 Penang, Malaysia.

All rights reserved.

ISBN: 1 84277 132 9 Hb (Zed Books)
1 84277 133 7 Pb (Zed Books)
983-9747-60-6 (TWN)

A catalogue record for this book is available from the British Library.
US CIP is available from the Library of Congress.

United Nations Development Programme

The United Nations Development Programme (UNDP) is the UN's largest source of grants for development cooperation. Its funding is from voluntary contributions of Member States of the United Nations and affiliated agencies. A network of 132 country offices — and programmes in more than 170 countries and territories — helps people to help themelves.

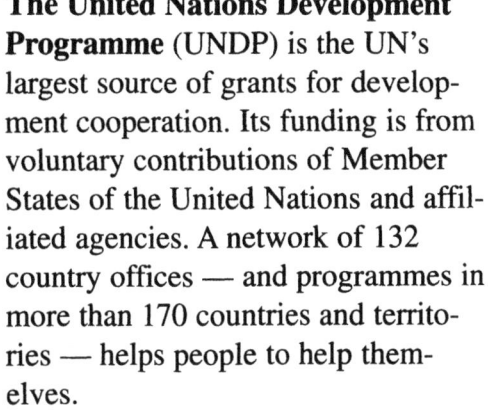

Special Unit for Technical Cooperation among Developing Countries

Technical Cooperation among Developing Countries (TCDC) is a means of building communication and of promoting wider and more effective cooperation among developing countries. It is a vital force for initiating, designing, organizing and promoting cooperation among developing countries so that they can create, acquire, adapt, transfer and pool knowledge and experience for their mutual benefit and for achieving national and collective self-reliance.

TWN
Third World Network

Third World Network (TWN) is a network of groups and individuals involved in bringing about a greater articulation of the needs, aspirations and rights of people in the Third World; a fair distribution of world resources and forms of development which are humane, are in harmony with nature and fulfil people's needs.

Contents

Preface
Introduction

Part I: Basic Needs and Social Services — *1*

1. Community-based health programs — *2*
2. Brazilian citizens taking action against hunger and deprivation — *22*
3. Disaster preparedness and management innovations in the Philippines — *32*
4. The Pani Panchayat: Water and equity — *51*
5. The SLU-SVP Housing Project — *60*
6. Housing co-operatives in Uruguay — *74*
7. Institutionalizing voluntarism: The University of the Philippines experience — *93*

Part II: Education and Information — *113*

8. Databanking and research for popular education — *114*
9. Pioneering gender awareness in the academe — *126*
10. The Other India Bookstore and Press — *146*
11. Theater for education and liberation — *158*
12. Alternative news agency as an instrument of social change — *177*
13. The Education Forum experience in alternative education — *191*

Part III: Social Rights and Advocacy *205*

14.	Consumers action in a Third World context	*206*
15.	Indonesian Legal Aid Foundation	*221*
16.	Defending indigenous women's rights	*232*
17.	Innovative policy advocacy for indigenous peoples in the Philippines	*249*

Preface

Despite the well-reported prevalence of social, economic and environmental problems and, in some cases, crises in countries of the South, there also exist many useful and valuable policies, practices and experiences in developing countries that have contributed to the well-being of their people.

Although these positive experiences may have evolved from the specific social and cultural conditions of these countries, they can also often provide valuable insights as well as lessons that people in other countries can learn from.

In some cases, the practice or policy of one country can be usefully replicated in other countries, of course with some modifications to suit the specific circumstances of the countries concerned.

It is, however, often difficult for policy makers or institutions from one country to obtain information about such positive experiences in other countries.

The United Nations Development Programme is convinced that the sharing of experiences among developing countries has a critical role to play in the search for, and application of, appropriate development policies and practices.

With this in mind, the Special Unit for Technical Cooperation among Developing Countries of the UNDP initiated a research project on 'Good practices and innovative experiences in the environment, social and economic sectors in the South.' The project was implemented by the Third World Network, whose international secretariat is based in Malaysia.

The aim of this project was to identify, collect information and describe practices and experiences by institutions and persons in developing countries that have been successful in solving environment, social and development problems.

The project covered practices and experiences in the governmental sector as well as in private and social institutions, non-governmental organisations, and local communities.

This book is one of the results of the implementation of the research project. It contains the third set of 17 case studies of good, innovative or appropriate practices, policies or institutions drawn from several developing countries.

The areas covered by this book are varied and include basic needs and social services, education and information, and social rights and advocacy.

What all the case studies have in common is that they have contributed towards sustainable development in one way or another.

There are two other companion volumes detailing more case studies covering other subjects.

The case studies presented in this book provide details of the policies or practices and how they operate, the needs or problems they address, the problems encountered, brief analyses on their replicability in other countries, and a description of the institution responsible for creating or adopting them.

It is my hope that this book (and the companion volumes) will catalyse awareness in the developing world about the existence of a wide range of innovative practices and policies that constitute an important component of the wealth of experiences in the South. I also hope that this increased awareness will lead to the eventual transfer and adoption of such innovative policies and practices in different parts of the developing world.

The implementation of the project and the preparation of the book was managed by the Third World Network, with the support and guidance of the Special Unit for TCDC of the UNDP. I would like to thank the Information Services Officer of the Special Unit for TCDC, Ms Atsede Worede Kal, and the Third World Network, especially its director Martin Khor, for conceptualising, coordinating and implementing the project and the book.

John Ohiorhenuan
Director
Special Unit for Technical Cooperation among Developing Countries
United Nations Development Programme

Introduction

This is the final volume of a series of three books arising from a research project on 'Good practices and innovative experiences in the environment, social and economic sectors in the South' which the Third World Network has been implementing with the cooperation of the Special Unit for Technical Cooperation among Developing Countries of the United Nations Development Programme.

The aim of this project was to identify, collect information and describe practices and experiences by institutions and persons in developing countries that have been successful in solving environment, social and development problems.

Research was conducted to collect information and analyse good practices and innovative experiences in developing countries. The project covers practices and experiences in the governmental sector as well as in private and social institutions, non-governmental organisations, and local communities.

The rationale for the project is as follows. The process of development requires appropriate policies and practices in a wide range of areas (economic, social, scientific, environmental etc.). In the developing world, there is a wealth of such policies and practices in the various countries and regions.

For example, a country may have a good system of public health, combining modern and traditional systems of health care, and combining preventive and curative systems. In another country, a municipal authority may have established a good and innovative system of urban management that emphasises environmental protection.

In many countries, there exist indigenous knowledge systems and practices (for example in the management of natural resources, in the use of medicinal plants or in dispute settlement systems) which are valuable components of sustainable development. There are also important examples of sustainable livelihoods, such as organic farming practices, fishing methods, and handicraft production, which are crucial for the task of poverty alleviation. Also, many non-governmental organisations have also established many interesting and innovative social, economic and environmental projects in line with promoting sustainable human development.

A crucial aspect of development is to learn from the experience of others, in order to prevent the inefficiency of 're-inventing the wheel', and to enable the avoidance of mistakes. In particular, the South-South exchange of information and experiences is a very valuable instrument for appropriate, sustainable and human development. Although there are many good practices and valuable experiences in each developing country, there is still much to be done to document these, and to make the information available to policy-makers, NGOs, social groups (farmers, women, indigenous people, small entrepreneurs, etc.) and scientists.

Ideally, there should eventually be a detailed inventory of good practices and innovative experiences in all major sectors and areas of activity. With this, a policy-maker or NGO or social group will be able to access and obtain information about good practices and experiences from different parts of the world, in an activity or area which is of interest to them. The South-South diffusion and transfer of such knowledge and information, and later of the practices themselves, should become one of the most important aspects of the development process. This project was intended to be a modest contribution to this important task.

The project, which started in the second half of 1997, has conducted research into innovative experiences, good practices and good policies in a range of social, economic and environmental issues. These experiences and practices have contributed or are contributing significantly to improving the quality of life, the social and physical environment and the status or position of people and communities in developing countries.

This book contains 17 case studies on three categories of policies and practices:

I: Basic needs and social services
II: Education and information
III: Social rights and advocacy

The first book contained 17 case studies on economic and environmental policies and management, community-based sustainable livelihoods and environmentally-sound practices and techniques.

The second book contained 16 case studies on social policies, indigenous and traditional knowledge and practices, and appropriate technology.

Summaries of most of the case studies arising from the research project will be made available on an on-line database, the Web of Information for Development (WIDE). In addition, CD-roms containing these case studies have been produced by the UNDP Special Unit for Technical Cooperation among Developing Countries.

The innovative experiences and good practices/policies investigated and described in this project meet one or more of the following criteria:
- they improve the position, welfare and quality of life of local communities or the general public
- they are innovative in meeting social needs
- they are environmentally sound and sustainable
- they have or can have significant impact on policy
- they promote local solutions, and make use of local materials and knowledge

Each of the reports has been compiled within a common framework, with information and analysis that includes:
- a description of the experience/practice
- a description of the institution responsible
- the problem addressed or the needs served by the experience/practice
- the effects of the experience/practice
- the problems and obstacles encountered and how these were overcome
- the possibility of upscaling
- the significance for (and impact on) policy-making
- the possibilities and scope of transferring the experience/practice to other communities and other countries

It is hoped that the reports provide concrete examples that show the wide range of good and innovative policies, practices and organisations that exist in countries of the South, and which people in other countries of the South can learn from.

I would like to thank Atsede Worede Kal of the Special Unit for TCDC (UNDP) for her great encouragement and ideas through the various stages of the project. Our deep gratitude also goes to Victoria Tauli-Corpuz (Tebtebba Foundation, Philippines) and Claude Alvares (The Other India Press, India) who played vital roles in helping to coordinate the project, and to Tewolde Berhan Egziabher and Sue Edwards (Institute for Sustainable Development, Ethiopia), Farhad Mazhar and Farida Akhter (UBINIG, Bangladesh), Yao Graham (TWN Africa Secretariat, Ghana) and Roberto Bissio (Third World Institute, Uruguay). Appreciation is also due to Lim Li Lin who managed the project at the TWN Secretariat in Penang, to Lean Ka-Min and Ong Beng Gaik who helped with the editing, to Raymond de Chavez and Martin Jalleh, and to Junie Tan and Linda Ooi for the production aspects.

Martin Khor
Director
Third World Network

Part I
Basic Needs and Social Services

1.

Community-based health programs

1. GENERAL INFORMATION

1.1 Title of practice or experience

Community-based health programs

1.2 Category of practice/experience and brief description

People's participation is the core principle of the community-based health program (CBHP) in the Philippines that differentiates it from the other health programs' approaches. Without people's participation, a CBHP would be just another "band-aid solution". CBHPs give primacy to the organization of the local people before they are implemented. Organizing the people would include activities such as education or consciousness-raising and leadership formation. It ensures people's participation in the planning, implementation and evaluation of the program. Thus, the success of any undertaking that aims at serving the people is dependent on the people's participation at all levels.

1.3 Name of person or institution responsible for the practice or experience

In the beginning, the Rural Missionaries organization of the Philippines was responsible for the practice. As the CBHPs increased in number, autonomous CBHPs were coordinated through the regional and national CBHP agencies. These included the following: Community-Based Health Services in Mindanao; Health Concerns (a pseudonym) in the Cordillera Region; National Ecumenical Health Concerns Committee for Protestant-based health programs; Rural Missionaries for Catholic-based CBHPs; and the Council for Primary Health Care (CPHC) for non-sectarian programs and overall national coordination. At present, the overall national coordination is managed through the Council for Health and Development (CHD).

1.4 Name and position of key or relevant persons or officials involved

Elconor Jara, head of the Council for Health and Development (CHD)

1.5 Details of institution

(a) Address: Religious of Good Shepherd Compound, 1043 Aurora Boulevard, Quezon City, Philippines
(b) Telephone: ++ (63) (2) 436 1830

1.6 Name of person and/or institution conducting the research

Erlinda Castro-Palaganas, RN, Ph.D. with the help of Tebtebba Foundation, Inc. (Indigenous Peoples' International Center for Policy Research and Education)

1.7 Details of research person/institution

Tebtebba Foundation, Inc.
(a) Address: Rm. 3B Agpaoa Compound, 111 Upper General Luna Road, 2600 Baguio City, Philippines
(b) Telephone: ++ (63) (74) 444 7703
(c) Fax: ++ (63) (74) 443 9459
(d) E-Mail: tebtebba@skyinet.net

2. THE PROBLEM OR SITUATION BEING ADDRESSED BY THE PRACTICE /INNOVATIVE EXPERIENCE

In September 1978, an international conference on Primary Health Care (PHC), jointly sponsored by the World Health Organization (WHO) and the United Nations International Children's Emergency Fund (UNICEF), attracted delegates from 134 countries to Alma Ata, the capital of the Kazakh Soviet Socialist Republic. The objectives of the conference were basically to define, promote and obtain universal endorsement of and commitment to PHC. Practically all nations became signatories to the Alma Ata Declaration.

The conference was a useful opportunity for representatives of different countries to exchange experiences on prior PHC-like programs. But probably the most salient result of the meeting was its unanimous endorsement of the PHC approach as envisioned by the WHO. PHC was identified as the key to attaining the goal of "Health for All by the year 2000". "Health for All" had been adopted as a goal by the World Health Assembly in 1977, and was defined as "the attainment by all peoples of a level of health permitting them to lead socially and economically productive lives" (WHO, 1981).

Not only was the WHO's definition of PHC ratified, but the conference appeared to put the stamp of expert and governmental approval on some of the operational modes supported by the WHO, notably the use of paraprofessionals or auxiliary health workers in lieu of physicians for the rapid extension of services in the Third World. This contradicted the physician-based models promoted by the Soviet Union and Cuba, but was deemed more appropriate in light of the constraints facing developing countries (WHO/UNICEF, 1978: p. 62). At its subsequent (1979) meeting, the World Health Assembly endorsed the Alma Ata Report and Declaration and approved a measure encouraging WHO member nations to formulate national, regional and global strategies of Health for All with PHC playing a central role, especially in developing countries (WHO, 1982: p. 5).

In the Philippines, the government as well as the non-governmental agencies rushed to launch PHC in recognition of the Alma Ata Declaration. The Commitment of the Philippine government to attaining the goal of Health for All in the year 2000 is embodied in the Letter of Instruction (LOI) No. 949 issued by the President of the Republic of the Philippines, the late President Marcos, on October 19, 1979. It mandated the Ministry of Health (MOH) to adopt PHC as an approach to the development and implementation of programs which focus on health development at the community level. This reflected the country's recognition of the inter-relatedness of health and development, expressed as follows:

"The attainment of health for all Filipinos is both a means and an end of the overall national development program of the New Society; ... health and health-related activities of the overall national development program ... (MOH's LOI 949, 1979)."

However, it has been claimed that PHC has had a long history in the Philippines even before the Alma Ata Declaration or the issuance of LOI 949 (CPHC, 1985; Galvez-Tan, 1987; Pesigan, Caragay and Lorenzo, 1992; Veneracion, 1993; Carabeo, 1994). Some medical practitioners from the private sector had been reaching out to the community from the late 1960s. A few examples of these were De la Paz of the Katiwala Program in Davao City, Viterbo of Roxas City, Macagba of La Union, Flavier of the Philippine Rural Reconstruction Movement, Campos of the University of the Philippines Comprehensive Community Health Program, Solon of the Paknaan Club Institute of Medicine Project and Wale of Silliman University. However, their efforts were limited to their own territories and they were not able to extend their programs on a national level (Galvez-Tan, 1987).

It was only when the Rural Missionaries of the Philippines launched their pilot community-based health programs (CBHPs) in 1975 that a nationwide movement commenced. The Rural Missionaries first studied the prototypes mentioned earlier and, using the Catholic Church network, initiated programs in Luzon (Isabela), Visayas (Leyte) and Mindanao (Lanao del Norte). Their experiences were eventually adopted by the Protestant National Council of Churches in the Philippines in 1977 and Alay Kapwa Kilusang Pangkalusugan (AKAP) in 1978, both of which established nationwide networks. At present, these CBHPs have national and regional coordinating bodies. The Council for Health and Development (CHD) oversees the national coordination.

The Ministry of Health commenced a Research and Development project in PHC in 1978 with technical and funding support from international organizations such as the WHO. However, it was only in 1981 that the nationwide implementation of PHC started. As of 1985, according to Department of Health documents, the "Primary Health Care approach [was] officially working in all barangays [communities] except for one per cent of these wherein there [was] an unstable peace and order situation."

Five years before the adoption of PHC in the country, the CBHPs already practiced its basic principles. Although the CBHPs have jointly worked with the government through the Department of Health in the propagation of PHC, it did not take long for them to feel that there was a lack of political will on the part of the government to correctly implement PHC. While CBHPs recognized the Alma Ata Declaration, they claimed that it fell short of accurately diagnosing the root of the health problems in the country. The comprehensive concept of PHC had reverted to selective PHC as a result of political, economic and practical factors. PHC became equated with episodic campaigns and basic services couched in child-survival rhetoric (e.g., Growth Monitoring, Oral Dehydration, Breastfeeding and Immunization).

The poor health situation of the Philippines is a reflection of the poverty of the people. The common health problems of the people include malnutrition, high infant mortality rate, poor environmental sanitation, lack of safe potable water supply, high incidence of communicable diseases, maldistribution of health personnel and facilities, and prohibitive cost of medical care.

The health-care system in the country as a whole has been and is still highly dependent on the West in terms of technology, organization, training, education and research. This kind of dependency has made the health system inadequate and ill-equipped to handle the health problems of a country (or a region) that is largely underdeveloped.

3. DESCRIPTION OF THE PRACTICE/INNOVATIVE EXPERIENCE AND ITS MAIN FEATURES

Guiding principles

The CBHP is one of the methods to address the health needs of the people. It does not provide the solution to health problems but assists and facilitates in laying the foundation of a health system that is governed by the people at the community level. CBHPs are programs that aim to respond to the basic health needs of the people through education, training and services. It is a method or process of giving or transferring knowledge, skills and power to the people so that they become more responsible for their health. It strengthens the people's resolve to demand their basic right to good health. Therefore, the CBHP is a method of health-care development with and for the people at the community level.

The CBHP accords primacy to the organization of the people before it is implemented. Organization would include activities on conscientization and leadership formation. It ensures people's participation in the planning, implementation and evaluation of the program. The organizing aspect encompasses the philosophy of the health program that is holistic, that is, the health problems of the community are recognized to be inter-related with the economic, political and cultural problems of the society. The philosophy of the CBHP is seen in the perspective of the realization of a transformed health system.

The formation of an alternative health system which has preferential options for the poor and deprived must be accompanied by the transformation of social and economic structures. The perspective of community health work assumes that the health problems of society are not merely technical but are inter-related with the economic, political and cultural structures of society. Thus, no health program can solve the problems; they can only help set up the conditions and prerequisites for the achievement of a transformed health system. The solution to the health problems would therefore be structural and long-term in nature. However, on the immediate range, a response to the health problems is by having a health program that has a health component, an organizing dimension, a philosophy of a structural approach to health problems and a community counterpart, a program that is a venue of exposure for health professionals to harness their special skills and training to serve the people.

In moving toward the laying of a foundation for a transformed health system, any health program should be holistic in its approach; be people-oriented; and encourage responsibility, confidence, initiative and primary decision-making at the community level. Its components should include organizing, education, health skills training and appropriate curative medicine, research, technology and self-reliance.

In the process of the implementation of a health program with the above-mentioned components, a transformed health system is foreseen, that seeks to serve the needs of the majority and encourages people's participation and one that is self-reliant.

Essential elements of CBHPs that have been recognized and described include the following:
(a) the community knows, feels and accepts responsibility for community health, not just the health of the individual;
(b) the community taps and develops its own resources to meet health needs, including personnel and material resources, organizations and institutions at all levels; and
(c) community priorities are the priority focus of the programs.

In a CBHP, the initial goals, objectives and plans are open-ended and flexible. It considers the community's felt needs and not those defined by the health professionals. The program staff try to inspire, advise, motivate and demonstrate, but do not make decisions for the community. The community is strongly involved in all areas where decision-making is needed. CBHPs are therefore built from the grassroots up and are not handed down by the medical doctor or by institutions.

Any program directed toward the community will not work without the essential element of community awareness and community involvement in its planning and implementation (Galvez-Tan, 1985; Quesada, 1985). It must involve those who suffer from disease and poverty, and it must let them take the decisions and responsibility for their own health care. Unless the people in the community comprehend what the program is all about, prior preparation and involvement with the people will be to no avail. The programs may work for a time, but they will not endure.

In CBHPs, the basic principle is one of working with, and not giving to, the community to improve health. Finally, health by the people, rather than health to the people, is aimed at. The communities will, therefore, be on their way to becoming self-governing, self-sustaining and self-reliant.

Evolution and growth

Since 1973, non-governmental CBHPs have been part of the Philippine health-care system. In the beginning, these programs centered mainly on teaching paramedics in far-flung, neglected rural communities. In due time, CBHPs learned to uphold, support and eventually become part of the common people's aspirations and struggles (Council for Primary Health Care or CPHC, 1985).

In 1973, three nuns from the organization Rural Missionaries of the Philippines commenced discussions on a developmental approach to health care. They envisioned a health program that would meet the most essential needs of the poor. At the same time, they wanted to turn away from the paternalistic orientation of previous programs (CPHC, 1985; Baboon, 1993).

In order to conceptualize a health program that is truly responsive to the health and development needs of the people, the nuns undertook a deeper study of the health situation and the existing health-care system. They saw that what was preventing good health for many Filipinos was poverty brought about by social inequalities. They realized that the existing public health-care system consisted mainly of charitable curative services, and was urban-based, medical doctor-centered and largely inaccessible to the most needy. Private medical services were way beyond the reach of the majority. Thus, the concepts and role promoted by the new health program reflected a deep dissatisfaction with the prevailing state of the health-care system.

In response to the health system's urban-centeredness, the program tried to reach out to the most remote and neglected rural communities. Instead of adopting a charitable orientation, it encouraged the people's acceptance of responsibility for their own health. It enabled them to recognize and be proud of their own resources. Rejecting the medical personnel-dependent concept of health care, the program trained local community members in basic health knowledge and skills. These were the first steps towards self-reliance in caring for their community's health.

In contrast to bureaucratic decision-making on health and related matters, the program advocated people's participation. Community members were encouraged to reflect on their health situation, to plan ways of improving it, and to take group action. In 1974, the Rural Missionaries' Health Team was formed. It was composed of two nurses and one chemist. They acted as a mobile team. Together with a few concerned health professionals, they gave paramedic training to local community leaders in rural and urban poor areas, mainly in Luzon. This was in line with their thinking that health education and prevention were more vital to health promotion than curative services.

The Team produced the *Community Health Worker's Manual* and *Trainer's Guide to Community Health*. The manual emphasized the "why's" and the "how to's" of treating common diseases in the community. This manual served as a valuable reference material to the health programs and health workers for many years. The Team visited existing non-governmental health programs throughout the country to find out how they were operating. At the same time, they actively promoted their idea of a self-reliant health program to different Catholic dioceses and groups.

What the Team attempted to do was to bring education and the wonders of modern medical science to the people in the barrios or villages. It took less than a year for them to realize the inadequacy of their mobile-services approach. The paramedic-training component was good as an advance on the previous system. But experience proved that it was not enough for a mobile team to visit communities periodically and offer such training. They saw the need for closer integration with the people at the village level and to know first hand the daily life of the people, their problems (including non-health ones) and how they viewed their situation.

This realization provided the impetus for the Rural Missionaries to set up pilot programs where staff could live in the community on a long-term basis. In July 1975, pilot programs were started in three dioceses in the three major areas of the country: Isabela province in Luzon, Leyte province in the Visayas, and Lanao del Norte in Mindanao.

In June 1976, the first joint staff meeting to evaluate the three pilot programs of the Rural Missionaries was held. The staff made use of structural analysis*. This strengthened the view that the health situation of the people was but an element of a bigger social situation and that it was influenced by, as well as influenced, the social context.

The recognition of the structural causes of ill health inspired the development of CBHPs to a new level. The structural approach to health problems was a step forward in that it exposed the interconnections of the health system with other social systems: economic, political and cultural. Thus, a more holistic and thereby more accurate picture of health emerged. Moreover, structural analysis introduced the idea of the health program as an agent of change, of "influencing rather than being influenced by". The analysis showed that concern should not just be directed to changing the health system but also to influencing all the other systems, to effect change in the whole social structure.

Alongside the use of structural analysis to analyze health problems, CBHPs, by this time, emphasized the need for strong community-organizing work complemented by the training of volunteer community health workers (CHWs). These trained CHWs, together with program staff who were closely integrated into the communities, would provide health services appropriate to the needs of the communities.

In terms of actual activities, this period saw the improved skills training of CHWs who were elected by the village people. Also, health surveys were undertaken in order to prioritize needs and to formulate plans of action. Case finding was done in order to give proper treatment and to directly follow up

---

* Structural analysis is a way of studying the organization and characteristics of a given society by looking into its economic, political and cultural systems and their interaction.

recipients of care. Coordination with government rural health units in terms of reporting disease incidence was intensified.

Through shared assessments and staff development activities, consolidation of the original pilot areas and expansion to nearby communities were undertaken. The Rural Missionaries assisted other dioceses in establishing their own programs and recruiting staff who were people-oriented and committed to community development work. The CBHP approach was also advocated for health professionals, priests, nuns and lay church workers by way of seminars and conferences. Philippine efforts were shared with other countries through attendance of CBHP staff at international conferences.

At this time, CBHPs were serving the purpose of testing alternative concepts of health and development. One aspect was the feasibility of a health program geared toward health promotion and disease prevention rather than toward cure. According to Galvez-Tan (1985),these were the questions confronting the team then: "Would the people accept such an approach with its inherently slow effects and quiet impact? To what extent would the program be able to mobilize local resources (material and human) without resorting to monetary rewards for CHWs?" (p. 3).

In 1977, the second evaluation workshop of the pilot programs was conducted. Its distinct outcome was the re-affirmation of the crucial role that community organizing played in CBHPs. Therefore, there was a need for CBHP staff, including health professionals, to undergo training in community organizing (Pagaduan and Ferrer, 1983; CPHC, 1985).

Community organizing at this time was still new to programs and organizations engaged in development work. Its application in the Philippine sociopolitical setting needed to be explored, considering that the concepts and methods of community organizing were originally applied in poor communities in the United States of America.

Community organizing taught a number of creative ways of organizing people around issues, identifying and developing local leaders, planning and preparing for small and eventually bigger mobilizations, and collective reflection on actions. But some essential questions were overlooked, such as: What do we want to change in present Philippine society? Towards what kind of transformation are we working? Community organizing lacked a longer-term perspective so that its creative methods could not be used by organizers to progressively heighten people's awareness and progressively build genuine people's organizations (Quesada, 1985; Population Center Foundation (PCF), 1990).

Despite the limitations of community organizing as understood and practiced at this time, the method did provoke critical thinking. In some areas, the health workers confronted local issues such as lack of health services or the absence of medicines. A few immediate demands were won. However, reaction to such efforts was swift. The CBHP, from the start, had been under a cloud of suspicion as a "subversive" program. With its revitalized organizing component, opposition heightened.

Some program organizers who were rigid in their application of community-organizing methods eventually became frustrated or stopped their programs altogether. Some tended to fall back on the health component, developing this more fully while the organizing work remained superficial. Other CBHPs forged ahead. With the help of other development programs which had learned their lessons earlier, and by the sheer dynamism of people's organizations, these program organizers learned in practice what genuine people's organizing meant (CPHC, 1985).

Because the programs facilitated more substantial integration of the staff with the most deprived lot in the communities, the social roots of ill health became more evident. The unfavorable health situation was seen to be caused by poverty which could in turn be attributed to such factors as landlessness, usury and the high price of agricultural inputs versus the low price of farmers' produce. There was no effective channel to voice the farmers' problems, much less to answer them. The seeming hopelessness of the situation bred fatalism and passivity. Superstitious beliefs only reflected the farmers' desperate search for palliatives (Carabeo, 1994).

The religious men and women and the health professionals behind the CBHPs arrived at a profound and far-reaching conclusion. The underlying causes of health problems in society were deeply embedded in the social, economic and political structures of that society. The way to lasting good health for the Filipino people was through a radical restructuring of unjust systems, through wide-ranging social transformation. Health programs alone, even those similar to the CBHP, were not the answer to health problems. But they could be of great value in initiating and contributing to the process of social transformation.

This period also included several historical landmarks:
(a) The National Council of Churches in the Philippines (NCCP) sponsored a consultation conference which paved the way for the establishment of the National Ecumenical Health Concerns Committee (NEHCC). The NEHCC, in turn, spurred the setting up of CBHPs by various Protestant churches and groups.
(b) Alay Kapwa Kilusang Pangkalusugan (AKAP), a non-governmental organization which advocated community-based tuberculosis control programs, was started.
(c) The first national consultation of health professionals working in CBHPs was held. It mandated the setting up of the non-sectarian Council for Pri-

mary Health Care (CPHC) to service and coordinate various CBHPs on a nationwide scale.

A substantial number of program documents and manuals were published and were widely disseminated in this period. These included:
(a) A report of the first staff workshop of diocesan CBHPs;
(b) Fr. Orlando Carvajal's *Of Myths and Realities: A Structural Approach to the Health Problem* (1976); and
(c) Jaime Galvez-Tan's series of articles, *Programa Han Katilingbanon Para Han Maupay Nga Panlawas (MAKAPAWA): A Community-Based Health Program; The Philosophy of Community-Based Health Programs,* and *Strategies and Methods in Building Community-Based Health Programs: The Samar-Leyte Experience* (1978).

In the succeeding years, CBHPs in various regions tried to find their own ways to maximize the use of the programs as support for genuine people's organizing while recognizing the concrete conditions in their regions.

CBHPs joined with other programs organizing along sectoral lines (e.g., organizing farmers, fishermen, rural women and youth). As an entry point, CBHPs provided valuable initial information about the communities. But in areas where the people had strong grassroots organizations, CBHPs acted as a support program. This meant that more time and effort was spent on improving the health component since basic organizing work had been accomplished (CPHC, 1985). For example, the people's organizations could be relied upon to select service-oriented and strongly motivated health workers from among their ranks. It was no longer necessary for the CBHP staff themselves to identify potential CHWs and to generate community support for them. Once the local people's organization agreed to establish a CBHP in their community, the staff could count on their cooperation and support.

More effort was also directed to increasing the awareness of medical and allied health professionals and students. First, there was the need to convince them of the structural causes of as well as the solutions to the problem of ill health. Second, there was the need to draw them toward sharing their special knowledge and skills with the people so that the health needs of the vast majority of Filipinos would be met.

The growth and strength of CBHPs were witnessed in the significant improvements in the content and methods of health and leadership seminars that contributed to the continuing consolidation of CHWs' knowledge, skills and attitudes in health and leadership. A sizable number of CHWs were now trainers themselves. They were a boost to understaffed programs since they could be relied upon to teach basic skills to new CHWs.

CHW associations were being set up at different levels – diocesan, subregional and regional. This was particularly evident in areas like Mindanao where most of the older and more advanced programs were located. These CHW organizations provided a venue for sharing and for mutual support in difficult times. These organizations were also proof that health care can be "in the hands of the people".

CBHP staff had expanded too, both in numbers and in the capacity to meet increasing and more complex requirements of the programs. Most important of all, the majority remained steadfast in their devotion to the cause of the people for whom they worked. Increased coordination of autonomous CBHPs was now made possible through the establishment of regional and national CBHP agencies. Some examples of these agencies included the following: Community-Based Health Services in Mindanao; Health Concerns (a pseudonym) in the Cordillera Region; the NEHCC for Protestant-based health programs; Rural Missionaries for Catholic-based CBHPs; and the CPHC for non-sectarian programs and overall national coordination. Such agencies serviced the training, education and research needs of CBHPs within their scope of responsibility. They monitored progress as well as facilitated exchange of experiences and resources.

Two developments external to CBHPs served to buttress the continued growth of the programs. One was the acceleration of organizing efforts among the grassroots in the rural areas. The other was the activation of institutional health workers, students and professionals in the cities to campaign for the CBHPs' interests, as well as to bring to public attention the worsening health conditions of the people (CPHC, 1985).

With the growing number of people's organizations in the rural areas, the CBHPs had been relieved to a large extent of the responsibility for undertaking basic organizing work. Their role now was to assist people's organizations in meeting the health requirements of their communities. This meant sharing with the leaders and their members the analysis of the national and local health situation. It involved helping them to choose their CHWs based on criteria mutually agreed upon by the community representatives and the staff. It entailed planning a series of health training workshops wherein knowledge and skills were gradually expanded. Health education and medical services were also undertaken. In this way, the CHWs became immediately useful to the community and they were able to apply their newly acquired abilities.

In some areas in the country, particularly in the Cordillera, the community health nurses (CHNs) played a key role in the establishment of CBHPs. In setting up a CBHP in the community, the CHNs utilized several strategies and implemented programs to contribute to the attainment of their collective visions, missions and goals. The approach adopted hinged on a development framework that locates health work in the wider context of development work. As such, it was viewed as a holistic and comprehensive approach. The core of such an approach revolved around organizing the poor and depressed communities they served. This involved the continuous and arduous process of making the people aware of their conditions and mobilizing them to take a direct hand in solving their own problems. The experiences of the CHNs revealed a wealth of insights, particularly in the use of the community-organizing process as a powerful tool in empowering the people.

In community organizing, the CHNs went through different phases, but not distinct steps, in establishing a CBHP. In the initial phase the CHNs evaluated the community's needs and planned an organizational structure composed of potential health workers who were eventually trained to service the community. Thus, the formation of a health organization eventually incorporated other community concerns as a result of continuing awareness-building by the community involved.

After the CHNs had identified the area or village where they could start their organizing efforts, they had to identify potential leaders, who were formed into a core group. A member of the team was given the role of a community organizer. In cases where no other member of the team had formal training in community development or organizing, the CHN accepted the role.

The CHNs guided the core group in carrying out their initial activities. Constant home visits were proven to be effective in ensuring accomplishment of their group and individually assigned activities. Planning was not the only activity that needed the guidance of the community organizer. In implementing the plans which had been agreed upon, the community organizer also had to be one with the core group. Other members of the team were also encouraged to participate in as many activities as possible. They served as role models for the core-group members. This facilitated the team's integration with the group and with the community. It assisted in showing their sincerity in helping the people. Also, an important activity in which the CHNs guided the core-group members was the timely evaluation of their actions and activities.

After the core group had been formed and trained, other members of the community were encouraged to form and join a community organization. This organization was envisaged to facilitate community participation in health and other development activities. The organization-building phase signaled the start of community self-management of the development program.

The organization-building experiences of the CHNs fell into two different approaches, namely: establishing a Barrio/Village Health Care Council without necessarily forming a community-wide organization, and establishing a community organization complete with a leadership structure at its helm. The determining factor as to which approach was adopted was the prevailing conditions in the community at the time the organization was being established. The ultimate aim was to form a structure or organization that would coordinate and become responsible for all the community-wide health and development activities.

By establishing a health organization prior to expansion into a community-wide body, community activities were centered at the committee level, thereby minimizing bureaucratic decision-making. On the other hand, the second approach, which involved the outright formation of a functional community organization, facilitated the dissemination of information, training of community residents and their mobilization to act on common concerns. Through the second approach, the community could be easily linked with other organizations at the municipal and provincial levels at a later time.

The CHNs worked on four major activities in this organization-building phase, namely: pre-organization-building activities; organizing and setting up the *barrio* health committee; training and education of the organization; and mobilization of the health organization.

4. DESCRIPTION OF THE INSTITUTION RESPONSIBLE AND ITS ORGANIZATIONAL ASPECTS

While the Rural Missionaries organization was initially responsible for overseeing the CBHPs, a number of regional and national CBHP agencies were subsequently set up to assume the role of coordinating amongst the growing number of autonomous CBHPs. Examples and brief descriptions of such agencies have been provided in the preceding section.

Twenty years after their founding, in July 1989, CBHPs formed their national consortium – the Council for Health and Development (CHD). Through the consortium, CBHPs have vowed to unite and work to build a people's health movement that will strengthen the broad movement for social change. They have formulated a declaration of their Vision, Mission, Goals, Strategies and Programs that should guide health work. With the formation of the national consortium, CBHPs look forward to better coordination and better services for their beneficiaries. The CHD continues to improve through better communication and utilization of resources among members.

5. PROBLEMS OR OBSTACLES ENCOUNTERED AND HOW THEY WERE OVERCOME

The problem of inaccessibility to health services has been solved by setting up health structures within the respective areas. Many communities have set up a cooperative Botika sa Barangay (Community Pharmacy) that stocks both chemical drugs and herbal medicines. Guided by the principles of rational drug use and traditional healing practices, the community pharmacy provided medicines to the people at a low cost. The money earned was then returned to the community fund. Even neighboring *barangays* benefited from the available drugs (Baboon, 1993).

In one instance, the CBHP in Ilagan, Isabela, set up a referral center. Here, CHWs diagnosed patients and referred those needing secondary or even tertiary health care to hospitals. The referral center became a venue for the CHWs' continuing education. With the guidance of health professionals with whom they discussed the cases, the CHWs were able to develop their diagnostic skills. The clinic also had laboratory facilities run by the CHWs themselves.

In another example, in Bonggao, Tawi-Tawi, the people themselves were able to convert a community surgical hospital into a primary referral hospital. The hospital used to cater for only a few residents who could afford the specialized services it offered. The CBHP helped reorient the hospital staff, including the administration, to primary care. From a purely Western mode of treatment, the hospital began to offer traditional modes of treatment such as acupuncture, herbal medicine, ventosa, moxibustion and pranic healing. The poor were able to afford the hospital's services.

At first, according to Sr. Eva, one of the pioneers of the CBHP, the bishop was against the hospital's reorientation. Later on, however, people began to see the advantages of this set-up. From its traditional role of giving "extension" services to the poor community, the hospital in Tawi-Tawi instead became an extension of the community. Its services are now determined by the needs of the people. There was better rapport between Christians and Muslims in that area as they got together and actively participated in finding solutions to their health and economic problems.

6. EFFECTS OF THE PRACTICE/INNNOVATIVE EXPERIENCE

Through the CBHPs, people began to discover their potential and power to effect changes in their communities. Through proper health education, people were able to manage common illnesses such as colds and coughs, measles, diarrhea, fever and tuberculosis, among others. They were also able to launch campaigns to prevent the onset of diseases endemic to their area such as malaria. Environmental sanitation and safe water supply were some of the projects undertaken by the communities.

The people became aware, not only of their health problems but, as a result of CBHPs' holistic approach to health care, also of their economic and political status in Philippine society. Hence, their heightened awareness led the people to challenge existing structures and to transcend "traditional" roles. Thus, peasants now confronted the landlord-tenant relationship and the urban poor confronted the national housing problem. Women now took on more decision-making roles in the community and encouraged their male counterparts to help at home.

Having evolved from the earlier concept of a paramedic-training program, CBHPs could take pride in health programs that attended to the health needs of the community members from the primary to the secondary and tertiary levels. CBHPs also developed a referral network where medical cases beyond the program's capacity were referred and transferred to other programs, health professionals or hospitals.

7. SUITABILITY AND POSSIBILITY FOR UPSCALING

After a community organization and/or a *barrio* health committee had already been established and the community residents were already actively participating in community-wide undertakings, the consolidation and expansion phase in the establishment of a CBHP followed. At this point, the different committees set up during the organization-building phase were already expected to function by way of planning, implementing and evaluating their own programs, with the overall guidance coming from their leaders. Any consolidation work strengthened the whole community organization, especially its working committees.

Consolidation referred to the process of molding the community organization into one cohesive unit (Health Concerns' *Annual Program Report*, 1993). It basically entailed strengthening the leadership group and uniting the membership in terms of the orientation, direction and objectives of the health program.

Expansion work referred to the activities of the community organization in widening the area of influence of the community development program. In expansion, the leaders and members of the community organization were able to apply and further develop their skills in development work, aside from assisting other communities in establishing their own health program.

Such upscaling prepared the community for the eventual phase-out of the CHNs and was achieved through various strategies such as education and training; networking and linkaging; conducting mobilization on health and development concerns; implementation of livelihood and related development projects; and developing "secondary" leaders.

The primary objective of education and training was to unify the members/residents on the goals, objectives, activities and methods of the program through regular planning and evaluation sessions, consultations, committee meetings and general assemblies, small group discussions and formal training sessions.

Networking and establishing linkages was another strategy found useful in consolidating the gains in organizing work. In this method, permanent structures in place of the non-governmental organization should take on the lead role of assisting the community organization once the CHNs have been phased out of the area. At this point, the linkages with service delivery agencies should have been formalized. Basic services could then continue even without the assistance of the nurses or the non-governmental organization.

Since community problems were only manifestations of issues that were of much wider scope, it was the social responsibility of the organization to join larger networks, municipality- or province-wide, with parallel goals and objectives. Among the activities and/or networks which community organizations could join were municipal/provincial CHWs' associations; region-wide CHWs' consultations with the Department of Health; region-wide health training; alliances in support of health issues such as the implementation of the Generics Act; and alliances to promote PHC and CBHPs.

Mobilization as a strategy was significant during this phase of the organizing process because of its proven effectiveness in developing the positive attitude of each organization member toward another and providing learning experiences related to the theories of leadership and management taken up during the leadership skills training. At this time, mobilization was not only limited to local health issues alone but included broader concerns. For example, the CHWs were involved in a province-wide campaign for immunization for control of tuberculosis. Mobilizations like these recognized the capabilities of the CHWs and leaders as incentives. Community-level mobilization was usually initiated and coordinated by the different committees of the organization or by the village health committees. The team at this point is preparing for its phase-out, and thus needs to develop the community residents' capability in managing the program by involving them in the different mobilization activities.

Another strategy employed was the implementation of income-generating projects. This component of the program was envisioned to generate funds for the community organization for use in implementing its various health activities. Under this scheme, the organization was given seed capital which members could lend to community residents for micro-enterprise investments or, collectively, for a consumers' agricultural or marketing cooperative. The proceeds of the lending activities or the profits of the community enterprise were accumulated and served, in turn, as seed capital for similar activities in other depressed communities at a later date.

The identification and development of "secondary" leaders or second-liners – people who could take on the role of the core-group members in the event that some became inactive – was another method adopted. In this method, the same principles that guided the formation of the core group and the barrio/village health committee were employed. Developing secondary leaders was usually not a separate activity from those in the organization-building and consolidation phases. It was easier to develop "secondary" leaders if they were included in all activities initiated or coordinated by the community organization.

Expansion work was less demanding than consolidation work; since the nurses and non-governmental organization had gained extensive experience in site selection, the task of looking for another project area should be less difficult. In searching for expansion sites, the same principles and processes applied in the initial search for project areas were followed. To facilitate project implementation in both the old and the new sites, the expansion area(s) needed to be contiguous to the old sites so as to facilitate mobility of the community organizer and the other staff. The expansion site(s) should be in the same Department of Health catchment area as the old site(s), so that political conflict would not exist between the new and the old project sites.

Expansion work was closely linked to consolidation work. Expansion was based on the strength of consolidation. Thus, no expansion was initiated if the community organization was not yet capable of planning, implementing and evaluating programs for the community's identified health needs. Furthermore, the expansion of the program to other communities was an opportunity for the team to consolidate the community organization established. Members of the barrio/village health committee acted as organizers, trainers or even consultants to the expansion communities.

8. SIGNIFICANCE FOR (AND IMPACT ON) POLICY-MAKING

The Alma Ata Declaration of 1978 was seen by many as a breakthrough, for it officially declared the pursuit of health as inseparable from the struggle for a fairer, more caring society. The Declaration was a response to the failure of Western medicine to meet the health needs of a large portion of the world's population. It adopted a comprehensive approach to meeting people's basic needs through Primary Health Care. The approach called for strong community participation, accountability of health workers and health ministries, and social guarantees to make sure that basic needs of the people were met.

The trend in health care has been toward focusing on the welfare and future of the whole community rather than toward individual health care. This trend can be traced to the experience of the CBHP, which grew from being a paramedic-training program to a community-based health program. Going by the vast and rich experience gained by the people in setting up a CBHP, it has been proven that with proper education, training and encouragement, the people can take care of their own health.

In transforming the health system to meet the health needs of the people, health programs should be comprehensive or holistic in their approach, people-oriented and self-reliant. Health is seen as only one component in the development of the community. Priority should be placed on using health as a way to motivate people to improve their standard of living and their quality of life rather than on emphasizing the acquisition of high-quality and sophisticated medical skills and treatment. The people should start to see that their health problems are related to food-production problems, nutrition, water supply, housing, education, income and its distribution, employment, communication and transport, and, ultimately, to political decisions. Physical health is not the only concern, as mental and social health should also be accorded due consideration. The total well-being of a community and its people is targeted.

Further, organizing and community development, which the people involved in the development of CBHPs nationwide already practiced, must be given importance. Though the development of CBHPs nationwide was initially slow, the CBHPs, implemented by health nurses, professionals and organizations, have expanded and strengthened to respond to the health problems of the people.

9. POSSIBILITY AND SCOPE OF TRANSFERRING TO OTHER COMMUNITIES OR COUNTRIES

Considering that many countries around the world endorsed the Alma Ata Declaration of 1978, it is thus possible for other countries to adopt the approach that the CBHPs in the Philippines have adopted to respond to the health needs of the people. The Declaration adopted a comprehensive approach, which called for active community participation to meet the people's health needs through PHC. This approach was also reflected in the development framework that guided the CBHPs. In countries where the existing health-care system falls short of meeting the needs of the people and lacks a community orientation, CBHPs could be utilized and developed. CBHPs are critical of the traditional approaches to health work and favor models based on empowerment and long-term solutions to social, political and economic injustice. They utilize a structural analysis of poverty and its effect on health. Using this analysis, poverty is viewed as a result of the inequalities of the socio-economic and political system rather than as a product of personal deficits. Thus, health problems and poverty cannot be solved through modifying health behaviors and individual lifestyles.

References

1. Cabaero, L., (1994) 'Philippine 2000: A Dream For Whom?' in *Migrant Focus* 1 (3).
2. Carabeo, J.M., (1994) 'The Fate of PHC with the Philippines 2000' in *TAMBALAN* January-April 1994.
3. Council for Primary Health Care, (1985) *Community-Based Health Program: An Alternative*, Council for Primary Health Care, Manila.
4. Galvez-Tan, J., (1978) 'Strategies and Methods in Building Community-Based Health Programs: The Samar-Leyte Experience' in *Selected Readings on CBHP*, 1978 Issue, Council for Primary Health Care, Manila.
5. Galvez-Tan, J., (1985) 'Participatory Strategies in Community Health' in *Council For Primary Health Care Series*, Council for Primary Health Care, Manila.
6. Galvez-Tan, J., (1987). 'Health in the Hands of the People' in *Restoring Health in the Hands of the People: Proceedings of Seminars Sponsored by the Bukluran Para sa Kalusugan Ng Sambayanan* (BUKAS), J. Co and M.L. Tan, (Eds.), Quezon City.
7. Pagaduan, M. and Ferrer, E., (1983) 'Working as Equals – Towards a Community Based Evaluation System' in *Community Development Journal*, 18, 2.
8. Pesigan, A.M., Caragay, R.N., and Lorenzo, M., (1992) *Primary Health Care in the Philippines: State of the Nation Reports No.3*, University of the Philippines – Center for Integrative and Development Studies, Quezon City.
9. Population Center Foundation, (1990) *Community Organizing: A Manual on the HRDP Experience*, PCF, Manila.
10. Quesada, M.L., (1985) 'Primary Health Care as a Social Development Strategy: A Focus on People's Participation' in *PHC Reader Series*, August 1985, Council for Primary Health Care, Manila.
11. Roemer, M.I., (1986) *National Strategies for Health Care Organization: A World Overview*, Ann Arbor, Health Administration Press.
12. Veneracion, C.C., (1993) *Initiatives and Strategies for Community Health Development: Case Studies of Four Philippine Rural Barangays*, Institute of Philippine Culture, Ateneo de Manila University.
13. World Health Organization-United Nations International Children's Emergency Fund, (1978) *Primary Health Care – Report of the International Conference on PHC*, Alma-Ata, USSR, 6-12 September 1978, WHO, Geneva.
14. World Health Organization, (1981) *Global Strategy for Health For All by Year 2000*, HFA Series, No.3, WHO, Geneva.
15. World Health Organization, (1982) *Review of Primary Health Care Development*, WHO, Geneva.

2.

Brazilian citizens taking action against hunger and deprivation

1. GENERAL INFORMATION

1.1. Title of practice or experience

The "Hunger Campaign": Brazilian citizens taking action against hunger and deprivation

1.2 Category of the practice/experience and brief description

Millions of Brazilian citizens design and carry out new and creative solidarity actions against extreme poverty and its roots, mobilizing an enormous amount of human and material resources against hunger on a scale that was previously unknown.

1.3 Name of person or institution responsible for the practice or experience

National Coordination of the Campaign against Hunger

1.4 Name and position of key or relevant persons or officials involved

Not available.

1.5 Details of institution

(a) Address: IBASE, Rua Visconde de Ouro Preto 5/7, Brazil
(b) Telephone: ++ (55) (21) 553 6097
(c) Fax: ++ (55) (21) 551 3443
(d) E-Mail: jcidadania@ibase.org.br

1.6 Name of person and/or institution conducting the research

Fernanda Lopes de Carvalho, researcher at the Brazilian Institute of Social and Economic Analysis (IBASE), advisor to the National Coordination of the Campaign against Hunger, and member of the Coordinating Committee of the Campaign for the State of Rio de Janeiro.

1.7 Details of research person/institution

As in 1.5 above.

2. THE PROBLEM OR SITUATION BEING ADDRESSED BY THE PRACTICE/INNOVATIVE EXPERIENCE

According to IPEA (a research office for the Ministry of Planning), there are about 32 million people living below the poverty line in Brazil, equally spread throughout urban and rural areas[1]. The largest concentration of people living below the poverty line is found in the northeast region and in metropolitan areas. Sixty percent of the rural poor live in the northeast. Even though the consumption of food on average is 7.5% greater in rural compared to urban areas, given the importance of non-marketable subsistence production in the former, malnutrition indices are worse for the rural population because of the lack of sewage facilities and health care.

Hunger in Brazil cannot be explained as stemming from a deficient food supply. Grain production (rice, beans, corn, soybeans and wheat) in 1993 reached a record level of 70 million tons. If we accept the Food and Agriculture Organization's (FAO) recommendation of a minimum daily diet of 2,242 calories and 53 g of protein, available supplies[2] of food are greater than required to cover the needs for calories and proteins of the population. The average grain production of the country for the last seven years (59 million tons) would still be able to supply 3,280 calories and 87 g of protein a day to every person.

Given its natural resources and its productive potential which is still largely unexplored, Brazil is actually able to produce food for internal consumption and still be left with a significant exportable surplus. Some estimates indicate that, even without technical innovations, it is possible to triple production. Deficient infrastructure in transportation, storage and handling causes losses estimated at 20% of output. If on the supply side, the problems seem solvable, it is the demand side that poses the toughest difficulty – lack of purchasing power affecting a large part of the population.

Unemployment is part of the problem, but disguised unemployment is much worse. Precarious and underpaid jobs do not allow a large number of people to rise above extreme poverty. Thus, even among those who have jobs, 19.7% earn less than the legal minimum wage (about US$80 a month), a value that is considered insufficient to cover the minimum requirements of decent living. In rural areas, the situation is even worse, where up to 41% of workers receive less than the minimum wage (in the state of Ceara). Precarious employment is indicated by the fact that 34.7% of employees do not have any formal contract and that 14.2% of children between the ages of 10 and 13 have to work, even though Brazilian labor laws forbid hiring children under 14 years of age[3].

There is a general consensus that extreme poverty in rural areas results mainly from the extremely concentrated structure of land ownership. About 1% of landowners hold 44% of the land, while 67% of owners own just 6%[4]. Forty-four percent of the families living under the poverty line are found in rural areas, even though three-quarters of the total population live in urban areas. A similar picture is produced from the data on earnings. In Brazil, average monthly earnings reach 4.1 times the minimum wage but this average is 4.9 times in the southeast against only 2.1 times in the northeast. And important as it is, land concentration is only one of the factors explaining income concentration. Gender and race factors are also relevant: average monthly earnings for males are 4.9 times the minimum wage, but only 2.8 times for females; white males earn, on average, 6.3 times the minimum wage, while black women earn 1.7 times the minimum wage.

3. DESCRIPTION OF THE PRACTICE/INNOVATION EXPERIENCE AND ITS MAIN FEATURES

The sudden emergence of a mass movement demanding the removal from office of President Collor, against whom evidence of corruption was piling up, was a turning point for Brazilian society. The Citizens' Action (CA) was born from this movement. The image of apathy, insensitivity and powerlessness that Brazilians had of themselves was broken. It was the new-found community spirit that allowed the Campaign against Hunger to thrive.

The Campaign has received broad coverage in the media since it was launched, which is essential for its success. Its organizers actively sought the collaboration of professionals in the field, in a very fruitful partnership. It provided the only means of widely disseminating the Campaign's message to a country with continental dimensions. TV networks broadcast publicity messages about the living conditions of the extremely poor, unemployment, hunger, as well as the meaning of solidarity and the need for concrete action to overcome these problems. TV shows and soap operas, which are very popular in Brazil, with the largest audiences among all shows, all mention the Campaign, eventually making it part of their plots. Radio stations also broadcast news about the Campaign and its results. Finally, the press coverage is also very large and useful.

The Campaign has an explicit strategy with respect to the media, to keep it permanently in the spotlight. A news service feeds the main papers, and TV and radio stations daily, with information sent through faxes. In addition, the animation group of IBASE (Brazilian Institute of Social and Economic Analysis) produces three-minute-long videos that are shown once every week on TV, showing local experiences of combating hunger and unemployment. The Campaign also had a weekly 30-minute show on public TV in Rio de Janeiro, hosted by Mr. Herbert de Souza and produced by IBASE. The Campaign has been able to count on the voluntary work of some of the best publicity writers and producers of the country, who organized themselves into a committee, very appropriately called the Ideas Committee. The Campaign also produces a bi-weekly newspaper, the *Citizenship Paper*, produced by IBASE and distributed all over the country to facilitate the spread of ideas, experiences and suggestions.

The Campaign is particularly effective with the public because of the active participation of showbusiness artists in most of its initiatives. Concerts, art exhibits and even auctions of paintings and sculptures have attracted the attention of large numbers of people. Concerts where tickets are obtained in exchange for given amounts of non-perishable food have multiplied in many states. A group of artists even organized a football team to play in games for which the entrance ticket is also paid for in food.

The participation of artists makes up the most visible part of the Campaign's public face. Its daily operations are, however, sustained by people representing practically all social groups. About 30 state-owned companies have created a committee that has contributed some of the most effective ideas the campaign has implemented. These initiatives involve the use or reallocation of the companies' resources and are especially notable because of the enthusiasm of their workers in offering new and creative solutions to the challenges the Campaign has put to them. Especially significant among these experiences is the use of idle land owned by these companies to raise new crops, through the joint initiatives of several firms, employees' committees and, sometimes, local municipalities. These committees organize the distribution of food, provide the opening of water wells, support the creation of bakeries, vegetable gardens, etc. Sometimes, programs to fight illiteracy are also implemented.

Such kinds of intervention have been multiplying throughout the country.

The solutions to their problems are mostly found by the committees themselves. Collaborations with local levels of government are particularly fruitful. When this is possible, the possibilities of permanently increasing income and employment are greatly improved. In these cases, new sanitation and housing projects that are labor-intensive have been implemented. Support for labor skills upgrading and to the small and micro firms is also provided.

Universities also joined the Campaign in a meeting of the Council of University Presidents in April 1993. A letter was signed by the members stating their commitment to working toward solving the problems of extreme poverty and social exclusion, identifying their causes and solutions, contributing to help communities in need through improving the productivity of their efforts and introducing new techniques of production that may be cheaper and better suited to their environment.

4. DESCRIPTION OF THE INSTITUTION RESPONSIBLE AND ITS ORGANISATIONAL ASPECTS

The Campaign sprang out of the Movement for Ethics in Politics (MEP), which gathered together individuals and organizations that assumed leadership in 1992 of a mass movement against alleged corruption in government and for the impeachment of then-President Fernando Collor. A wave of indignation then took over the country when the extent of corrupt practices was revealed, leading to a general call for ethics and justice, and new ways in thinking about and acting in politics.

When President Collor resigned, the MEP's discussions concluded that nothing threatens democracy more than the existence of extreme poverty. On the view that democracy and extreme poverty are completely incompatible, the Citizens' Action (CA) was launched, led by Mr. Herbert (Betinho) de Souza, the secretary-general of IBASE, to confront the state of deprivation in which a significant share of the population was living.

An appeal was made to all individuals, institutions and organizations all over the country to create committees to take the initiative to fight hunger and poverty. The committees were urged to devise suitable means for concrete actions in their area of operation, concentrating their efforts on the urgent and immediate need for reducing hunger without losing sight, however, of the need for structural changes in Brazilian society and economy in order to avoid the perpetual renewal of the causes of deprivation and hunger.

The response to this call was overwhelming, giving rise to perhaps the largest mass movement in Brazil's recent history. Committees were organized practically everywhere, gathering together people of different ages, religions, political views and social origins. The movement was joined by institutions other than those usually dedicated to philanthropy, such as trade unions, professional and entrepreneurs' associations, private and state companies, grassroots groups, municipalities, universities, churches, NGOs, etc. Committees were organized by area, workplace, professional affiliation, schools, etc. Each committee is free to choose the ends and means to act, while establishing partnerships and upholding the general principles of CA of autonomy, decentralization, accountability to the community and responsibility. CA thus operates as a catalyst, to increasingly awaken the sense of solidarity among the population, inducing and publicizing new proposals for the operation of committees, and giving support to existing initiatives.

Parallel to this movement, the Workers' Party in 1993 proposed the adoption of a food security program to President Itamar Franco. The President accepted the suggestion and ordered his Cabinet to elaborate a Plan to Fight Hunger and Extreme Poverty. He also created the Council for Food Security (CONSEA), constituted by nine ministers of state and 21 members representing society. CONSEA was chaired by the President himself and has Bishop Dom Mauro Morelli as its secretary-general.

CONSEA was a partnership between the state and society in the search for means to overcome extreme poverty. It is also a space for society to exert pressure on the state toward changing the latter's form of operation in favor of greater sensitivity toward social demands. Because of these pressures, some agility was imparted to the decision-making process of the federal government in the distribution of stocks of food to the population in the northeast of the country, stricken by a lengthy drought. Some families have benefited from programs of family settlement in rural areas. Among other results is the improvement in the distribution of food for schoolchildren.

The Campaign against Hunger thus runs along two channels: CONSEA, which concerns actions by the state; and CA, where private individuals and organizations organize themselves to fight hunger and, beginning in 1994, to support the right to work and a decent living standard for all. The main result of the Campaign was doubtless to give hunger, extreme poverty and employment a central place in the political agenda of the country, awakening in the population the will to participate in the process of change that Brazil is experiencing. Solidarity and the discovery of new dimensions in the politico-ethical question that make explicit the link between a new politics and a new, less unequal social structure must lead to the end of a long-established feeling of indifference with respect to the living conditions of the poorer social groups in the country. The campaign has so deeply marked Brazil's recent history because it allowed the feeling of powerlessness in relation to the social situation in Brazil to be overcome.

5. PROBLEMS OR OBSTACLES ENCOUNTERED AND HOW THEY WERE OVERCOME

Brazil has the tenth largest Gross National Product (GNP) in the world, and it is the third largest food exporter. The economy is also characterized by deep social inequality, expressed in (but not restricted to) a very skewed structure of income distribution. Social and political inequalities are, in large part, inherited from the country's past of colonialism and slavery, and are strengthened by the ways in which agriculture has been modernized and by the accelerated advancement of urbanization and industrialization.

The CA movement has gone very far in the mobilization of Brazilian society because it gives concrete meaning to abstract claims for human rights and for ethics in politics, and at the same time opens up a space for participation in a country long accustomed to alienation and passivity. The Campaign against Hunger has opened up to a large part of the population the new possibility of participation and of understanding basic community links.

6. EFFECTS OF THE PRACTICE/INNOVATIVE EXPERIENCE

The power to mobilize has been overwhelming. Even convicts have contributed to the Campaign after female inmates in Rio de Janeiro took the initiative of donating the equivalent of one day's food rations a week. Unfortunately, the strength of the movement, which is its decentralized character based on self-organization and local accountability, is also the greatest impediment to a more adequate assessment of its results. It is practically impossible to calculate the amount of resources that have been utilized to this day in the Campaign even if the time and effort of all the volunteers are not taken into account. For example, just the publicity inserts on Globo Network, which reaches 80% of the TV audience in Brazil, would have cost about US$5 million in six months.

According to opinion polls by IBOPE (one of the largest Brazilian public opinion institutions), conducted in December 1993 and, again, in July 1994 among those 16 years or older, 62% of the population was informed about the Campaign against Hunger; 32% declared their intention to participate or to contribute to the Campaign in some form; and 11% were members of a Committee of Citizens in Action. This degree of participation would be very significant in any community, but it is particularly meaningful in Brazil given its social and political situation.

7. SUITABILITY AND POSSIBILITY FOR UPSCALING

By the end of 1993, the Campaign was undeniably successful in conveying the message that hunger had to be combated immediately, and in mobilizing the population to do it. It was then thought that a step forward could be taken toward finding more permanent solutions to extreme poverty. The urgent nature of the Campaign in 1993 was explicit in its slogans, such as "Hunger Can't Wait", but it has always been clear that a definite solution to the problem could not be restricted to merely distributing food, but required creating jobs. A new slogan was then offered to summarize the next stage of the movement: "Food Against Hunger; Jobs Against Misery". Action should turn both to supporting initiatives to resume economic growth with income distribution and to defining means of stimulating the communities to find local employment for their unemployed, supporting the creation of cooperatives, small firms, etc. This new form of the movement is still in the initial stages but there are already many successful initiatives to its credit.

While the movement maintained its urgent nature, the kinds of measures that had to be taken were relatively easier to identify. It was largely a matter of redistributing food in favor of those below a certain level of income. Initiatives in this direction could be taken by anyone. However, when the creation of jobs is the goal, the only possible course of action is exerting pressure on the government, in the normal course of politics.

As a matter of fact, many committees had already advanced solutions to the emergency hunger problem that involved creating possibilities for the communities themselves to open up definite opportunities for income generation, utilizing the unemployed or "disguised" unemployed. Projects such as organizing production of consumption goods that involves labor rather than capital goods were already being implemented. Small plants to manufacture clothes, shoes and sandals, processed food, construction materials, furniture, etc., were created in many communities. Groups of workers were organized to supply services like plumbing, house painting and office services. The creation of community vegetable gardens and courses to help improve the skills of workers is also within reach of the movement. These efforts can be very effective in instilling and cultivating in the people the need to fight against social exclusion, to practice solidarity and to build citizenship bonds.

One important concept has been consolidated in all these actions: partnership. It helps cooperation not only among citizens, but also with the government and with all kinds of institutions, like private and state-owned firms, non-governmental institutions, etc. Again, as with the first stage of the campaign, the quantification of its material results is not possible for the moment.

8. SIGNIFICANCE FOR (AND IMPACT ON) POLICY-MAKING

The initiator of the campaign, Mr. de Souza, used to insist that one of the principal goals of CA is to change the way in which politics is understood and engaged in, by changing the conscience of the public as to how society should be organized. To give priority to the fight against inequality, exclusion and misery is to create a society that is safe and stable because all of its members recognize it as their own. The goal of the Campaign is to awaken the sense of responsibility of those who are members of Brazilian society as well as to awaken in those that are excluded, a consciousness of their rights. The degree of social exclusion and indifference reached in Brazil threatened to paralyze it. A new opportunity for Brazilian society was introduced with the struggle for clean and ethical politics. CA hopes to be able to help keep the torch lit by opening up spaces for the building and exercise of citizenship, to ultimately contribute to the creation of a democratic culture in the country. Even if all the other initiatives of CA were to go awry, at least one of its banners would be successful; the dimension of the problem of social exclusion is now public knowledge.

Some left-wing groups have criticized the alleged "assistencialist" character of the Campaign. The criticism is, in fact, deeply misguided. The campaign is actually an exhortation to society to look the problem of exclusion in the face and to understand the need for change. The traditional left tends to see the state as the only solution to every problem. CA believes that society, not the state, is the solution. Citizenship is born when one sees one's neighbor as a bearer of rights, not when the state declares him or her so. If society changes, the state sooner or later will also change. CA relies on the power of society to organize itself and has not been disappointed.

It is particularly important to stress that CA is not just a solidarity movement of the privileged toward the needy. Its central concept is partnership. It is not just a question of donating, but of organizing. Many of the most significant initiatives the Campaign has inspired involve the poorer communities organizing themselves to improve awareness of the use of their resources, with or without the help of higher-income groups.

CA believes that it is, in fact, combating a form of paternalism that has been deeply rooted in the minds of the traditional left that only sees the state as the solution to social problems. However, recent history has shown that the alienation of society itself is a more serious and difficult problem.

9. POSSIBILITY AND SCOPE OF TRANSFERRING TO OTHER COMMUNITIES OR COUNTRIES

CA has already reached nationwide dimensions in Brazil. While it is a concrete reaction to Brazilian circumstances, its main principles can be valid for many other countries in similar conditions.

Notes

(1) The poverty line is defined by the level of family income that allows the purchase of a minimum food basket that covers, for the whole family, the minimum nutritional requirements set by the Food and Agriculture Organization (FAO)/ World Health Organization (WHO).
(2) Available supplies include initial stocks of food, plus additional production, and imports less exports.
(3) Data for 1990, taken from *Mapa do Emprego* (Employment Map), produced by the Central Statistical Office of Brazil (IBGE).
(4) The 18 largest rural establishments occupy an area equivalent to the whole of Portugal, Switzerland and Holland put together. Of the around 400 million hectares that are privately owned in rural Brazil, only 15 million ha. are officially considered idle, and thus potential targets for redistribution.

3.
Disaster preparedness and management innovations in the Philippines

1. GENERAL INFORMATION

1.1 Title of practice or experience

The Citizens' Disaster Response Center: Disaster preparedness and management innovations in the Philippines

1.2 Category of practice/experience and brief description

The experience documented here deals with how a Philippine disaster response center focuses its efforts in preparing both "less vulnerable" and "most vulnerable" sectors in coping with and getting over disasters via education. The experience also shows the efficiency of relying more on community folk's own talents, skills and resources in disaster preparation, mitigation and rehabilitation. In the process, community folk learn management and organizational skills which benefit them even beyond situations of disaster mitigation and rehabilitation.

1.3 Name of person or institution responsible for the practice or experience

Citizens' Disaster Response Center (CDRC)

1.4 Name and position of key or relevant persons or officials involved

Zenaida G. Delica, Executive Director

1.5 Details of institution

(a) Address: 72-A Times St., West Triangle Homes, P.O. Box 2893 CPO, Quezon City, Philippines

(b) Telephone: ++ (63) (2) 924 0386
(c) Fax: ++ (63) (2) 924 0386

1.6 Name of person and/or institution conducting the research

Tebtebba Foundation, Inc. (Indigenous Peoples' International Center for Policy Research and Education)

1.7 Details of research person/institution

(a) Address: Rm. 3B Agpaoa Compound, 111 Upper General Luna Road, 2600 Baguio City, Philippines
(b) Telephone: ++ (63) (74) 444 7703
(c) Fax: ++ (63) (74) 443 9459
(d) E-Mail: tebtebba@skyinet.net

2. THE PROBLEM OR SITUATION BEING ADDRESSED BY THE PRACTICE/INNOVATIVE EXPERIENCE

The Philippines is a disaster-prone country. An average of 20 typhoons ravage the country each year, affecting millions of Filipinos and leaving a trail of deaths, injuries and damage to property worth billions of pesos (millions of US dollars). Typhoon casualties and damage are brought about by floods, landslides, and wind-battered homes and farm crops. In 1996, eight typhoons brought heavy rains and destructive winds which adversely affected some 1,669,643 people. Over 3,600 families lost their homes while 35,000 families had partially ruined homes. The typhoons left 94 people dead, 75 injured and 25 reported missing.

The country also lies within the Pacific Ring of Fire where 80% of the world's earthquakes occur. At least 21 of the country's 220 volcanoes are considered active and are scattered all over the archipelago populated by 68 million Filipinos.

The situation is worsened by the wanton degradation of the country's environment and natural resources. The main culprits of such large-scale environmental destruction in the country are factories, mining companies and loggers. The worst fishkill in Manila Bay happened in October 1996, during which an estimated 30,000 kilos of dead fish were found floating in the bay's shallow shores. This prompted the Bureau of Fisheries and Aquatic Resources (BFAR) to probe the disaster. The Bureau's findings: the fish died of low oxygen levels and internal bleeding when their internal organs absorbed toxic chemicals. The chemicals were traced to the industrial refuse various factories had been dumping in Manila Bay. The fishkill disrupted the livelihood of thousands of fishing families.

The country's worst mining disaster in recent history happened in March 1996 when the Filipino-Canadian Marcopper Mining Corporation's mine tailings spilled into the Boac River in Marinduque in central Philippines. The spill practically killed the river which supplied the local folk's drinking water, farm irrigation and freshwater fish.

Another fact of life in the Philippines is another human-made disaster: militarization. The problem of militarization began under the late Ferdinand Marcos's martial law regime (September 1972 – February 1986). This problem has bred what the Citizens' Disaster Response Center (CDRC) calls "internal refugees". These are villagers, including women and children, forced out of their homes because of militarization.

Also in the countryside, villagers are vulnerable to forced evictions by private firms. Residents of 16 villages in 1996 were displaced in Davao Oriental Province in Mindanao island in southern Philippines, for example, to give way to the tree plantation of a timber company.

Yet another human-made disaster occurs from time to time in the heart of Manila: urban poor dwellers forced out of their shacks to give way to development projects such as condominiums, megamalls, factories and other commercial establishments. In Manila alone in 1996, CDRC documented 72 incidents of demolition, rendering some 193,326 persons homeless.

CDRC also considers as disastrous the economic dislocation resulting from factory lockouts and deadlocks in collective bargaining agreements (CBAs) between workers and employers. In 1996, CDRC listed at least 69,789 workers, upon whom some 369,882 family members depend, who lost their jobs because of CBA deadlocks and shutdown or closure of firms.

All these natural and human-made disasters plus the acute poverty among most Filipinos create a magnified disaster situation. This complex situation gave birth to the establishment of CDRC in 1984.

CDRC recognizes that a developing country like the Philippines faces greater difficulty in coping with both natural and human-made disasters. This is because poverty-stricken victims lack the means to cushion the effects of disasters. Recovery is also difficult and tedious.

CDRC has thus focused on developing disaster management programs to help prepare community folk in wrestling and coping with the impact of disasters and to help hasten their recovery. It also ensures that assistance to beneficiaries is geared toward improving their economic condition to make them less vulnerable to disasters. The teach-them-how-to-fish-rather-than-giving-them-fish approach is CDRC's formula. Otherwise, disaster victims would become dependent on handouts.

CDRC's disaster response and management programs are thus anchored to the following needs of beneficiaries: economic capacity-building and more participation in decision-making.

CDRC's programs also affirm the right of people to a healthy environment and equal access to the country's abundant natural resources.

3. DESCRIPTION OF THE PRACTICE/INNOVATIVE EXPERIENCE AND ITS MAIN FEATURES

The key to CDRC's disaster management program is education. CDRC has thus evolved education modules for disaster preparedness and management in the grassroots. Developed with the help and participation of several disaster response groups and of its provincial networks nationwide, CDRC's disaster education course, or what CDRC calls Disaster Management Orientation (DMO), consists of four modules.

Module 1

Module 1 tackles the physical characteristics and features of the Philippines which render the country vulnerable to disasters. Included here are scientific explanations and the social bases of disasters in the country. The whole module actually offers a comprehensive overview of the Philippines' national disaster situation, on which CDRC's disaster management work is based.

Like one of the rules in Sun Tzu's *Art of War,* Module 1 can be summarized thus: Know your enemy and yourself. The "enemy" includes the various disasters and the "self", the country itself with its physical and geographical features. Participants are thus informed that the country, for example, has a 28,962-kilometer coastline (one of the longest in the world) and 7,000 islands. It also has 421 rivers, 58 lakes and 100,000 hectares of freshwater swamp. Sixty percent of the country's landforms are mountains.

Module 1 briefs participants on typhoons, tornadoes, floods, tidal waves, drought, volcanic eruptions and earthquakes. Basic information on these are culled from the country's weather bureau and the Philippine Institute of Volcanology and Seismology (PHIVOLCS), which monitors earthquakes and volcanic activities.

Module 1 also includes an inventory of the country's natural resources. Participants can appreciate, for example, that 55% of the country's over-60-million population live off the sea's resources. They are also enlightened on the role of other marine environmental resources such as coral reefs and mangroves. Basic information about other resources are also given: forests and the country's remaining forest cover, and mountains and their role as windbreaker, for example.

Also included in Module 1 are environmental problems and their causes: soil erosion, landslides, "red tide" pollution, and pollution on land, in the air and in the water. All these are included in the module because they also bring disasters such as ailments, injuries and deaths.

Module 2

Module 2 looks into the relation between the impact of disasters and poverty. This module strives to answer the following questions: What was the day-to-day life situation of the victims before the disaster happened? Do they have the capacity to cope with the adverse effects on their livelihood of an earthquake, drought or militarization?

Module 2 includes a whole general orientation on the country's economic situation. The course analyzes, for instance, the implication of the country's huge foreign debt to the International Monetary Fund. It looks into how the loan conditionalities influence the government's policies on trade liberalization, reduction of the budget on social services, tax hikes, currency devaluation and oil price hikes, among others.

Other parts of the course include briefings and analysis of other related issues such as inflation, low wages, prohibitive cost of education, lack of decent housing for the poor, public health woes (malnutrition, sanitation), transportation problems and other social service deficiencies.

Still another part of the module is an orientation on the roots of the armed conflict in the country. The longest insurgency war in Asia, the country's Left-led armed struggle, is directly rooted in a clamor for change toward a social and economic order where the powerless majority is empowered. Still another insurgency war is being waged by Muslim secessionist rebels in Mindanao island in southern Philippines.

Ever since the time of the Marcos regime, the government has instituted counter-insurgency policies. For every automatic rifle fired and bomb dropped in rural communities, thousands of families get caught in the crossfire. CDRC, for example, documented 1.4 million civilians or 256,905 families who became "internal refugees" from 1986 up to 1992. The number of refugees who leave their communities as a result of natural disasters pales in comparison to counter-insurgency-driven "internal refugees". Most vulnerable to this kind of disaster are the aged, women and children.

Module 2's concluding part is called Capacities and Vulnerabilities Analysis (CVA). CVA assesses and analyzes three aspects in a community:
(a) the physical aspect;
(b) level of social organization of each community member; and
(c) attitudes of and motivating factors for community members.

The physical aspect refers to the community's location, and the community folk's livelihoods or occupations, type and structure of houses, skills and training. This aspect also includes a look into who is benefiting the most from the community's natural resources.

The second aspect takes a look at the various formal and informal political organizational structures in a community, which also include community members' level of unity, the family and neighborhood support system, and the decision-making process among community leaders and members.

The third aspect assesses the community members' common and differing worldviews, philosophies in life, and attitudes toward change.

CDRC acknowledges that disasters can victimize all people from all walks of life. But CDRC similarly recognizes that there are those who can easily rise up, pick up the pieces and start life anew, and there are those who can hardly recover. This is where vulnerability and capacity come into play.

CDRC cites an Intensity 7.7 earthquake that battered northern Philippines in July 1990. All were affected, but there were those who recovered faster than others. There were sectors whose livelihoods were badly hit, but they had the capacity to even help others.

Assessing a community's capacities and vulnerabilities enables disaster management handlers to strategize and prioritize their disaster preparedness and disaster response programs.

Included in CVA is how to size up the hazards brought about by both natural and human-made disasters. Disaster management orientation participants are briefed about three types of hazards: natural (typhoon, earthquakes, volcanic eruptions, tidal wave, tsunami and floods), hazards brought about by human activities (wars, fire caused by negligence or congested house structures, nuclear fallout accidents and the like), and a combination of both (environmental destruction due to logging, mining and other activities can magnify the effect of natural disasters: forest destruction, for example, leads to floods, siltation and landslides). All these dangers lead to loss of lives and property, injury and grief.

In incorporating these points, Module 2, in a way, not only helps raise the participants' level of disaster awareness; the module also introduces them to an appreciation of environmental protection as a major and long-term approach in cushioning the impact of disasters.

Module 3

Module 3 tackles the rudiments of Disaster Management or DM. DM has three goals: to prevent or minimize loss of lives and property, to reduce personal suffering and grief of victims, and to help speed up rehabilitation and recovery of victims.

For effective DM, CDRC lists at least six vital elements to bear in mind in responding to disasters:

(a) Risk management

This considers the following:
(i) type of risk or hazard;
(ii) frequency, time and duration of hazard;
(iii) estimate of hazard's impact or effect on the community; and
(iv) possible ways and means to lessen or cushion effect of hazard or risk.

(b) Loss management

This involves a thorough study of the damaging effect of hazards on people's lives, livelihood, infrastructure and property. Based on this study, possible preparations are identified before danger happens. Flood-threatened communities, for example, must be evacuated before a heavy monsoon or typhoon comes. Also included under loss management are the foreseen tasks that must be done after a disaster happens. Preparing ahead for post-disaster tasks will continue to lessen the effect of the disaster.

(c) Control of events

This refers to control of events during and after an emergency. This can be achieved if:
(i) the nature of the disaster and its effect on a community are immediately identified;
(ii) mitigating measures are carried out to lessen a disaster's effects;
(iii) the community has organized and synchronized preparation;
(iv) there is sufficient information on which to base responses;
(v) responses are appropriate;
(vi) responses are prompt;
(vii) responses are morale-boosting and can encourage action and initiative from the community; and
(viii) responses are systematically done.

(d) Equity in relief and rehabilitation programs

Relief and rehabilitation aid must be based on the actual situation and the actual damage wrought by the disaster. The volume of relief aid, for example, must be based on the size of a family, or on the gravity of the damage.

(e) Relief aid management

This is related to item (d). Those in charge of relief goods and rehabilitation materials need some management skills and systems, especially in big disasters where there are tons of goods and supplies to distribute. Management skills must come into play, for example, in determining what and how much is enough for each particular victim. The volume of aid also depends on the cost estimate of damage of each victim.

(f) Lessening the impact of disaster

Many opportunities, lives, livelihoods and property are lost during disasters. But the impact of disasters is much worse in a country like the Philippines. For example, the country spends so much on relief and rehabilitation, but spends proportionately less on raising the economic lot of disaster-vulnerable folk. CDRC believes that a more economically empowered community is less vulnerable to or can recover faster from disasters.

Aside from the vital elements of disaster management, there are the various tasks for each phase of the disaster:

(a) Pre-disaster phase

The pre-disaster phase has two sub-phases: preparedness and mitigation.

Tasks in relation to preparedness include a thorough study of the type of disaster which may hit a community and what action plans to take. Prepared with these tasks, community members can synchronize and organize their response.

More specific examples of preparation include these steps:
(i) getting ready with CVA and hazard map;
(ii) evacuation drills; and
(iii) training or briefing on how to manage an evacuation center.

Specific examples of action include the following:
(i) preparing a counter-disaster plan;
(ii) readying warning device systems;
(iii) preparing communication and transportation facilities; and
(iv) organizing disaster response machineries.

Mitigation tasks aim to help lessen damage or loss of lives and property and displacement. Mitigation measures, if all in place, can also help cushion the magnitude of a disaster.

The following are examples of some mitigation measures:
(i) repairing infrastructures that need to be fixed;
(ii) building protective dikes;
(iii) reinforcing posts of houses;
(iv) establishing livelihood programs;
(v) reforestation;
(vi) establishing a system of food storage; and
(vii) campaign and advocacy for laws to address disaster issues.

(b) Emergency period

Tasks during an emergency aim to help disaster victims recover fast and dampen the magnitude of, if not avoid, any worsening of their situation. Relief operation, for example, is done to stave off hunger and death during disasters.

Relief operation includes food and clothing aid, health aid, search and rescue, temporary shelter, first aid, evacuation, and fast repair of important facilities such as communication and transportation systems, electricity, roads, bridges and others.

(c) Post-disaster phase

Post-disaster tasks stress on how survivors can pick up the pieces, start life anew, and move on. Tasks at this stage focus on rehabilitation. Rehabilitation work stresses on economic recovery, such as livelihood programs (e.g., seed and animal dispersal, and setting up communal farms), and infrastructure and house repairs.

But there is one important point to consider: disaster survivors must actively participate in all stages of disaster management, including rehabilitation. In the process, the community's capacity (in terms of preparedness, mitigation and rehabilitation) is strengthened and enhanced, and the community's vulnerability to disasters lessened.

In disaster management, community members are the primary actors. Community members, not outsiders, know best what they need most. It is they who decide what kind of help is appropriate for them. This framework debunks the general misconception that disaster "victims" are miserable beggars. It is true that disaster "victims" need outside help. But the task of decision-making (i.e., what type of appropriate help), for example, rests solely on community members. Any outside help given to disaster survivors must enable them to get on with their lives, and not to permanently depend on some charity. Thus CDRC's management framework is basically one of helping disaster survivors help themselves.

The gauging of the effectiveness of a disaster management program is also based on this same framework. That such a program is effective can be gauged further by changes in the capacity, outlook and organizational strength of a community. There is change, for example, if a community which used to totally depend on outside help during disasters can now rely on its own capacity. Capacity includes the community's ability to prepare for disasters (via training and setting up of disaster response networks) and mobilize local resources during the three stages of disaster.

Another key element in sizing up effectiveness is whether or not there has been some change in the community folk's outlooks, attitudes and even values. After the disaster management program, for example, how do the community folk view outsiders who help out in disasters? There is some change if outsiders are not viewed simply as "donors", but as "facilitators" to help disaster survivors recover, stand on their own two feet and move on. There is some change if the community folk view disaster response as a collective responsibility of all sectors such as governmental, non-governmental and people's organizations, the victims themselves, the disaster agency and international organizations, and not the sole responsibility of just one disaster agency.

Module 4

Module 4 tackles what CDRC calls a Citizenry-based and Development-oriented (CBDO) strategy to guide community disaster response networks in their ultimate mission. This CBDO strategy asserts that in the long run, disaster response interventions, alongside the active participation of the community, can help improve the socio-economic lot of the community.

The CBDO strategy has two main aspects:
(a) how to mobilize both the non-vulnerable or less vulnerable and the most vulnerable as partners in preparing for and responding to disasters, and
(b) how to help the community help themselves in charting their own development goals.

The first aspect aims to enable the community to stand on its own by utilizing its own talents and resources in preparing for, responding to and coping with disasters. If both the non-vulnerable or less vulnerable and the vulnerable fully grasp the nature and demands of the various disasters, both can share each other's burden. Those who are less vulnerable and who have more in life (in terms of material resources, for example) can help out the more vulnerable and disadvantaged. This kind of collaboration can go beyond disaster management, and has, as its ultimate aim, the attainment of real progress for the community or country.

The second aspect seeks to use the whole disaster management program as a way by which to help raise the local capacity of the community and thus lessen its vulnerability to disasters. Because disaster response requires active participation from the community, the community folk, in the process, are being trained to think and decide for themselves. To CDRC, the key to "people empowerment" is developing the ability and confidence of community folk to decide and chart their own development direction, which includes capacity-building programs against disasters.

But building up the community folk's confidence to decide for themselves is not enough without disaster response machineries. CDRC cites its experience with the communities of Mount Pinatubo, a volcano in Central Luzon 70 km north of Manila.

After it erupted in 1991, Mount Pinatubo spewed out lahar (volcanic mudflow) which practically buried many communities. The community-based disaster response committees and organizations CDRC and other disaster agencies helped set up led the way in helping victims recover from the impact of the volcanic eruption.

In the face of despair and confusion, it was these grassroots machineries that led in planning and facilitating mitigation and rehabilitation programs in the affected communities.

A disaster response machinery can take the form of a community-based committee, organization, association or even simply a volunteer team. Highly trained, this community-based machinery can synchronize and coordinate local efforts to prepare for, cushion and heal the effects of disasters via an organized and systematic approach.

CDRC'S four modules under its Disaster Management Orientation (DMO) have been patterned both from the experiences of other disaster survivors overseas and from the rich experiences of CDRC's provincial networks and field workers. CDRC, along with its 17 other provincial networks in the Philippines' key islands, continues to conduct DMO seminars, training and workshops for community-based non-governmental and people's organizations and community folk. The rich experiences and ideas of grassroots organizations and villagers also continue to enrich CDRC's DMQ modules.

Aside from the DMO, CDRC has evolved similar modules for its Emergency Response Workshop and Disaster Preparedness Training which have since been used to educate community folk around the high-risk areas around Mount Pinatubo and in the island communities around the Taal Volcano in Batangas Province, also in Luzon island south of Manila.

CDRC's modules are now easily accessible and made handy through its 80-page disaster management handbook, *Bagyo, Lindol, Bulkan at Iba Pa*

(Typhoons, Earthquakes, Volcanoes and the Like).

Participants and beneficiaries of CDRC's disaster education programs come mostly from government-neglected communities and people's organizations being served by CDRC's strategically located provincial networks. CDRC has nine networks in Luzon island in northern Philippines, five networks in the Visayas islands in central Philippines, and three networks in Mindanao island in southern Philippines. In 1996, CDRC also tapped the Catholic Church network, giving disaster education training to workers and volunteers of the Church's social action centers (SACs) and some representatives from among farmers, fisherfolk and other sectors served by the SACs.

Special training has also been designed for urban poor dwellers who suffer from both human-made and natural disasters. Urban poor dwellers in Metro Manila, who daily face the threat of demolition and are, at the same time, vulnerable to flooding and fire, for example, are given special training. Aside from the usual DMO, human rights education is also given to urban poor dwellers. They must be made aware, for instance, that their rights are protected under the Philippine Urban Poor Law. This law requires the demolishing outfit to first provide relocation sites before urban poor dwellers can be ejected from their homes.

Through the DMO, urban poor residents are also encouraged to identify their capacities and vulnerabilities. In a training program conducted in an urban poor neighborhood in Pasig City, part of Metro Manila, for example, participants identified the following as their capacities: determination and readiness to face challenges, livelihood and technical skills, operation of a daycare center, existence of roads, and active membership in people's organizations. Their vulnerabilities: absence of water supply and electricity, lack of health facilities, health hazards posed by nearby factories, dangers posed by the nearby Pasig River when it swells during the typhoon and monsoon season, and the distance from schools. Another training phase involved the participants in preparing their communities' hazard map and counter-disaster plan.

This example shows how flexible CDRC is in its disaster management programs. In areas where villagers are dislocated by militarization, CDRC also has to be creative and resourceful in employing other means. Take the case of 164 farmer families in Davao Province in Mindanao island in southern Philippines whose community a real estate developer wanted to take over in 1996.

Harassed by armed men, the residents opted to stay on their land. But they had a problem: they were restricted from going in and out of their village. Their livelihood already hampered and with armed men hounding their neighborhood, the villagers worried about their safety.

On its own, CDRC's Mindanao Field Office would have been unable to conduct emergency relief operations under such a tight situation. Neither could it mobilize the villagers, whose community had practically been transformed into a well-guarded fortress. CDRC's only solution was to mobilize other groups in the region. In planning the actual relief operations, CDRC tapped the support of a local farmers' association, which, in turn, tapped its own networks, for the actual relief delivery operations.

Forming part of CDRC's disaster management program is its Food Security and Nutrition Improvement Program (FSNIP). The program seeks to attain for a community "sustainable, accessible, quality, sufficient and equitable food supply".

Implemented within the context of disaster preparedness and mitigation, FSNIP goes beyond sustainable agriculture and feeding projects. The program also educates community folk about the roots of "food insecurity" or hunger and malnutrition. It therefore cuts through issues such as landlessness, unequal distribution of food supply, market and trade policies, and the impact of global economic policies under the General Agreement on Tariffs and Trade (GATT) and the World Trade Organization (WTO). To CDRC, these issues have significant impact on the capacity and vulnerability of community folk to cope with disasters.

But while CDRC collaborates with other sectoral groups in advocating for strategic programs such as agrarian reform to combat landlessness, the Center's FSNIP has also facilitated short-term projects in key areas nationwide to help communities become self-sufficient in food. These projects include distribution of livestock, seedlings and farming tools, provision of nursery sheds and fences, and feeding programs for severely malnourished children. Also taught are various skills such as food preservation, farming techniques, food and nutrition tips, how to manage a project, and more. All these are integrated with training on disaster management.

CDRC cites a successful pilot project in Compostela town in Cebu Province in central Philippines. Hardly provided with government social services such as health facilities, potable water and schools, Compostela's farming families earned meager incomes. The Cebu Relief and Rehabilitation Center, a CDRC provincial network, introduced to the community folk skills such as putting up a plant nursery, vegetable raising, peanut production, and raising swine and cattle.

In the community nursery, Compostela residents are encouraged to plant seedlings of various fruit-bearing trees, leguminous crops and medicinal plants. Since some of the nursery's seedlings can be sold, individual or family participants also earn additional income. The nursery also gives the community readily available seeds which they do not have to buy from commercial farm supply stores. The plant nursery's long-term goal is to help rehabilitate the community's depleted natural resource base and sustain farm production there.

Also trained in health and nutrition, organizational management systems and disaster management, Compostela residents can now stand on their own two feet come typhoon or storm.

If there is one word to describe CDRC's disaster response and management program, it is "holistic". CDRC's holistic approach to disasters is based on its comprehensive grasp not only of the country's natural and human-made disasters, but also of the country's political and socio-economic problems which, more often than not, are the more devastating disaster.

4. DESCRIPTION OF THE INSTITUTION RESPONSIBLE AND ITS ORGANIZATIONAL ASPECTS

Since its establishment in 1984, CDRC has sought to address four main concerns: increasing poverty, natural and human-made disasters, the worsening ecological crisis and the problem of "internal refugees". (Internal refugees, as pointed out earlier in this research, refer to those who are forced out of their homes and villages because of military operations against armed rebels. Internal refugees, all innocent civilians who include the elderly, women and children, have nothing to do with the armed conflict still raging in the Philippine countryside.)

Over the years, CDRC has developed disaster management programs which seek to help raise the people's capacity in preparing for the impact of disasters and thus hasten their recovery. Any assistance CDRC extends to or facilitates for communities is always geared toward improving the beneficiaries' economic condition to help make them less vulnerable to disasters.

Its disaster management programs, as detailed above, provide beneficiaries with skills that are necessary in responding to the demands of rehabilitation work. The programs are also geared toward strengthening people's collective spirit in coping with the effects of both human-made and natural disasters.

It is in this context that CDRC envisions "a just, humane and prosperous society". Under this society, "people ... equitably share in the nation's wealth, have access to basic services, and are self-reliant; ... are free to chart the course their society takes, meaningfully participate in decision-making, and enjoy a credible government; ... pride themselves in their cultural heritage and positive values; ... enjoy the blessings of a healthy environment and abundant natural resources; and ... possess utmost capacity to cope with hazards, both natural and human-made."

Based on its vision, CDRC aims to help increase the vulnerable sectors' capability to address the issues of poverty, environmental degradation and armed conflict. The approach toward this mission: a citizenry-based and development-oriented disaster response. How? Through the organization and development of a nationwide movement of similarly minded institutions and people's organizations.

Working within the framework of sustainable development, CDRC stresses on rehabilitative and ecologically sound interventions. Since disaster response and preparedness requires the involvement of every citizen, CDRC works with the vulnerable sectors or the marginalized who have little capability to cope with disasters because of their poverty. But it also works with the less vulnerable sectors who have the means to overcome the damaging effects of disasters. As pointed out earlier, the less vulnerable can share and tap their surplus resources in helping the more vulnerable sectors during disasters.

CDRC has five major programs and services: Field Operations; Local Partnership Development; Training and Education; Research, Documentation and Public Information; and Overseas Partnership Development.

The Center's Field Operations include assistance to regional centers during relief operations, appraisal and monitoring of rehabilitation and disaster-preparedness and mitigation projects, and consultancy and technical assistance for project management.

Local Partnership Development covers networking and campaigns, local resource generation and mobilization, and volunteer organizing.

Training and Education include the following:
(a) development of community-based disaster management training programs and other related training curricula;
(b) training courses on disaster management orientation, disaster preparedness and emergency response;
(c) training support for the formation of Barangay or Village Disaster Response Organizations and Committees; and
(d) training management consultancy.

Its Research, Documentation and Public Information program focuses on research and databanking on disaster events, disaster management and on development work. Aside from coming out with publications, this program is also involved in disaster monitoring, information dissemination and advocacy.

The Overseas Partnership Development program is concerned with establishing and strengthening ties between CDRC and various international governmental and non-governmental organizations involved in the rehabilitation of disaster victims.

CDRC has 17 regional or provincial networks strategically situated nationwide. It has nine networks in Luzon island, five in the Visayas islands, and three in Mindanao island.

5. PROBLEMS OR OBSTACLES ENCOUNTERED AND HOW THEY WERE OVERCOME

One problem CDRC encountered was the difficulty in getting funding support for victims of human-made disasters. In 1996, for example, CDRC had its hands full during the rash of demolitions of homes in Metro Manila's urban poor communities during the preparation for the Asia-Pacific Economic Cooperation (APEC) Summit which Manila hosted. Some 10,444 shanty homes were torn down. Communities unsuccessfully contested in the courts the demolition orders and tried to defend their homes with barricades. In many cases, relief and resettlement assistance was not provided.

CDRC responded to the situation by circulating a major emergency appeal. But only two European church-based disaster support groups responded. CDRC made do with the support the two international groups extended. CDRC was able to deliver services ranging from food and non-food relief to disaster training and advocacy.

Some 2,722 homeless families received the standard food relief pack and non-food relief items like emergency shelter materials, water and kitchen utensils. All these items were based on the damage-needs-capacities assessment of CDRC and the victims. The prompt arrival of the external support enabled CDRC to respond to the victims' plight within 24 hours amid rainy weather.

But in its many years of disaster response and management work, CDRC found that response to human-made disasters was virtually nil. Most foreign donor agencies and local sources like corporations do not empathize much with demolition victims as much as they do with victims of volcanic eruptions, typhoons and earthquakes.

From this experience, CDRC thought of a way out: setting up a "standby fund". This fund is programed to help CDRC respond promptly to human-made disasters. But in the long term, CDRC has a more apt solution: educate the less vulnerable sectors of Metro Manila. By educating them, CDRC hopes that they will not hesitate to help out individuals affected by human-made disasters such as demolitions.

Another human-made disaster which hardly generates sympathy and support is the hazards caused by big commercial mining. CDRC and other advocacy groups who bring to the public's attention the perils of large-scale mining have often been misunderstood. They, for instance, have been perceived as "politically inspired" groups out to sabotage the mining industry.

But CDRC found one effective way of getting to the bottom of the problem. Once in 1996, CDRC presented the hazards of big mining through a nine-day photo exhibit at a shopping mall in Makati City, Metro Manila's business and financial district. One of the photographs, for example, showed a former footbridge construction worker who has become paralyzed after suffering from aplastic anaemia because of prolonged exposure to toxic mine tailings in the Boac River in Marinduque Province in central Philippines. The province is where the Filipino-Canadian Marcopper Mining Corporation has been operating for decades. In March 1996, the company's mine tailings spilled into the river, rendering it biologically dead.

Subsequently, a rich foundation offered CDRC a space in which to display further its photo exhibit. The exhibit, which the media also featured, helped induce public opinion and debate about the Marcopper tailings. CDRC and the media, which also sufficiently reported on the mine-tailings spill, all helped in pressuring the government to make the company accountable for the damage done. Aside from suspending the company's operations, the government also fined Marcopper.

Another common problem CDRC and its regional networks often encounter in the field is the dole-out mentality of some community folk. CDRC acknowledges, however, that this problem is understandable in many communities where such dole-out mentality has been fostered even by the government.

But through sincerity and developing a good rapport with the communities, CDRC has been able to turn such a mentality upside down through its holistic disaster response and management education.

6. EFFECTS OF THE PRACTICE/INNOVATIVE EXPERIENCE

The practice has helped CDRC's target groups brace themselves for disasters. Because CDRC has always stressed on tapping local resources (human and material), the practice has, in a way, helped and continues to help empower communities. The practice has helped communities to stand on their own two feet.

Through CDRC's disaster education program, community-based disaster management handlers can strategize and prioritize disaster response programs. The education program has also helped reinforce traditional community values such as self-help, resourcefulness and cooperativism.

7. SUITABILITY AND POSSIBILITY FOR UPSCALING

CDRC seeks to upscale its operation through its 17 regional and provincial networks nationwide. The Center continues to expand by building new alliances at the community level. Its priority target in expansion, however, is the more vulnerable communities, which are often neglected by the government.

8. SIGNIFICANCE FOR (AND IMPACT ON) POLICY-MAKING

In a country where the government's response to disasters is by and large reactive, CDRC's disaster preparedness and management program cannot be ignored. Through a holistic disaster preparedness and management approach, the government's resources can be maximized and wisely utilized.

More often than not, millions of pesos in calamity funds end up being siphoned off through graft. These resources cannot be laid to waste if they are put to use where they should be – in the affected communities. But as CDRC's experience shows, these communities must be well-versed in disaster preparedness and disaster management. They must be well-organized. Through organized disaster response machineries, these communities can effectively demand from the government what is due to them. Once organized, they can tightly guard every cent the government allots for calamities.

The government's smallest political unit, called the *barangay* (village), which has its own set of officials, can also adopt CDRC's disaster education program. Municipal and provincial governments can actually make disaster preparedness and disaster management a permanent policy. But they must not forget one important facet: they must work hand in hand with the communities.

CDRC's disaster preparedness and management program also poses another challenge to the government: how to make community folk less vulnerable to disasters by addressing the roots of their vulnerabilities. The roots of their vulnerabilities, which are often more disastrous than typhoons, earthquakes and volcanic eruptions, include unequal access to the country's wealth and resources and political powerlessness.

9. POSSIBILITY AND SCOPE OF TRANSFERRING TO OTHER COMMUNITIES OR COUNTRIES

The practice can be replicated in any disaster-prone community or country which lacks disaster preparedness strategies. The lack of preparedness to disasters often magnifies the impact of typhoons, quakes, volcanic eruptions and other calamities. Preparedness via education, training and organization can help save lives and property.

Disaster preparedness and management can also bring out the best in people: their leadership, managerial abilities and resourcefulness can be unearthed and put to good use. Once prepared, communities can anticipate disasters in the same way that they can anticipate the changing of the seasons.

10. OTHER COMMENTS

If there is one key element in disaster preparedness, it is, as CDRC has shown, reliance on the capacities of people. Disaster preparedness does not simply require funding and material support. Funding and material support are necessary. But it is the people's managerial abilities, creativity, innovation, outlook and values which make the real difference. This is the reason CDRC stresses on disaster education. Unless properly educated, a community will most likely put to waste, if not mismanage, enormous amounts of funds and other material support intended to help ease the pain of disasters.

References

1. Bagyo, Lindol, Bulkan, (1994) *At Iba Pa* (A Disaster Management Handbook), Citizens' Disaster Response Center Foundation, Inc.
2. Citizens' Disaster Response Center Foundation, Inc., *Annual Report 1996*.
3. Citizens' Disaster Response Center Foundation, Inc., Brochure.
4. Interviews.

4.

The Pani Panchayat: Water and equity

1. GENERAL INFORMATION

1.1 Title of practice or experience

The Pani Panchayat (Water Council): Water and equity

1.2 Category of practice/experience and brief description

In an era of increasing water scarcity, a committed engineer has worked out a radical new set of technological and social innovations that not only helps repair and restore degraded watersheds (thereby increasing water harvests), but, by guaranteeing each family within the community an equal share of the water harvested, meets goals of equity as well. Rarely do technical projects like watershed-management schemes or irrigation projects meet the demands of equity. The Pani Panchayats (Water Councils) set up by Vilasrao Salunkhe do.

1.3 Name of person or institution responsible for the practice or experience

Gram Gourav Pratisthan

1.4 Name and position of key or relevant persons or officials involved

Vilasrao Salunkhe

1.5 Details of institution

(a) Address: Khalad village, Saswad, Pune District, Maharashtra, India
(b) Telephone: ++ (91) (21152) 2462, (91) (21152) 2577

1.6 Name of person and/or institution conducting the research

Claude Alvares, Editor, Other India Press

1.7 Details of research person/institution

    (a) Address: Above Mapusa Clinic, Mapusa 403 507, Goa, India
    (b) Telephone: ++ (91) (832) 263 306, 256 479
    (c) Fax: ++ (91) (832) 263 305
    (d) E-Mail: oibs@bom2.vsnl.net.in

2. THE PROBLEM OR SITUATION BEING ADDRESSED BY THE PRACTICE/INNOVATIVE EXPERIENCE

In 1972, the state of Maharashtra went through a severe drought crisis. The drought hit several hundred villages with a combined population of more than 400,000 people. During his travels around the drought-affected areas, Vilasrao Salunkhe was struck by the fact that in several areas, there was no water available for agriculture of any kind. Villagers had no means of survival. The government of Maharashtra had determined that the villagers should continue to work by preparing road construction materials to enable them to receive a subsistence wage from it under its employment schemes.

Salunkhe found that though farmers owned land, they could do nothing with it without access to a guaranteed source of water for cultivation. This was the principal cause of their poverty. Since there was no water, they could never employ themselves on the land and earn an assured income. In drought-prone areas, this was the fate of both large and small landowners.

No villager wanted to be on the dole as it were: they wanted water so they could cultivate. At the moment, they were not asking for water all year round. They wanted water supply guaranteed every year for at least one single crop. Since there was no prospect of this happening, people were leaving the villages and migrating to cities like Mumbai where they could at least eke out a living on the pavements or in the slums.

Salunkhe found that the problem could be solved if attempts were made by the farmers themselves to conserve the scanty rainfall that the region receives every year. His primary task was to perfect a watershed-management plan which he first put into effect on land gifted to him by the villages. Through well-established schemes of water conservation and afforestation, Salunkhe was able to harness enough water to transform the area into a green oasis.

This was his technical success. The more significant aspect of the development work was the social aspect, relating to the problem of equity. Historians have pointed out that not only were the older water-harvesting systems for which India is well known communally owned but the benefits were shared far more equitably than they are nowadays. In certain regions like south India, even lands were rotated among peasants by lots every few years to enable everyone in the community to get access to the most fertile of the village lands. But this principle of just access was not incorporated into policy. Even today, despite the fact that the government agencies have accepted the idea that watersheds must be developed holistically, equity considerations have not been addressed in the implementation of programmes.

In fact, every development project in India today continues to suffer from the problem of equity or rather the lack of it. Invariably, while some people benefit from a project installed, often with public funds, other people pay. Some receive water from a dam, others are displaced in the process. Even in the command areas of irrigation schemes, those with large landholdings get copious quantities of water, whereas those with small holdings and those at the margins of the command get little of it. Salunkhe was determined to end this state of affairs. He resolved that in the schemes he started, the equity problem would be tackled from the inception. This he ensured by insisting that every person in a development area in which a water-harvesting project was coming up would get an equal share of the water. This principle of guaranteed water shares would apply whether the person owned land or not. The innovation had profound implications, for it gave the landless an economic (and, therefore, bargaining) power that had always been denied them because they did not own land. Two other major problems were associated with water. First, available supplies in well-endowed areas were unjustly distributed. Water supplies from large dams and irrigation projects, including lift irrigation schemes, invariably benefited largely the richer farmers. Rich farmers could also command resources with which to undertake lift irrigation projects in which they alone benefited while the rest of the community was left to fend on its own. In addition, most of the good water available even in drought-prone areas was being used for water-intensive cash crops like sugarcane instead of for the growing of food grains. Salunkhe's technological and social innovations provided neat solutions to some of the most serious of these problems and are therefore seen as one of the really useful and significant contributions made to rural development and welfare.

3. DESCRIPTION OF THE PRACTICE/INNOVATIVE EXPERIENCE AND ITS MAIN FEATURES

Vilasrao Salunkhe was one of the first people within the country to begin thinking of environmental regeneration in terms of watersheds. And there was no better place to test his ideas than the drought-prone areas of Maharashtra where the rainfall fluctuates between 250 mm and 500 mm per year and where even drinking water is sometimes not available. Salunkhe first tried out his ideas on a 16-hectare plot of hillside in Naigaon village in the Purandhar *taluka* of Pune district. The land belonged to the temple trust of the village and had remained barren and uncultivable for several years. However, since it was offered to him by the villagers, he decided to accept it and got down to work. He signed a lease with the trust for use of the land for 50 years and also paid the trust rent. He also constructed a hut on the plot and began to live there with his family.

He reasoned that if his experiments in water conservation worked here, they would work almost anywhere else. When he commenced work, the plot could not produce more than 2-4 bags of grains a year. Salunkhe began the restoration work by first attempting measures to conserve the soil and harvest the scarce rain water. First, a series of contour bunds were raised to trap water runoff and also to protect the soil from erosion. A percolation tank was constructed at the base of the hillslope which he saw was a micro-watershed. He estimated the capacity of the percolation tank at one million cubic feet of water. A well was dug below it and water pumped from here up the hillslope for irrigating the fields.

More than 4,000 trees were planted amid the rocky areas and around 2,000 fruit trees were raised on and around the more fertile bunds. Grass and shrub were allowed to grow on land that was not being cultivated. The area was protected from animal grazing for a while to enable the vegetation to gain strength. Eventually, as the general health of the watershed improved as a result of these measures, production from the land increased to 100 quintals (1 quintal = 100 kg) of foodgrains and the employment generated on the 16-hectare farm enabled five households to survive with 15 head of cattle. The entire exercise of environmental regeneration of the watershed took a whole five years. When it was completed, Salunkhe was able to prove that what could be grown on half an acre of irrigated land was sufficient to support one individual's food requirements for a complete year. Having worked out the technology necessary, Salunkhe now attempted to multiply it and apply it in adjoining areas. But with an important difference. At the Naigaon temple trust farm, the problem of equity had not arisen because this was land held in trust.

But the problem of equity was bound to emerge in a major way in the projects which he was going to help duplicate with the cooperation of farmers who had seen his work at Naigaon in other parts of the region. Therefore, when he commenced the application of these new techniques of micro-watershed management to the first new scheme in Naigaon itself, he proposed a strikingly new idea: that the water resource gained as a result of the project would be allocated to each farmer in proportion to the number of family members (the maximum share per family unit of five members being two and a half acres) rather than in proportion to landholdings. In this way, the benefits of each irrigation scheme would be equitably distributed. Overall agricultural production would also increase because water would be allocated to a large number of small farmers and it is well recognised that small farms are able to work at higher levels of productivity than large farms.

The idea Salunkhe proposed was that as water is a common property resource, all the villagers should have equal rights and access to the utilisation of the water harvested in the area. This was translated into practice by offering membership of the lift irrigation schemes to landless villagers. By doing this, the landless could become sharecroppers in the lands of the larger landholders who had excess land but could do nothing with it. This also solved the problem of employment within the village itself. But for all this to happen, the lift irrigation schemes must be collectively undertaken by farmers as a group rather than on an individual basis. Collective control over a lift irrigation scheme can also enable the group to ensure that scarce water is judiciously used and allocated not for water-guzzling crops like sugarcane but for seasonal crops, including foodgrains, since these do not require large quantities of water. The water rights of a family were also detached from land ownership, which meant that if a piece of land were sold to a new owner, then the water rights reverted to the group and the new owner would not automatically get rights to water. Salunkhe also worked into his schemes scope for farmer participation in the design and investment proposals related to lift irrigation schemes they wished to install in their area and insisted that the water management committees take full charge of the lift irrigation schemes. He insisted that at least 20% of the investment in lift irrigation schemes must be put in by the members of the scheme. But his principal insight was to insist on equity and to be able to prove that once the equity problem was taken care of, society as a whole improved its prospects, whereas in the conventional system supported by the government, only those with vast resources benefited in proportion to their assets and landholdings while the rest of the community was left to fend for itself, a permanent guarantee for increasing disparities among different sectors of the population.

4. DESCRIPTION OF THE INSTITUTION RESOPNSIBLE AND ITS ORGANISATIONAL ASPECTS

For the purpose of applying his social innovations, Salunkhe initiated the Gram Gourav Pratisthan Trust in 1974. All the experiments in watershed management and the later multiplication of more than 50 lift irrigation schemes in the area were carried out with the support of the GGP. The GGP itself was supported financially by donations received from industrialists, Salunkhe's own industry, and from several international aid agencies. The GGP played a catalytic role in supporting groups of farmers from different areas who wished to carry out programmes for water harvesting and lift irrigation schemes. It provided money in the form of interest-free loans to enable farmers to meet the costs of such schemes. It also trained young boys from the state at its campus at Khalad, employing a syllabus which consisted of 20% theory and 80% practice. These young men were soon equipped to handle the technical problems connected with the lift irrigation schemes. At present, the GGP continues to train such "barefoot" managers, civil engineers and personnel from non-governmental organisations (NGOs).

The GGP also made a policy decision that no scheme would be implemented unless it had two components:
(a) it came from a group of farmers and not from individuals; and
(b) they were ready to put up 20% of the cost of the scheme. This invariably brought about greater cohesion in the village set-up, since it forced villagers to work together and maintain their schemes in their own interests.

5. PROBLEMS OR OBSTACLES ENCOUNTERED AND HOW THEY WERE OVERCOME

The principal problem encountered by the organisation was the lack of concern sometimes shown by government bureaucrats in the different departments dealing with agriculture, electricity and irrigation. When Salunkhe, for example, first approached the agriculture department for carrying out water conservation plans in the villages of the *taluka*, he was told that technicians were not available to either prepare the plans or carry out any surveys. Eventually, Salunkhe had to draft students from an Engineering College to carry out the work.

After several lift irrigation schemes were approved by the government and even the subsidies had reached the farmers, the electricity department did not want to consider the demand for power to energise the sets. Electricity proved to be a more difficult proposition than finances. The farmers threatened a boycott of the elections and during a protest agitation, 200 of them were put in jail for eight days. Finally, their demands were met.

Other problems were caused by the political instability of the period which often delayed arrival of subsidies, created such hurdles that farmers could not procure subsidies, or delayed electrical connections for lift irrigation schemes until years after such schemes had been paid for and ready for use. In most cases, the gap between the time the villagers approached the authorities and the time they got the support that was legally due to them was approximately five years!

The second major problem was the non-availability of civil engineers, who refused to work in the villages, preferring the cities instead. This problem was eventually solved by creating a cadre of young men who were trained as "barefoot engineers", equipped with basic civil engineering skills so that they could assist farmers with technical aspects of lift irrigation schemes and other water-harvesting projects.

6. EFFECTS OF THE PRACTICE/INNOVATIVE EXPERIENCE

The impact of the successful innovations introduced by Salunkhe and the GGP is truly astonishing. Barren lands that had produced little or no food were gradually producing one good seasonal crop, which helped farmers survive the year with dignity. In some areas, as water availability increased, farmers could go on for two crops. The 50-odd schemes co-sponsored by the GGP eventually enabled 3,000 acres to be brought under protective irrigation, benefitting a population of some 10,000 people from 1,500 families.

The availability of water made possible through conservation schemes and percolation tanks meant that drinking water for the village population was accessible and close at hand and villagers, women especially, did not have to trudge across long distances for water in the hot sun any longer.

7. SUITABILITY AND POSSIBILITY FOR UPSCALING

The innovations described above are of two kinds:
(a) The techniques of micro-watershed management can be upscaled, though with variations for different eco-regions. Basic techniques of contour bunding, digging of percolation tanks in the lowest point of watersheds, etc. are well known and can be found in any textbook on irrigation though they are rarely applied. No technique available will be of any assistance, however, unless the engineer is able to grasp the unique feature of the

watershed and of the ecosystem in which it is supposed to function. This can only come about from acute study and observation, including consultation with people in the immediate environment.
(b) The social principles involving the guarantee of equal water shares to villagers on a per family basis, and the setting up of the structure of the five-member Pani Panchayat or Water Council (*Pani* = water; *Panchayat* = five-member council) which takes charge and leadership of the schemes, can be and are now being applied in other areas of the country as well.

8. SIGNIFICANCE FOR (AND IMPACT ON) POLICY-MAKING

Several of the principles behind the organisation of the Pani Panchayat ought to be made part of public policy. First, the principle that people should have equal shares in common resources, if adopted, would revolutionise society in far-reaching ways. Today, a landless person in the village is seen as a person who has no right to resources just because he has no land. Because of this, he often also does not have political power since it is assumed he is poor and therefore his views need not be taken into account when decisions concerning his survival or that of the community are being made.

The Pani Panchayat guarantees him the right to a share of water even if he has no land. He can then dispense with this right as he wishes, particularly if he has no land on which to use the water. He can use it as an input on the lands of large landowners: both together can thus produce output where none could before individually. Present policies dictate that those who have large landholdings get larger quantities of water and those nearest the water source get more water than those who are far away. Such policies should not form the basis of democracies based on the idea of equality and equity. The technical aspects of watershed management and the lessons of Naigaon have been incorporated by the government in the conception and planning of its comprehensive watershed-development programmes.

9. POSSIBILITY AND SCOPE OF TRANSFERRING TO OTHER COMMUNITIES OR COUNTRIES

There is every scope for transferring Vilasrao Salunkhe's ideas to other communities and countries, as both the technical and social innovations are such that they can be readily understood and implemented with appropriate adaptations to suit local circumstances. The idea of planning development on the basis of watersheds in place of piecemeal development projects which are conceived in isolation is now well-established and has become a routine plank of public policy, at least in a country like India. The government now routinely issues development grants for the purpose of watershed development. The second attractive aspect of Salunkhe's work, the principle of equal shares in water sources, can also be adopted with minor variations in different situations with significant impacts on human welfare.

5.

The SLU-SVP Housing Project

1. GENERAL INFORMATION

1.1 Title of practice or experience

The SLU-SVP Housing Project

1.2 Category of practice/experience and brief description

The Saint Louis University (SLU)-Saint Vincent Parish (SVP) is one of the few successful private housing cooperatives in the Philippines and in the world. At the Habitat II Non-Governmental Organization (NGO) Forum at Istanbul, Turkey, on June 3-14, 1996, the SLU-SVP was presented as a case study of one of the world's best examples in cooperative housing. The success of this housing project can be attributed largely to the revitalization of an ancient Filipino tradition of collective work, called *bayanihan*. The dynamic cooperation of institutions like the church Congregation of the Immaculate Conception of Mary (CICM), NGOs, governmental organizations (GOs) and individuals was also crucial to the success of the project.

1.3 Name of person or institution responsible for the practice or experience

The Saint Louis University (SLU) and Saint Vincent Parish (SVP) Housing Cooperative, which was initiated by Fr. Paul Zwaenoepoel, CICM and former President of Saint Louis University.

1.4 Name and position of key or relevant persons or officials involved

The CICM priests: Fr. Paul Zwaenoepoel, CICM, former President of Saint Louis University in Baguio City; Fr. Paul Bohlen, CICM
Prominent Baguio residents: Dr. Marcelo Cabato, Dr. Antonio Adorable
The SLU-SVP Cooperative Officers

1.5 Details of institution

(a) Address: Old Site Bakakeng, 2600 Baguio City, Philippines
(b) Telephone: ++ (63) (74) 442 8821, 442 7560

1.6 Name of person and/or institution conducting the research

Raymundo D. Rovillos, Assistant Professor of History, University of the Philippines College in Baguio, for Tebtebba Foundation, Inc. (Indigenous Peoples' International Center for Policy Research and Education)

1.7 Details of research person/institution

Tebtebba Foundation, Inc.:
(a) Address: Rm. 3B Agpaoa Compound, 111 Upper General Luna Road, 2600 Baguio City, Philippines
(b) Telephone: ++ (63) (74) 444 7703
(c) Fax: ++ (63) (74) 443 9459
(d) E-Mail: tebtebba@skyinet.net

2. THE PROBLEM OR SITUATION BEING ADDRESSED BY THE PRACTICE/INNOVATIVE EXPERIENCE

Shelter is a basic need that any human being aspires to fulfill. The Filipino, for one, would work himself ragged, even to the extent of leaving his loved ones for greener pastures abroad, if only to someday own his own house and lot. The Filipino's concept of a house assumes a psycho-social dimension, and not just a physical one, as can be gleaned from the synonyms of the word *bahay* (house). The Filipinos' *bahay* is their *tirahan* (a place to stay in), their *tuluyan* (a place to go to), their *uwian* (a place to return to), their *tahanan* (a place to rest in) (Constantino, 1987:1). Owning a house connotes economic security which, in turn, brings about peace of mind. Unluckily, the realization of this cherished dream has been elusive not only for the Filipinos but also for many people all over the world. The following facts can bear this out:
(a) According to United Nations statistics, more than one billion people live in very poor housing, in unhealthy environments. Of this number, 100 million are literally homeless. They sleep in the streets, in vacant lots, or huddled against inclement weather under bridges and alleys.
(b) Still according to UN statistics, around one-half of the urban population live in slums.

(c) *IBON Facts and Figures* of September 15, 1987 cites official estimates that 3.5 million families or roughly 21 million Filipinos are homeless and that 10.8 million (out of a total 12.9 million) households are in need of better housing, almost 84% of the Philippine population.
(d) In Metro Manila alone, there were 425 slum colonies as of 1981 with a total squatter population of 1.6 million; that is to say, more than one-fourth of Metro Manila's population were squatters. And this phenomenon is not confined to only Metro Manila; all major cities of the country have slum areas in which large numbers live. In Bacolod, 30% live in slums; in Davao City, the figure is 33%; in Cotabato City, 34%.
(e) In Baguio City, an additional 26,800 units need to be constructed to meet the growing population's housing demand by the year 2000 (Boquiren, 1991).

The SLU-SVP Housing Project was indeed a timely response to the need for housing not only for the lower-income group, but also for the middle-income professionals in Baguio City, like Attorney Ruben A. Corpuz. Corpuz narrates his experience thus:

"Way back in 1971, I was just employed as an instructor in St. Louis University, Baguio City. I had been married for only a year then and my first child was born. With a salary of P380.00, I could only afford to rent one room for everything – it served as a bedroom, kitchen and dining room. Like many others in Baguio, I was in need of better housing.

"My case was no better than that of the parishioners of St. Vincent Parish who were living around a lagoon whose waters rise every time the typhoons come. Every year during typhoons, I hear over the radio people around the lagoon being rescued by volunteers. The parish priest was concerned with procuring a better housing facility for these parishioners."

The housing problem in the Philippines is of course a result of poverty. With around 60% of the Filipino people living below the poverty line, with 14% of the workforce unemployed and 22% underemployed, with a minimum wage that consigns even those who have jobs to living below the poverty line, one can only expect slums to expand. There is also the natural population growth rate to swell the slum population. Moreover, there is the continuous flow of migrants from the countryside escaping from the depressed rural economy and hoping for a better chance in the urban economy (Constantino, 1987).

There is also the basic problem of land – not so much its scarcity, but more the "monopoly ownership that gives the appearance of scarcity and consequently pushes land prices beyond the reach of the poor or even the not-so-poor".

Finally, the housing problem can be directly linked to misguided government policies, and, where policy is sound, the absence/lack of proper implementation of such policies.

3. DESCRIPTION OF THE PRACTICE/INNOVATIVE EXPERIENCE AND ITS MAIN FEATURES*

The SLU-SVP *barangay* is a private low-cost housing scheme of the SLU-SVP Housing Cooperative in Bakakeng. Approximately 15 minutes away from the city proper by public utility jeepney, the area is divided into two: SLU-SVP Old Site (6 hectares) and SLU-SVP New Site (5 hectares). The *barangay* has 11 *puroks* with 282 dwelling units and 330 households. Such a relatively small number can be attributed to the fact that most of those staying in the *barangay* are connected with Saint Louis University, Saint Vincent Parish and/or the Congregation of the Immaculate Conception of Mary.

The SLU-SVP Housing Cooperative was established in 1971 under the initiative of Fr. Paul Zwaenoepoel of the CICM order who also became President of Saint Louis University. The cooperative, which was initially meant for SLU employees only, later expanded to include residents of Saint Vincent Parish.

Through the help of M + R (Philippines) Foundation and the endorsement of the CICM Missionaries, the cooperative was able to obtain a "soft" loan from Misereor Foundation of Germany. The amount would be sufficient to put up 50 housing units. At the same time, the CICM fathers offered to sell several hectares of land at a "token" price. The land is 3 kilometers from the Baguio City Hall and, at that time, was thick with pine trees and overgrowth.

Since the initial funding for the housing scheme came from the CICM fathers, it was also decided that membership be opened to CICM employees. Support from outsiders, including prominent Baguio residents like the late Dr. Ernesto Abellera, Dr. Marcelo Cabato and Dr. Antonio Adorable, to name a few, helped to establish the cooperative. The construction of the first houses came to fruition with the purchase of 3-4 hectares by the cooperative. It was considered a "simulated sale" for it was practically a donation from the CICM fathers. The construction of the first 50 houses was further facilitated with a

---

* This section is lifted from a study entitled: *Urbanization In Medium Sized Towns In Third World Countries: A Comparative Study Of The Philippines, Thailand And Kenya: A Report On Baguio City, Philippines* (1993). The study was conducted by the Cordillera Studies Center of the Social Sciences Division, University of the Philippines College in Baguio, through its faculty, namely: Gladys A. Cruz, Fe Marie A. Gacad, Lourdes A. Hamada, Raymundo D. Rovillos and Florence T. Salinas.

grant from Belgium. The area where these 50 houses were built is now known as the Old Site. At present, the housing project encompasses 13.4 hectares. The cooperative acquired it from the CICM at a cost of P7.00 per square meter in the Old Site and P17.00/sq. m in the New Site. The whole area where the housing project is located used to be owned by the Parisas, a family of Ibaloi descent, who sold it to the Palispis family at P1.00/sq. m. The Palispis later sold it at P1.20/sq. m to the Milo family who sold it to the CICM at P2.60/sq. m.

To be a member of the cooperative, applicants must have the following qualifications:
(a) they must have been an SLU or CICM employee for at least three years or a resident of SVP for at least five years;
(b) have a per capita income of not less than P1,500.00;
(c) not own any lot anywhere in the country; and
(d) attend a two-day educational seminar.

Applicants for membership are required to pay a down payment of P5,000 (minimum) and must participate in the *bayanihan* where cooperative members render community services for free. Landscaping, site development, cleaning, road building, etc. are the most common activities in the *bayanihan*. A cooperative member's participation in these activities earns him/her points, which are a major factor considered in awarding houses and lots. But apart from the points that one earns from participating in the *bayanihan*, there is the spirit of community that is inculcated in each member even before he/she is awarded a house and lot. By working side by side with other members (who are one's prospective neighbors), friendship, a sense of belonging and the community spirit are instilled. From the perspective of the cooperative, this contributes to the relative stability and peacefulness of the community. The cooperative also reserves its right to evict members who become a nuisance to the community.

Other criteria for the award of house and lot include the following:
(a) duration of membership in cooperative;
(b) time when down payment was given;
(c) attendance in seminars;
(d) per capita income of member;
(e) *bayanihan*; and
(f) payment of capital build-up (a member must own a minimum of at least four shares (P200)) which can be increased later.

The above criteria correspond to a certain amount of points all of which will add up to 100%.

At present, no *bayanihan* is taking place because there are no awardable lots yet. In addition, the housing cooperative is being transformed into a multi-purpose cooperative. The cooperative feels that it has already largely satisfied the major need of its members, that is, housing. Although there are plans to look for additional land, lack of funds has forced the cooperative to shelf these in the meantime. Amortization payments are spent mainly on the construction of new housing units. Although grants were its initial funding source, the cooperative aims for greater self-reliance in the future.

As a whole, the SLU-SVP is considered to be one of the more successful housing schemes in the country. As a community, the SLU-SVP *barangay* has put up its own church and multi-purpose hall. Being a private housing scheme, it can be said that the responsibility for planning of the area fell on members of the cooperative themselves. This was facilitated by the fact that some of the residents have professional degrees such as in engineering, architecture and the like. The development of the area has been mainly under the initiative of the cooperative's members and this is part of the *bayanihan* practice in the area.

Transportation services are not a problem, although residents are in favor of more public utility jeepneys. Most of the roads are concreted with funds from the local government (the SLU-SVP Housing Project just recently became a *barangay* separate from Bakakeng Central). Electricity, water and sewerage services are generally adequate.

While the value of houses and lots acquired through the cooperative is generally reasonable, the value of real estate in the vicinity of the SLU-SVP *barangay* has been rising. The fact that a number of private subdivisions, namely Eagle Crest, Rich View, Santo Nino and De Castro Subdivision, are located around the *barangay* has made property within the cooperative prime property. City Hall appraises the cost of land in the area to be from P1,000 to P2,000 per square meter.

The SLU-SVP *barangay* is a purely residential area inhabited by housing cooperative members who have been awarded their house and lot. Awardees are given 20 years to complete their amortization payments, upon which the land titles are awarded to them. At present, only 10% have titles.

Ownership of property in this *barangay* is purely private, and the cooperative has adopted policies which will ensure that only the awardees will be the ultimate beneficiaries of the housing scheme. Although some of these rules which limit the rights of awardees to use and dispose of their house and lot have undergone revisions recently, they were imposed to maximize the benefits derived by the community members. Some of these rules are as follows:

First, the cooperative prohibits members from renting out any part of their house and lot. Data, however, show that there are households in SLU-SVP who merely rent. Although the incidence of this is relatively low (4%), the fact that there are members who lease out either rooms or an entire storey of their house implies that this rule is not strictly enforced. Members who migrate out of Baguio typically leave their houses in the care of relatives instead of renting them out to strangers. Rights to the house and lot, however, remain with the cooperative member.

Second, until recently, cooperative awardees were not allowed to sell the rights to their house and lot, except to the cooperative. Today, this legal encumbrance has been dropped: an owner is given a clean title and he/she has the option to sell to anybody; the property can likewise be used as a collateral. A Deed of Transfer can also be issued by the owner provided that his/her name (as original owner) is indicated.

In general, therefore, the awardees of houses and lots are required to reside in the *barangay*. The fact that in order to qualify for membership, one must not own land anywhere in the country accounts for their high compliance. Also, this ensures that awardees will not sell their house and lot once it is awarded to them.

The lots awarded by the cooperative to its qualified members have an area of 246.12 square meters on average. Old Site awardees were given 250 square meters while New Site awardees got smaller lots ranging from 200 to 248 square meters. The houses built by the cooperative consist of two bedrooms, a comfort room, a living room and dining room. Awardees have 20 years to pay, with monthly amortization payments varying between P115 (for those awarded in 1972) and P1,100 (for those awarded in the 1990s). The difference in monthly amortization rates is determined by the construction cost of the house awarded to the member. On average, monthly amortization is P424.96 (standard deviation – 306.13), an amount that is cheap compared to regular rents in other parts of the city.

TABLE 1		
Year house and lot was awarded to respondent, SLU-SVP		
Year	**F**	**%**
1971-75	13	27.1
1976-80	9	18.7
1981-85	9	18.7
1986-90	15	31.3
1991-92	2	4.2
N*	48	100.0

* Number of Valid Cases

Table 1 shows that 31.3% were awarded their house and lot between 1986 and 1990 while more than one-fourth were awarded in the early 1970s. Although the houses have retained some part of the original design, 92% of the sample have undertaken renovations and improvements in their houses. Many of the original one-story structures (with floor size of 42 square meters) have been renovated and expanded into two-story structures with a wider floor space which accommodates more and bigger rooms. These renovations explain the large difference between the acquisition value (Table 2) and the present value (Table 3) of these properties. Table 2 was derived by adding the awardee's down payment to his total amortization payments for 20 years. This reflects the value of the house and lot before improvements were made. The values shown in Table 3 are the estimates of the respondents themselves as to the highest price at which they will sell their property.

The acquisition values of property in the SLU-SVP *barangay* range from a low of P28,600 (for a house built on a 250-square-meter piece of land and acquired in 1971) to as high as P270,500 (lot size of 250 square meters acquired in 1987). The property awarded in 1991 has a value of P269,720. When compared to the present market value of these properties, it can be noted that values have naturally increased. The average present market value of property in SLU-SVP is P463,522.73, almost 4.5 times higher than the average

TABLE 2						
Acquisition value of house and lot according to year when it was acquired, SLU-SVP						
Acquisition Value	Year When Acquired					
(In Pesos)	1971-75	1976-80	1981-85	1986-90	1991-92	TOTAL
50,000 and Below	12 (25.0%)	4 (8.3%)	–	–	–	16 (33.3%)
50,001-100,000	2 (4.2%)	5 (10.4%)	5 (10.4%)	–	–	12 (25.0%)
100,001-150,000	–	–	5 (10.4%)	2 (4.2%)	–	7 (14.6%)
150,001-200,000	–	–	–	7 (14.6%)	–	7 (14.6%)
200,001-250,000	–	–	–	3 (6.2%)	–	3 (6.2%)
250,001-300,000	–	–	–	2 (4.2%)	1 (2.1%)	3 (6.2%)
N*	14 (29.2%)	9 (18.8%)	10 (20.8%)	14 (29.2%)	1 (2.1%)	48 (99.9%)

Mean Acquisition Value: P105,806.47
*Number of Valid Cases

TABLE 3

Present (1992) market value of house and lot according to year it was acquired, SLU-SVP

Present Value (In Pesos)	Year When Acquired					
	1971-75	1976-80	1981-85	1986-90	1991-92	TOTAL
100,000 and Below	2 (4.4%)	2 (4.4%)	1 (2.2%)	1 (2.2%)	–	6 (13.3%)
100,001-250,000	3 (6.7%)	1 (2.2%)	2 (4.4%)	6 (13.3%)	–	12 (26.7%)
250,001-500,000	3 (6.7%)	3 (6.7%)	3 (6.7%)	2 (4.4%)	1 (2.2%)	12 (26.7%)
500,001-750,000	1 (2.2%)	–	–	3 (6.7%)	–	4 (8.9%)
750,001-1,000,000	2 (4.4%)	3 (6.7%)	2 (4.4%)	3 (6.7%)	–	10 (22.2%)
1,000,001-1,250,000	1 (2.2%)	–	–	–	–	1 (2.2%)
N*	12 (26.7%)	9 (20%)	8 *17.8%)	15 (33.3%)	1 (2.2%)	45 (100%)

Mean Acquisition Value: P105,806.47
*Number of Valid Cases

acquisition value. This reflects not only the improvements made by the awardees but also the increasing value of property in the Bakakeng area where several large subdivisions are located. The generally favorable condition of social services like water, electricity, garbage collection and transportation services also accounts for this.

Impact of the SLU-SVP Housing Project**

Community-building

The housing cooperative is unique, in the sense that unlike other shelter programs, SLU-SVP did not only build roofs. It has built a community with strong bonds and a cooperative spirit.

** This section is based on an article, "A village built by a cooperative", by Maurice Malanes, Philippine News and Features, published by *The Sunday Chronicle*, March 17, 1996. Mr. Malanes is currently a staff member of Tebtebba Foundation.

The community bond is deeply rooted in the *bayanihan* (cooperative self-help) principle which the SLU-SVP stressed at the very beginning. Through what they call "sweat equity", the cooperative's pioneering members, many of them bringing their families along, would take part each Sunday in site development such as building roads, digging, drainage and laying down culverts. They even dug up and constructed the septic tanks through "sweat equity".

Attorney Corpuz, one-time cooperative president explains:

"*Bayanihan* is a principle of self-help which is of a rural value but which the cooperative believes can have an urban application. It's being cultivated as a primary value in the newly emerging community which has been motivated by sound principles, namely,

(a) through *bayanihan* work, the future awardees would be evolving a real community, not a mere collectivity, and
(b) through bayanihan work, they would be lightening each other's burden of paying a higher cost of development.

The *bayanihan* sweat equity enabled the first awardees to pay a minimal monthly amortization of as low as P115 to P116. "The amount was so small that I would even forget to pay it because my water and electricity bills were even bigger," says Corpuz.

The Bakakeng housing awardees were lucky to get their lots at almost giveaway prices from CICM priests who had bought wide tracts of land in the area for a seminary. The awardees were also able to get grants and soft loans from Catholic-based funders in Europe.

But SLU-SVP liaison officer Renato Fernandez says outside funding was not the key factor behind the success of the housing program. "The key factor is our having internalized the principles of cooperativism," he notes. He cites many "fly-by-night" cooperatives that have failed although they received multi-million-peso seed funds from government lending institutions.

The *bayanihan* spirit and community bonding can be seen in every aspect of the *barangay*'s life, in disaster situations or during festivals. In the aftermath of a killer quake in 1990, for example, the community moved as one in rebuilding damaged homes. Attorney Corpuz writes:

"The pioneers narrate how they had to be united to be able to meet emergency cases. When an intruder was sighted loitering in the area, one would immediately make the corresponding signal, like striking an iron post to produce the warning sound, so that almost simultaneously, everyone came out to chase and apprehend the intruder."

One source of pride for the Bakakeng residents is that they helped fulfill the dream of Fr. Luc Colla, a Belgian CICM priest assigned to the area, of putting up a chapel. While they humbly call what they built a chapel, it actually looks like an imposing cathedral. They built it through collective sweat equity and by raising funds for it through raffles.

In no time, Bakakeng became a new *barangay* with two sets of officers: the cooperative's board of directors and the *barangay* council. It also became a full-fledged Catholic parish.

Community development

In the process of building their shelter, the members of the SLU-SVP Housing Cooperative accomplished projects that would enhance the holistic development of the emerging community. They planted trees around the village, implemented a continuing education program among officers and members, conducted seminars and workshops for women and youth sectors of the community, and sent members to participate in various cooperative housing seminars both within the country and abroad (Alterplan, undated:8).

To respond to the various needs of the community, the cooperative has transformed itself into a multi-purpose cooperative. It has branched out into the establishment of credit, consumer and transport operations, thereby making cooperativism a virtual way of life for the members (Alterplan, undated: 9).

Improving the quality of life through self-development

The impact of the cooperative on the members' lives is evident. Many former ordinary teachers and employees at SLU have become lawyers, or masteral and doctorate degree holders. Some lawyers have become judges, and others have succeeded in business. "Since they no longer have to worry about high rentals, they can now focus on their self-improvement," explains Attorney Corpuz.

4. DESCRIPTION OF THE INSTITUTION RESPONSIBLE AND ITS ORGANIZATIONAL ASPECTS

The SLU-SVP Housing Cooperative was born out of the union of the dreams of two institutions, namely Saint Louis University and Saint Vincent Parish. Sometime between 1967 and 1971, as Fr. Zwaenoepoel, CICM, then President of SLU, was figuring out what he could do to help his employees, Fr. Paul Bohlen, CICM, was likewise concerned about the plight of his parishioners at the lagoon area. During the summer period of 1967, SLU opened two programs: a Seminar-Workshop on Cooperatives and Community Development, and a college course entitled "Town and Country

Planning"(unpublished report by the SLU-SVP Housing Cooperative).

As a result of the seminars and workshops, some participants who were employees of SLU and parishioners of SVP gathered to look into the possibility of operationalizing a housing cooperative. Six committees were created to prepare the various studies needed to work on the project. M + R (Philippines) Foundation, Inc., then based in SLU, was called upon to aid the group, to study the administrative, technical, organizational, educational and financial aspects of the undertaking. This initial group became the coordinating committee.

To facilitate the organization and registration of the housing cooperative, the coordinating body invited a representative of the Bureau of Cooperative Development Authority (BCOD) to sit in with them. A pre-membership seminar was held. Then a general assembly was organized to elect the first Board of Directors. On February 10, 1971, the SLU-SVP Housing Cooperative, Inc. came into being (Corpuz, undated:56).

At present, the cooperative has transformed itself into a multi-purpose cooperative, with credit, transport and consumer components. The leadership is composed of professionals: lawyers, teachers and clerks of SLU and SVP.

5. PROBLEMS OR OBSTACLES ENCOUNTERED AND HOW THEY WERE OVERCOME

The housing cooperative encountered a few problems in the course of implementing its plans and realizing its dreams. There was the problem of inflation, and consequently, the increase in the price of construction supplies, which almost halted the implementation of Phase IV of the project. The cooperative solved this problem by obtaining soft loans from local as well as foreign lending agencies.

Then, there was also the problem of scarcity of land for expansion. After the completion of Phase IV, around 100 applicants hoped and prayed that they too would be awarded a house and lot. They continued to attend *bayanihan* works and joined in the educational and socio-cultural activities of the cooperative. But because they were aware of the fact that there was no more land on which to build more houses, many of them were losing hope. Even some members of the board were contemplating putting an end to the housing project, and dissolving the cooperative. But the majority of them opposed the idea. With great concern, the Board of Directors thought of remedies. They decided to venture into an entirely new, practically self-help scheme, to start a new phase financed by housing loans being offered by the government (PAG-IBIG).

Again, they succeeded in purchasing a two-hectare lot in Ambiong, La Trinidad, Benguet, with a loan from PAG-IBIG (SLU-SVP Cooperative Report, undated).

6. EFFECTS OF THE PRACTICE/INNOVATIVE EXPERIENCE

The experience has brought about tangible and intangible, and immediate as well as long-term effects on the cooperative members, their families and their dependents. The effects are summarized as follows:
(a) The housing project has built a community with strong bonds and a cooperative spirit. The value of cooperation is something that pioneers of the project will treasure and pass on to succeeding generations.
(b) Integrated community development: The residents of Bakakeng learned that building a roof over their heads was not the only key to social development. Hence, they ventured into credit, consumer and transport operations, skills training and seminars, and the like.
(c) Improvement in the overall quality of life: The ultimate result of the housing cooperative was an increase in the community's overall quality of life. Once the basic need for housing was fulfilled, the people were able to afford better food, pursue higher education and engage in leisure.

7. SUITABILITY AND POSSIBILITY FOR UPSCALING

The SLU-SVP Housing Cooperative has shown that with cooperation, perseverance and networking/linkages, the hitherto elusive dream of owning a house can be achieved – and it is teaching other people how this can be done.

The SLU-SVP has sustained its concern for the growing housing needs of the Cordillera Administrative Region. It is engaged in the continuing efforts to address the housing shortage. It also recognizes that its experience is a critical tool in helping the government address the human settlement problem (Alterplan, undated:10).

The SLU-SVP community has been very supportive and accommodating of other visiting cooperatives that participated in the study tours conducted by various non-governmental and governmental organizations. They have willingly accepted them into their homes during interviews and gladly entertain questions. From time to time, housing advocates from Canada, USA and Manila come to visit the community and study the SLU-SVP Housing Cooperative scheme.

8. SIGNIFICANCE FOR (AND IMPACT ON) POLICY-MAKING

The success of the SLU-SVP Housing Cooperative has inspired policy-makers tremendously. National and regional government and non-governmental institutions have tapped the cooperative's wealth of experience and know-how in addressing the human settlement problem. The officers of the cooperative have served as resource persons, consultants and advisers to housing bodies in the Philippines and abroad.

9. POSSIBILITY AND SCOPE OF TRANSFERRING TO OTHER COMMUNITIES OR COUNTRIES

The experience can be replicated by GOs and NGOs in other communities and countries provided the following basic requirements are met:
(a) Potential beneficiaries and partners should be organized and reminded, if not taught, of basic principles of cooperativism.
(b) The price of amortization for a land grant or sale (from private and public institutions) should be within the means of the beneficiaries.
(c) If it emphasizes the idea of partnership and cost-sharing, the project must target people with the capacity, no matter how minimal, to pay. This suggests that potential beneficiaries must be gainfully employed or at least have regular sources of income. The point to emphasize here is that the problem of housing should be seen within the broader context of fundamental policy concerns such as employment and alleviation of poverty.
(d) The practice of inter-agency linkages and networking for sharing of financial, technical and other resources should be emphasized.

References

1. Constantino, Letizia R., (1987) "The Housing Problem" in *Education Forum-Teacher's Assistance Program* (TAP), Vol. VI, SM 122, 15 October 1987.
2. Corpuz, Ruben A., *The Pioneers: A Brief History of The Beginning*. (leaflet, undated)
3. Cruz, Gladys; Gacad, Marie; Hamada, Lourdes; Rovillos, Raymundo; and Salinas, Florence; (1983) *Urbanization In Medium Sized Towns In Third World Countries: A Comparative Study Of The Philippines, Thailand and Kenya: A Report On Baguio City, Philippines*, Cordillera Studies Center, U.P. College in Baguio, March 1993.
4. Malanes, Maurice, (1996) "Barangay Bakakeng: Housing Miracle in Baguio City" in *The Sunday Chronicle*, March 17, 1996.
5. *The Forces That Shape The SLU-SVP Experience*. (photocopy)

6.

Housing co-operatives in Uruguay

1. GENERAL INFORMATION

1.1 Title of practice or experience

Housing co-operatives in Uruguay

1.2 Category of practice/experience and brief description

The Uruguayan Co-operativist Centre (CCU) has been working for 30 years implementing innovative ways to solve the housing shortage in the country, particularly for the low-income bracket of the population, channelling low-cost State loans and helping communities organise as co-operatives to solve the problem collectively and through self-help, self-building organisation of the work.

1.3 Name of person or institution responsible for the practice or experience

The Uruguayan Co-operativist Centre (CCU)

1.4 Name and position of key or relevant persons or officials involved

Sr. Juan José Sarachu

1.5 Details of institution

    (a) Address: Eduardo Victor Haedo 2252, C.P. 11200, Montevideo, Uruguay 11200
    (b) Telephone: ++ (598) (2) 400 9066, 401 2541
    (c) Fax: ++ (598) (2) 400 6735
    (d) E-Mail: ccu@chasque.apc.org

1.6 Name of person and/or institution conducting the research

Cristina Canoura

1.7 Details of research person/institution

(a) Address: Quijote 2523/1002, Montevideo, Uruguay
(b) Telephone: ++ (598) (2) 480 7344
(c) Fax: ++ (598) (2) 401 9222
(d) E-Mail: ccanoura@chasque.apc.org

2. THE PROBLEM OR SITUATION BEING ADDRESSED BY THE PRACTICE/INNOVATIVE EXPERIENCE

As a result of the economic crisis of the sixties, home-building had dropped in 1963 to half the 1956 figure. Housing loans from the State-owned mortgage bank (Banco Hipotecario del Uruguay – BHU) had dropped from 10 billion pesos in 1955-58 to only 350 million in 1968. There was an estimated shortage of over 100,000 houses, in a country of less than three million inhabitants.

3. DESCRIPTION OF THE PRACTICE/INNOVATIVE EXPERIENCE AND ITS MAIN FEATURES

In 1965, a group of members of the CCU (the Uruguayan Co-operativist Centre, an institution promoting the development of agrarian and credit co-operatives since 1961) decided to create a housing section within the organisation. Three pilot projects were set up in the towns of Isla Mala, Fray Bentos and Salto.

From 1965, the CCU created an interdisciplinary team to research, draw up and develop co-operative housing programmes aimed at satisfying the housing needs of low-income brackets of the population, although not exclusively for them, and facilitating access to social credits.

The main objective was to achieve efficient administrative management of the co-operative undertaking by training its members to plan, make suitable decisions, control and evaluate management.

Apart from the actual building of homes, the mutual aid mode implies taking on business management, requests for services – electricity, water, drainage, telephones – and the establishment of links with others who are working towards similar goals.

Another objective deals with consolidating the group, strengthening links between the members and establishing fluid relations with the surrounding neighbourhood and interaction with the popular movement.

Towards this end, the CCU accompanies the group from when it is set up through the land-buying negotiations and legal registration, the loan request transaction, the completion of works, control of finances, internal consolidation, the awarding of homes and group preparation for living together and the organisation of complementary services. In order to regulate operations, the co-operative, backed by the technical advisors, draws up and approves both a contract and regulations for internal operations.

This is no small challenge. True business organisation is needed to complete the work within a set deadline (of between 18 and 30 months), personnel must be contracted and supervised, and resources administered. When the work is completed, the financial panorama has to be restructured in order to meet payment of the BHU loan and cover other types of needs arising from cohabitation.

One of the most difficult obstacles faced by advisory institute staff is to make the members understand that once the home is completed, they are only the user of the premises and not the proprietor of the real estate.

In fact, the User System, created by law No. 13,728, introduces a novel conception of the issue of occupation and renting of housing, maintaining this as an asset for use and not commercial gain.

The co-operative awards its members a home – exempt by law from the payment of all property tax – after signing a usufruct agreement, whereby it grants the co-operative member the right to reside in this home with his/her family for an unlimited time as long as they fulfil the obligations established in the Housing Law and respect the other statutory norms and internal regulations.

The co-operative is the proprietor of the homes. The users are members of the co-operative and are, collectively, its owners, meaning they can neither sublet nor cede the deeds of the home except in cases of marital disintegration or the death of the title holder. In the case of sudden unemployment, illness or any other misfortune which affects the member's ability to pay, the debt generated on the quotas must be directly negotiated with the co-operative. The law itself establishes the creation of an Assistance Fund, which the member can fall back on if necessary.

Over the last 30 years, the CCU backed half of all housing co-operatives of different sorts, promoted the law for housing co-operatives, and, as well as creating the Single Federation of Housing by Mutual Aid (FUCVAM), stimulated the creation of the Housing Co-operatives Federation (FECOVI), which draws together users of the savings and loans mode. By 1989 alone, it had handled loans worth $90 million with the BHU.

According to Teresa Buroni, present co-ordinator of the advisory body's Unit of the Planning and Execution of Services in the Housing Area, the CCU receives 9% of the total cost of the co-operative.

The first housing co-operative was started in Isla Mala, later renamed Estación 25 de Mayo, a small town of 1,700 inhabitants, mainly rural workers (who have to be away from home for long periods) and their families.

Work was started in November 1968, with an initial group of 28 families. Isla Mala was practically a town of female-headed households as the men worked on the land during the week. Given this situation, the CCU technicians started a series of organisational experiments and the statutes were drawn up.

With a block-making machine donated by the Centre, work could continue moving ahead even though there was no money to pay for materials. The need for fundraising led members of the management commission to organise a lottery and sell chocolates and a local savoury snack. The money raised was used to buy cement to make the blocks, which were cast during the week. At the same time, this experiment was copied in Salto for 42 railway workers' families and in Fray Bentos with 25 municipal workers' families.

According to Daysi Solari, the only social worker participating in this experiment, the women played a fundamental role in making the roof tiles and they carried out most of the building work.

The chocolate-selling proved to be the catalyst for future organisation. The co-operative members often bemoaned the lack of interior fittings and decorations for their new homes. The only skill they could offer in order to earn even a meagre income was washing clothes for the nearby dairy establishments. Consequently, the women later organised themselves into a co-operative to sell and export their handicrafts.

The completion of the works in the 25 de Mayo Co-operative showed the experience to be not only valid but also possible. FUCVAM was founded during its inauguration, on May 25, 1970.

The Salto Mutual Aid Housing Co-operative (COSVAM), with 42 homes, and Exodo de Artigas, in Fray Bentos, with 25 (built through an agreement between the CCU, the National Institute of Economic Housing (INVE), IDB and the Municipal Council of Rio Negro), were completed in 1971.

The National Housing Law (No. 13,728) was approved in 1968, through the efforts of deputy and architect Juan Pablo Terra. The Law included a special chapter on housing co-operatives – drawn up with CCU advice – under which new legal modes and mechanisms were created to promote construction of these.

Similarly, the foundation of FUCVAM was a fundamental factor in the consolidation of the mutual aid co-operatives as a social force, rapidly being transformed into one of the most powerful social movements in contemporary national history.

From the beginning, the federation made important achievements which contributed to the expansion of the co-operative movement. Greater and speedier availability of land and the acceleration of administrative procedures for approving legal status, were amongst its "conquests".

These were the other merits of law No. 13,728:
(a) unification of all the public financing mechanisms aimed at socially conscious housing;
(b) establishment of the need to plan housing production in Five-Year Plans and annual adjustments;
(c) creation of the National Housing Department (DINAVI) with responsibilities for planning, promotion, financing, evaluation and supervision of the actions of bodies operating in the housing field along with everything pertaining to fulfilment of the law;
(d) creation of a DINAVI assessment commission made up of 14 members representing all sectors with direct interests to operate both during the planning stages and in the supervision of the Plan;
(e) establishment of the definition of a "housing minimum" which must be fulfilled by all housing built in the nation;
(f) confirmation of the need to offer subsidies allowing access to housing, taking into account the composition of the family nucleus without excessively affecting income;
(g) creation of the National Housing Fund through the imposition of a 2% income tax (1% contributed by the employer and 1% by the Social Security Entities) aiming to subsidise housing for the lower-income bracket;
(h) creation of a readjustment mechanism for loan financing guaranteeing the return in real values of the amounts awarded and impeding the liquidation of the Fund, as had occurred previously as a consequence of inflation. Thus, a unit was formulated which was index-linked to the Average Index of Wages, with the production of this index being the responsibility of the Statistics and Census Office. On September 1, 1968, the value of the Readjustable Unit (UR) was set at $1,000, to be readjusted annually every September 1. At the same time, a safeguard was built in for debtors. In the case of family incomes not keeping pace with the Average Index of

Wages, the families could choose either a longer payment period or complementary subsidies;
(i) installation of new mechanisms and legal practices for access to housing such as co-operatives, social funds and private promotion; and
(j) initiation of the Technical Assistance Institutes, made up of non-profit-making multidisciplinary teams whose commitment was to providing co-operative education and technical assistance to the co-operatives and social funds.

Law No. 13,728 dictated precise norms for the housing co-operatives:
(a) The housing co-operatives are companies ruled by the co-operative principles. Their main objective is to provide suitable and stable housing to the associates, through their own efforts, mutual aid, direct administration or through contracts with third parties, along with offering complementary services to housing.
(b) The bodies ruling over them are the General Assembly, the Fiscal Commission and the Co-operatives Development Commission.

Housing co-operatives are classified according to various criteria:
(a) The Co-operative Housing Units are groups of homes which can have between 10 and 200 partners. The Parent Co-operatives, meanwhile, can have between 20 and 1,000 members without housing awarded, having affiliates whose character is that of the co-operative units, being ruled by the same dispositions as them.
(b) Affiliation can be open or restricted to the members of a neighbourhood, trade union or workplace.
(c) The co-operativists contribute in the form of prior savings or with work during construction.
(d) The co-operative can either change over to a regime of horizontal property once construction is completed or once the debt is settled, or continue indefinitely as a co-operative. In the latter case, the co-operative continues to be the proprietor of the housing. The usufructuary right of each member to his/her housing unit is transmitted by inheritance and can be ceded according to the legal dispositions in force.

The combination of all these variables led to 20 different types of co-operatives. The CCU has prioritised the mutual aid co-operatives for its advice where the members are users and not proprietors of their homes, a mode assumed for the most part by the salaried sectors of low to middle income. A large percentage of the middle-income bands advised by the CCU opted to be users, even though they had made their contributions in cash and had considered other options to be valid as long as they respond to co-operative principles.

Shortly after the Housing Law was passed, there was a co-operativist "boom". Following the experiences in Isla Mala, Salto and Fray Bentos, between 1970 and 1976, the CCU advised 24 housing groups across the country, including the five inter-co-operative boards of Montevideo which involved almost 1,200 families, the parent co-operatives from the textile trade union and the first territorial or neighbourhood ones. During the same period in Paysandu, the first four housing nuclei of the Sanducera (meaning "from Paysandu") Housing Co-operative (COVISAN) were built – the fifth was to be completed in 1978 – along with the first Municipal kind. In the space of seven years, 217 homes were built in this department.

During this stage – which coincided with the darkest years of the military dictatorship – the co-operative organisation showed its potential as a channel for participation not only in the housing area but also in crafts and production. These experiences became genuine "islands of freedom", allowing for the channelling of collective participation from daily life, neighbourhood and community ambits.

4. DESCRIPTION OF THE INSTITUTION RESPONSIBLE AND ITS ORGANISATIONAL ASPECTS

The CCU technical teams

Architects, promoters, social workers, lawyers and accountants – supported by a hardworking team of assistants and secretaries – form the technical team which works on the consolidation of the housing co-operatives in their different forms.

From within the institution and throughout the process until the home is inhabited, they are the immediate referees in the advisory process. They are turned to by co-operativists seeking resolution of the numerous doubts and inconveniences which present themselves over the years. They also bear the brunt of the barrage of moans, complaints and criticisms.

One of the basic concerns which have guided the actions of the CCU since its inception has been to make the technicians aware that their priority function is to effect the active participation of the co-operative group not only towards satisfying its basic needs but also to consolidate self-management and efficient organisation.

On this front, they are conscious that training in business management and co-operation will enable the people they advise to undertake new associated projects that have the potential of improving their quality of life.

Accounting and Legal departments

The Accounting Department, made up of four women and one man, specifically advises treasurers and fiscal managers in the first stage of transactions for the co-operative and on the administration mechanisms of the funds collected. This means that, from the outset, they are able to save on purchases and control spending.

Once the works are underway, the CCU accounting experts work alongside the treasurers, administrators and Work Commission which they teach how to calculate hours.

Often with no training in company management, those co-operativists elected to carry out this function must suddenly confront the management of large sums of money for purchases, payment of salaries, contracting of personnel, balances, set deadlines and current accounts. They have to be taught how to organise the paperwork, how to work with the banks, to decide whether cash deposits or the storing of materials is more profitable, not forgetting the reserves they must maintain for meeting set commitments, like social contributions. All the documentation is processed in the CCU, where they close the balances and cash up.

In the post-construction stage, the same work is continued in trying to maintain consciousness of the need to not sever connections with administrative responsibility for the co-operative as the co-operativists still have to pay the likes of the bank and for the water, and take charge of maintenance and the assistance funds – which help the co-operative avoid going into debt when one member cannot pay his or her quota. A considerable number of housing complexes remain linked to the CCU in this area through specific contracts for advisory work.

In the Legal Department, lawyer Uruguay Ortiz is almost a co-operative "constitutionalist". In fact, one of his main tasks is to advise on and guide the fulfilment of the statute – a constitution which includes the norms ruling the actions of the co-operative – pointing out which is the domain of the Directing Council and the various commissions, and the powers of the General Assembly.

Furthermore, members of the Legal Department accompany the management in acquisition of the land and loan before the competent bodies, which, according to Ortiz, generally becomes a rite "where the entire bureaucracy becomes involved in a transaction which goes to and fro from one office to another".

The most serious problems they handle include difficult relations between members arising from such causes as drunkenness, aggression – situations which have been experienced and are being reported more frequently – sexual harassment and non-fulfilment of work obligations.

In these cases, stresses Ortiz, it is essential that the co-operativists recognise the sanctions the wrongdoers expose themselves to, and the situations in which a warning, suspension or exclusion is applied.

Excluding a member – an issue which is in general decided in the Assembly – is always a traumatic matter. Many co-operativists opt to abstain from the vote, understanding that their decision could cut off that person's opportunity to have his/her own home. This sanction is reserved for serious cases, including failure to fulfil obligations with the co-operative, neglect of management, undue appropriation of funds, encouraging fights which "come to blows" and "duly proven" sexual harassment.

The issue of non-fulfilment of contracts and subcontracts for works made with specialist personnel or builder's yards is another of the big responsibilities assigned to the CCU Legal Department.

Social workers: promoters, educators and technical advisors

In Montevideo and the interior of the country, a team of social workers makes up the CCU Socio-educational Area, previously known as the Housing Promotion Sector.

Depending on the circumstances, this team also incorporates other technicians like a social communicator, a teacher and, more sporadically, social psychologists, while always maintaining a stable group of social workers and promoters.

Within the CCU, the social workers have been enjoying the same functional categorisation as other professionals like architects, lawyers and accountants, which for them shows "a valuing of our professional task which in some way has been modifying the known devalued image of social work, the origin of which stems from the university academic conceptions and structures themselves" and which is also suffered by other professions with a high index of female participation.

The CCU works with co-operative groups from the salaried sectors, made up of between 30 and 50 families with an average size of four people, predominantly the type of nuclear family with an income of between $400 and $800 per month. With a middle to low educational and economic level, this sector of the population often is employed in unstable paid work, often of a seasonal nature or working in several jobs.

The co-operative for them is not a lifestyle choice, but a way, and probably the only one, to resolve their housing problem. The dream of having their own home is practically the only common denominator among the applicants.

Few know the co-operativist philosophy and only some have acquired organisational experience in union campaigning or parish groups. Among the working-class sectors, especially, there is scarce contact with public administration, which makes the process of their transformation into valid negotiators with the authorities and state hierarchies more difficult.

The social workers are conscious that this transition must be carried out. Their task is to smooth the way for this, providing the co-operativists with the instruments to strengthen and train themselves.

Fundamentally, in the construction stage, the human relations established between the co-operativists are conflictive, not only because of the socio-economic difficulties of the situation but also because of the physical and emotional burden of dividing time between the demands of construction itself, the extensive dedication to work outside, the complex transferral to the co-operative and mutual aid participation.

On another front, intra-family links are weakened on some occasions, leading even to conflict and marriage break-ups due to the demands of co-operativist work and campaigning. One of the consequences of this is a fall in mutual aid yield levels.

According to the social workers, a strong sense of individualism, the absence of practice in working as a group, the lack of alternative collective solutions to deal with the various problems of daily life, along with the economic impossibility faced by many family nuclei in meeting mortgage payments on the loan once construction is completed, are issues which crop up repeatedly amongst participants in projects assessed by the CCU.

"In the co-operatives, the social workers play the multiple role of promoters, educators and technical advisors. Our professional action is built on three basic pillars, which are the active protagonism of the end users, the resolution of the basic need through interdisciplinary technical support and self-management," they explain.

Active protagonism of the participants is the fundamental element aimed at by the technical advisory team. To achieve this, they use suitable methods for the group to develop self-knowledge, identify its needs and resources and visualise the socio-political context in which it is inserted. It is also important to stimulate the group's capacity to set objectives and find suitable solutions for any problems which may crop up.

Training, organisation and the extension of private and individual spaces of power or decision-making into collective ambits are the basic elements in developing the self-management process.

Beyond the co-operativist members knowing their rights and obligations, and the powers of the General Assembly, the operational mechanisms of the

Directing Council, the Fiscal, Development or Electoral commissions, or the Works and Labour sub-commissions, "it is necessary that they get practical experience to understand and learn about collective work relations. Only then will they be able to develop an awareness of the possibilities presented by their own strengths, sometimes positive, sometimes negative, but which make it possible for them to confront the difficulties which will crop up," stress the social workers.

In practice, the social workers participate in the co-operative meetings advising the Directing Council and the Works Sub-commission, in charge of monitoring the performance of the mutual aid workforce. They also offer technical help to the Fiscal and Development commissions and supervise preparations for the General Assemblies.

Architects

"We are exactly on the boundary between what the Architecture Faculty prepares theoretically and the real demands posed by mutual aid," says architect Danilo Azpiroz – who has worked with the CCU on and off since 1970 – in defining the essence of a professional function which had to be adapted to a mode of construction with its own peculiarities.

Co-operativists are not like the traditional clients who contract an architect to design and plan the house of their dreams. Nor are they the classic entrepreneurs who engage the services of these professionals to carry out commercial projects. However, they need to incorporate some of the characteristics of both to be able to take hold of the reins of an experience which belongs to them.

One of the first barriers which must be breached is learning the new language of symbols used on plans. Few people are generally able to make much sense of these plans, which show an image of what their house will be like on a scale that is difficult to transfer to reality, with its esoteric sections, heights and dimensions.

5. PROBLEMS OR OBSTACLES ENCOUNTERED AND HOW THEY WERE OVERCOME

At the beginning of the 1970s, there were already more than 10,000 families in mutual aid co-operatives, which managed to build some 8,000 units. And several advantages fed the explosion of this mode. These included the lower cost and better quality of their homes compared to those produced both by the State – until then through INVE – and by the private companies. The BHU would lend around 90% of the value of the housing project and the remaining percentage would be contributed by the members in the form of obligatory mutual aid. This implied 21 hours' work a week, the cost of which was calculated on the basis of a study on the yield of non-qualified workers with no previous experience. In the interior of the country, the hours of work offered by the nuclear family were – and continue to be – higher than the contribution of members in the capital, in some cases exceeding 24 hours per week.

The first co-operative groups were created in the union ambit – textile, printing, metallurgical, transport workers – but they later began to crop up in neighbourhood or territorial bases. In Montevideo, three large parent groups were set up, two by textile and railway workers (COVIMT and COVICAFE respectively) and the other being the territorial Nueva Esperanza (COVINE).

At that time, most of the land available to the co-operatives was in outlying or suburban zones, with poor service infrastructure, including even education and supplies. This, in the majority of cases, meant extending the water, electricity, drainage and telephone networks in a self-managed manner or in association with the State entities.

The creation of a Supply Centre allowed for mass purchasing of materials by the hundreds of construction co-operatives, considerably reducing costs. Similarly, the installation of a prefabrication plant contributed to making the production of these types of elements more technical and flexible.

In 1975, one of every two loans requested from the BHU for house-building came from the co-operative regime, either in mutual aid mode (more than two-thirds) or in the prior savings schemes.

Despite having been conceived as a means for the worse-off classes to realise their human and constitutional right to decent housing, the co-operative mode was not well received by various union, political and university sectors who saw mutual aid as contributing to the overexploitation of the working classes, who had to add hours of free work to their paid working hours. The use of unpaid workers would create unemployment amongst construction workers, who, in fact, were replaced by co-operative members, argued representatives of the Single Construction Workers Union (SUNCA).

Over the years, this view changed and many unions encouraged the creation of co-operatives amongst their members. The first of these sprang from the textile workers and was called COVIMT.

The architect, Miguel Cecilio, both technical advisor and member of COVIMT, says the size of the project (30 homes) represented the ideal typology. "For above this quantity, construction becomes complicated for the non-expert workforce," he says.

Despite this, from 1973, mutual aid co-operativism moved on from small groups to large inter-co-operative complexes or "boards", of which five were built between 1973 and 1976, with a total of 1,758 homes.

According to Cecilio, it was not only the scarcity of land suitable for the construction of small groups which led to the move to join various co-operatives together in the same space but also that at that time, DINAVI "was up against large complexes of private promoters and could not compete on a small scale".

The prefabrication techniques oiled the way to a much larger scale of construction, rationalising the labour of an inexperienced workforce. The architectural design incorporated duplex houses, built on different levels, along with spaces for a community room, child-care centre, shops and social services.

The team of CCU technicians, made up originally of some 12 people, increased five-fold in size in order to keep up with monitoring of the boards.

They were dealing with hundreds of people working, and coming from different experiences and situations in a very complex historical context. Everything was mixed up: contract specialist workers were being helped by inexperienced co-operativists, who were in fact their employers. The site supervisors, meanwhile, wanted to work as they did on traditional building sites, but had to adjust themselves to completely different working styles and rhythms.

The qualitative jump from traditional co-operativist construction to a larger scale put to the test not only the cohabitation and organisational capacity of thousands of inexperienced people but also the professionals who advised them, who rapidly had to modify the architectural prototypes to adapt them to the new dimensions and larger sites. In Montevideo, four of the five inter-co-operative boards were built at the same time, with thousands of people working simultaneously in self-construction.

Even today, Miguel Cecilio maintains that the construction was only completed due to "the tenacity and conviction that this could really be done". In the case of Board 1, however, the original deadline of 18 months was finally extended to 30.

"No one knew anyone else in a group of 1,000. Few felt taken up by the final objective. This is the difference between the mass and craftsmanlike approaches," says Cecilio.

A nursery, a public school and a health centre were built by the co-operative as part of the services offered to the neighbourhood. A social and sporting club, which included activities like baby football, bowls, yoga, drawing classes, a library and a meeting venue for senior citizens, was also established.

To satisfy the demands of an area which saw its population multiply in a short period of time, the public transport system improved its services, increasing the number of lines and frequencies of buses. Similarly, a neighbourhood market was installed, the co-operatives opened a road to a nearby rubbish dump, and with the assistance of the neighbourhood commission, the road lighting was extended.

For collective decision-making, each of the five co-operatives operated with a Directors Council which met once a week. Once a month, these met in a plenary session. An Executive Board, made up of a delegate from each co-operative, carried out the decisions of the plenary.

However, the five co-operatives in general have had a membership turnover of around 40%. The veterans claim "the new ones are only interested in resolving the problem of getting a roof over their heads" and say that the "CCU must continue the co-operativist training courses it gave at the beginning." The new members do not always integrate into co-operative life and, in most cases, feel that if they keep their quotas up to date, then they have met their obligations.

This perception is a generalisation which could apply to nearly all the co-operative variants, not only mutual aid. As far back as 1985, the late architect, Juan Pablo Terra, evaluated mutual aid, saying once the preparation and construction phase of the co-operative was over, the intensity of participation fell visibly. Its continuity depended "on the existence and operation of common services and activities, on the physical conformation of the complex and on the social strata of its members, as apparently integration into neighbourly life is greater in the lower strata than amongst the middle class".

State and institutional factors

In mid-1974, more than 70% of investments in the Housing Plan had been aimed towards the public system of which 57% corresponded to co-operatives, a little over 20% to mutual aid co-operatives and the rest to the savings and loans mode.

Under the military government (1973-1985), State stimulation of the co-operatives diminished notably. In the 1974-76 period, while investment in housing was low (less than 3% of Gross Domestic Product or GDP), rents increased, producing a profitability of 15.5%, a percentage of almost speculative proportions. Concomitantly, the progressive implementation of new economic policies with restrictive consequences on loans for housing contributed to a worsening housing situation.

Two decrees from 1975 established that DINAVI should be the body charged with giving final approval to loans, in order to plan the allocation of the scarce resources available. In practice, this meant a large reduction in loans to co-operatives. New loans to co-operatives fell and interest rates on existing ones increased from 2% to 4%.

In 1977, under law No. 14,666, the BHU's role in relation to housing was widened. From then on, its hitherto exclusively financial role expanded to encompass administration, recovery, building, selling, planning, executing, evaluating and even social education. Through legislation, the social criteria guiding the National Housing Plan were substituted by banking profitability criteria.

In fact, during this period, the BHU had to take charge of the design of the housing programmes, and of operational regulation of the various mechanisms along with the reception, evaluation, approval and financial supervision of the projects. Furthermore, it had to advise the Executive Power on issues relating to the provision of co-operative and social education to the housing groups.

On July 25, 1979, the BHU approved service resolution No. 7,000, an internal regulation disposition by which it was made possible for those co-operatives which had had their legal status approved to get access to loans.

However, in accordance with the restrictive policy on the co-operative system of the time, this service resolution limited the number of homes to be built to 50 per housing complex from 200 previously. That same year, the BHU imposed even harsher credit conditions on loans for housing, increasing interest rates on these from 4% to 5%. The amount of the loan would reach up to 85% of the rating value of the programme and the remaining 15% would be financed by previous savings (5%) and a minimum contribution of mutual aid labour equal to 10%, with possibilities of this reaching 12%.

With these conditions, the brakes were applied on access to credit benefits for housing for 40% of the population in the lowest income bracket, ironically the very group the system was originally aimed at.

Conversely, in 1978-79, an increase was seen in private promotion in the construction of housing units to the detriment of the co-operatives. Thus, the co-operative mode, which in the preceding nine years had represented 40% of the total number of houses built, saw this figure dwindle to little more than 10%. Meanwhile, the private promoters almost doubled their participation, from less than 30% in the 1969-1977 period to 59% in 1978 and 53% in 1979.

In the three-year period from 1980 to 1982, the co-operativist mode as a solution to the housing problem continued to shrink and its participation in the total number of new houses built was lower than 5%. In 1982, it represented barely 2.3% of the total investment. In 1983, 35% of the population of Montevideo and more than 40% of the country's total population had no access to any of the BHU credit lines.

In December 1983, the Executive Power sent the State Council a message and a bill proposing that the homes making up the mutual aid co-operative complexes be passed over to "the regime of individual and exclusive property", leading to the rejection of large sectors linked to co-operativism. In a campaign for a plebiscite to abolish the law, more than half a million signatures were collected in just a few hours. The decree was repealed in 1986.

At the end of the dictatorship, in 1984, there was a stock of 800,000 houses in the country of which 40,000 were unoccupied and 66,000 were summer homes. Out of the total, 104,600 were in a state of serious deterioration and a further 14,000 were in slum conditions or in ruins. The First Five-Year Plan (1985) aimed to prioritise sectors with an income lower than three minimum salaries. Encouragement of the co-operatives, social funds and self-build schemes was also announced.

In order to respond to the difficult situation of debtors, an agreement was made granting the possibility of extending the mortgage repayment deadline, coupled with a reduction of interest rates and the granting of supplementary subsidies. The construction of 68,000 homes was planned, with the private sector expected to build a further 54,000 with its own resources.

According to data from the BHU, 904 homes were built in the period with 4% of the total investment of the institution.

In 1988, requests for loans were allowed from co-operatives having legal status since before 1986. Thus, 138 new co-operatives with 3,800 members applied, 75% of them mutual aid, mostly of proprietors, as the BHU itself said users would not get loans.

Of the total number of co-operative homes built in the 1969-1992 period, 63.3% were built in the first eight years to 1976. The corresponding figure from 1977-1984 was 23.6%, and in the 1985-1989 period, barely 6.3% of the total were built.

In 1994, the Ministry of Housing, Territorial Ordering and the Environment was created and was given exclusive responsibility for the planning, execution, supervision and control of housing policy. At the same time, the National Housing Law was modified. All articles referring to subsidies were repealed, and this area would in future be defined by the Five-Year Plan and executed by the Ministry of Housing and not by the BHU.

In this period, new subsidised housing started to be built – including the so-called Basic Unit for Development aimed at the low-income families – which no longer had to conform to the previously considered minimum levels of quality and size.

Meanwhile, the Movement for the Eradication of Unhealthy Rural Housing (MEVIR) got a strong boost. Although it did not adopt the co-operative mode, it built more than 5,000 homes by mutual aid.

Between 1990 and 1995, the BHU recovered its financial position, no longer only attending to the lower-resource sectors. Half of the 23,500 planned loans were for the purchase of used housing and not for the construction of new units.

MVOTMA, meanwhile, only completed 22% of the 31,000 homes it should have built in accordance with the 1990-95 Plan, due mainly to the design and operation of the Plan. Thus, at the end of the period, as a corollary of this failure, resources were once again assigned to the co-operatives.

For the 1995-1999 Plan, MVOTMA estimated demand to be at 80,000 homes of which 30,000 corresponded to the low-income sectors. Of the 28,161 homes MVOTMA expected to hand over in this period, only 7,135 are really new. Only 300 of them are co-operative. Another 3,029 housing co-operatives initiated in the previous five years are expected to be completed before the year 2000.

"Shell" projects

At the beginning of the nineties, the CCU was faced with a new situation that put to the test its resourcefulness and improvisational capabilities. The popular sectors, natural "clients" of co-operativism by mutual aid, were notably pauperised and unable to gain access to housing with the traditionally promoted architectural characteristics. It was necessary to "invent" new typologies which would permit a reduction in costs and mutual aid time, explained Teresa Buroni.

Under an agreement with the Ministry of Housing and the Montevideo Municipal Authority (IMM) and with external funding, the CCU began to build the so-called "shell" projects, and wood was incorporated in the structure of the evolutionary homes. Thus, a "minimum" home was conceived, a "shell" with outer walls and a roof suited to backward extension, which was aimed at sectors with low family income and no savings capacity. The reduction in costs was achieved through interior terminations and a lower work input in time, and at the expense of the equipping of exterior spaces.

The external "shell" – walls and roof – is the same as that historically built by the co-operatives. Improvements must be carried out in a second stage in terms of floors, bathroom and kitchen tiling, and interior doors. Finally, non-essential paths are laid, equipment installed and community constructions built.

"This product is a highly valid and incomparable alternative from the architectural and social point of view in relation to the evolutionary modules built by the Ministry of Housing. It costs 1,150 UR, with nearly 60 square metres of construction, while the basic unit built by MVOTMA measures 30 metres," says Buroni.

For Buroni, the experience, which was originated by Martinez Reina, revealed to a certain degree the articulating role played by the CCU in striking a balance between the popular movement, the needs of the people and the

State. "With the 1,000 UR the State has for each Basic Unit for Development, something better could be done incorporating mutual aid," she says.

The COVIHON 3 and CIVITRIVIC co-operatives, completed in 1997, are examples of both construction systems.

6. EFFECTS OF THE PRACTICE/INNOVATIVE EXPERIENCE

After 27 years of involvement in housing co-operativism, on May 24, 1997, FUCVAM reported that more than 10,000 families of the near 300 federated co-operatives had benefited from mutual aid co-operatives at a time when 37 co-operatives were in the building process and another 40 awaiting land.

The CCU offered advice to 68 of these, including the five inter-co-operative boards, which benefited 4,535 families. Paysandu and Montevideo were the departments with the greatest concentration of co-operatives advised by them, with 14 and 23 respectively, but the Centre also worked in Mercedes, Fray Bentos, Trinidad, San Jose, Pando, Canelones, Colonia, Tacuarembo, Florida, Salto and Minas.

7. SUITABILITY AND POSSIBILITY FOR UPSCALING

"[Changes in the international arena could mean] we will soon no longer have credit funds from abroad. In the national ambit, support for co-operatives has been increasingly restricted. Previously the building land was included in the loan and many sites were granted by DINAVI itself or the BHU. Now it is the co-operatives themselves who have to find it, which indirectly means more work for the CCU," says Teresa Buroni.

In her view, the challenge for the new millennium, on the technical front, relates to finding building systems which improve parameters of cost and construction time.

"Our traditional advisory role, in the terms we have worked with up until now, is tending to disappear in Uruguay. From hereon, a package will have to be put together covering the whole process from the funding and the obtaining of land to construction. We must have, on one side, land, and on another, access to forms of financing which do not depend exclusively on the Housing Ministry," says Buroni.

The appearance of the Private Pension Funds (AFAPs) on the national scene suggests, according to Buroni, the possibility of bringing investment into housing. If this were the case, the obtaining of loans would no longer be exclusively at the mercy of the political oscillations of the State institutions.

"We must start to motivate ourselves to readjust the institutional profile. This does not mean the CCU will become a loan financier but an institution with the capacity to direct these investments towards co-operatives," she concludes.

8. SIGNIFICANCE FOR (AND IMPACT ON) POLICY-MAKING

The concept of housing as a right and a public asset, and not as a market commodity, can be implemented in practice, even within the framework of a country with a liberal market orientation throughout the economy.

The building option of mutual aid co-operatives has had an impact on the socio-economic structure of the country and changed the urban physiognomy of the neighbourhoods where these co-operatives are found. They had the wisdom to employ architectural models and construction procedures that take advantage of skills passed down from one generation to the next while also using prefabricated elements – like the flooring and roofing tiles – which simplified the task and facilitated the incorporation of an inexperienced but enthusiastic workforce.

In nearly three decades of existence, hosts of parquet-layers and tilers have been trained – a large percentage of them women – along with first-rate builder's mates, bricklayers and officials.

For the middle- and lower-income sectors, who are normally unable to save, this practice has shown itself to be a viable alternative route to getting a decent home.

9. POSSIBILITY AND SCOPE OF TRANSFERRING TO OTHER COMMUNITIES OR COUNTRIES

The Uruguayan co-operative housing experience is already being used as a model in similar experiences in Brazil. The lack of systematised research and evaluation and of literature on this is, however, a major obstacle to the international dissemination of what is a successful development and empowerment experience.

7.
Institutionalizing voluntarism: The University of the Philippines experience

1. GENERAL INFORMATION

1.1 Title of practice or experience

Institutionalizing voluntarism: The University of the Philippines experience

1.2 Category of practice/experience and brief description

The practice shows how academic institutions like the University of the Philippines can directly engage in volunteer work. The University's involvement in voluntarism calls for the rendering of free service by its constituents – faculty, students, alumni and non-teaching staff – to communities in greatest need. U.P., as a state-subsidized university, owes its existence to the people who support it. Through voluntarism, the University is making a concrete contribution toward helping people help themselves. Involvement in voluntarism is also beneficial to the University, for it enhances the academic institution's fourfold function of instruction, research, extension and public service, and transmission and preservation of culture.

As shown by the U.P. experience, the institutionalization of voluntarism becomes effective only if it is backed by policy at the university level. In the case of U.P., policy was operationalized with the formation in 1994 of the volunteer service program called the Ugnayan ng Pahinungód/Oblation Corps (UP/OC) in all the autonomous units of the University. Volunteers are given training, assured of benefits (such as minimal allowance and insurance) and are properly recognized by the University. Since then, the University has served 40,000 Filipinos, which has involved the services of 4,500 volunteers from the different U.P. units.

1.3 Name of person or institution responsible for the practice or experience

University of the Philippines System
University of the Philippines – Diliman
University of the Philippines – Manila
University of the Philippines – Los Banos
University of the Philippines – Visayas
University of the Philippines – Mindanao
University of the Philippines – Baguio

1.4 Name and position of key or relevant persons or officials involved

Dr. Emil Q. Javier, President, University of the Philippines System
Director, Ugnayan ng Pahinungód/Oblation Corps-System
Director, Ugnayan ng Pahinungód/Oblation Corps-Diliman
Director, Ugnayan ng Pahinungód/Oblation Corps-Manila
Director, Ugnayan ng Pahinungód/Oblation Corps-Los Banos
Director, Ugnayan ng Pahinungód/Oblation Corps-Visayas
Director, Ugnayan ng Pahinungód/Oblation Corps-Mindanao
Coordinator, Ugnayan ng Pahinungód/Oblation Corps-Baguio
The Ugnayan ng Pahinungód Volunteers

1.5 Details of the institution

(i) Ugnayan ng Pahinungód/Oblation Corps-System
    (a) Address: Basement, Quezon Hall, U.P. Diliman, 1101 Quezon City, Philippines
    (b) Telephone: ++ (63) (2) 920 5301 loc. 4710/4713
    (c) Fax: ++ (63) (2) 929 2550

(ii) Ugnayan ng Pahinungód/Oblation Corps-Diliman
    (a) Address: Coral Bldg., Lakandula St., U.P. Diliman, 1101 Quezon City, Philippines
    (b) Telephone: ++ (63) (2) 920 5301 loc. 8962, 924 7722

(iii) Ugnayan ng Pahinungód/Oblation Corps-Manila
    (a) Address: 2nd Flr. Old NEDA Bldg., Ermita, Manila, Philippines
    (b) Telephone: ++ (63) (2) 526 4346
    (c) Fax: ++ (63) (2) 526 4363

(iv) Ugnayan ng Pahinungód/Oblation Corps-Los Banos
  (a) Address: International House Bldg., U.P. Los Banos, Laguna, Philippines
  (b) Telephone: ++ (63) 536 0505
  (c) Fax: ++ (63) 536 5362

(v) Ugnayan ng Pahinungód/Oblation Corps-Visayas
  (a) Address: Main Bldg., U.P. Visayas, Iloilo City, Philippines
  (b) Telephone: ++ (63) 337 8591
  (c) Fax: ++ (63) 335 0106

(vi) Ugnayan ng Pahinungód/Oblation Corps-Mindanao
  (a) Address: Ladislawa Avenue, Buhanging, Davao City, Philippines
  (b) Telephone: ++ (63) 222 5302, 221 0343, 221 0082, 221 3912

(vii) Ugnayan ng Pahinungód/Oblation Corps-Baguio
  (a) Address: U.P. College Baguio, 2600 Baguio City, Philippines
  (b) Telephone: ++ (63) 442 3888
  (c) Fax: ++ (63) 442 3888

1.6 Name of person and/or institution conducting the research

Wilfredo Vidal Alangui*

1.7 Details of research person/institution

Not available.

2. THE PROBLEM OR SITUATION BEING ADDRESSED BY THE PRACTICE/INNOVATIVE EXPERIENCE

The University of the Philippines will turn 100 in the year 2008. Despite its proud tradition of academic excellence and service to the nation, the premier State University continues to strive for greater relevance as an educational institution. Thus, in recent years, U.P. has embarked on a rethinking of its vision, mission and goals. Central to this critical self-evaluation are re-

---

* Alangui is assistant professor of mathematics at the University of the Philippines College Baguio, Baguio City, Philippines. He served as the first coordinator of the Ugnayan ng Pahinungód-Baguio and held that position for two years (1995-1997). He is at present the head of the U.P. College Baguio Extension Program. Prof. Alangui has been with U.P. College Baguio since 1986.

flecting on the true meaning of U.P. education, and assessing how the University has played, and continues to play, its role as a social critic, catalyst and agent of change.

As an institution supported by the people, U.P. has a commitment to social transformation, which means empowering the people and improving the conditions of the poor majority. The U.P. faculty, students and alumni have the knowledge and skills that can be harnessed to help transform Philippine society. With the majority of the Filipino people still grappling with problems of survival, the University is expected to mobilize its constituents to realize their social responsibility and commitment.

The ideals of nationalism and democracy promoted at the University, coupled with strong adherence to academic freedom, have instilled among many of its constituents the desire to be of service to the people. Through the years, many among the U.P. faculty, students, alumni and even the non-academic staff have involved themselves in different kinds of voluntary work in various ways.

Although many individual members of the University have practiced voluntarism, their involvement did not really benefit from concrete institutional support. For the most part, the many voluntary activities of the U.P. faculty, students, alumni and non-teaching staff were done in the volunteers' individual capacities. There was, in general, no institutional involvement and support to speak of.

In February 1994, under the initiative of U.P. President Emil Javier, the University launched its volunteer service program called the Ugnayan ng Pahinungód/Oblation Corps (UP/OC). The program was envisioned as a way of "institutionalizing the spirit of social commitment and service that has marked the U.P. since it was founded in 1908" (Flores, 1996).

Why institutionalize a volunteer service program? What good does it do the University? Why should U.P. as an academic institution engage in voluntarism? President Javier provides the answer, in expounding his concept of a modern university:

"A modern university has four main functions: instruction, research, extension and public service, and the preservation and transmission of culture. Voluntarism can be most clearly seen as performing the third function, that of extension and public service. In the actual act of serving, the university would be similar to other volunteer programs. It is in its conscious connections and contributions to the performance of the other three functions and in its rationale and capacity to perform public service that a university program is distinguished from all other forms of voluntarism."

In other words, while voluntarism is directly related to a university's function of extension and public service, a university's involvement in volunteer work can also enhance its three other functions.

Voluntarism and the function of extension and public service

Voluntarism is one mechanism in the performance of a university's task of extension and public service. A university engages in extension and public service in order for it to share with society what it has analyzed and discovered. More than this, state-run universities like U.P. must engage in extension and public service because they owe it to society, which supports them. In performing extension and public service, a university can tap its vast resources, embodied in its faculty, students and alumni.

Voluntarism and the function of instruction

Voluntarism enhances instruction. Universities engaged in volunteer work may be able to validate theories taught inside the classroom. In the process of voluntary work, the university is able to get feedback on whether its theories work and are applicable in real life. At the same time, universities can look at voluntarism as "an object of study and discourse" (Javier, 1995). A university's involvement in volunteer work can promote voluntarism and related topics as a subject of scholarship and instruction.

Voluntarism can also teach the young ethics and values like selflessness, human dignity, social justice, love of country and service to others. Moreover, older members of the academe already engaged in volunteer work might find further strength in pursuing their involvement with institutional support, while others may rediscover the psychological rewards that go with voluntarism. Hence, voluntarism may help in molding the character of universities' constituents, especially among the students, which is one role of education. Universities engaged in voluntarism have the edge in equipping their students with not only the needed skills and knowledge to prepare them to become competent leaders of the country, but also important ethics and values that would inspire them to truly work for the betterment of the people.

Voluntarism and the function of research

Voluntarism offers a fertile ground for research. The experience and knowledge generated from actual volunteer work can be used in the formulation of new theories on the role of voluntarism in society.

Voluntarism and the function of culture preservation and transmission

There is a cultural basis for universities to engage in voluntarism. Across cultures, there are practices that may be classified as voluntary involvement of communities working together for the common good. In the Philippines, for instance, we have the *bayanihan* in the lowlands or the *ub-ubbo* in the Cordillera region, both of which call for the sharing of work among community folk. As Javier asserts, voluntarism may be inherent to all cultures, because "it is a means of affirming one's sense of community with fellow humans." This means that as universities engage in voluntary work, they are at the same time promoting the time-honored tradition of voluntarism in society.

All these point to the idea that pursuing and promoting voluntarism within a university is a good in itself not only because it enhances and helps the university in performing its functions as an academic institution. More than this, voluntarism may help bridge the gap between the academe and the community in general. It is one way of making universities truly sensitive and responsive to the needs of the people.

3. DESCRIPTION OF THE PRACTICE/INNOVATIVE EXPERIENCE AND ITS MAIN FEATURES**

The volunteer service program of the University of the Philippines is called the Ugnayan ng Pahinungód/Oblation Corps (UP/OC). It institutionalizes voluntarism among the faculty, students, alumni and non-academic staff through the rendering of free service to communities in greatest need. This is in recognition of the fact that the University has a stake in the welfare and development of the country.

"Pahinungód" is a Cebuano term in widespread use throughout the islands of Visayas and Mindanao. It is the closest Filipino word equivalent to "oblation", which means offering or sacrifice. The term "Ugnayan" is used to signify the linkages that are forged between the University and the volunteers, who are called "pahinungóds", with the community and society. "Ugnayan ng Pahinungód" therefore means a network of volunteers and partners.

The mission statement of the program reflects the desire of U.P. to get involved in the life of the nation:

"To make the University a more caring academic community that is bound

---
** Based on the Ugnayan ng Pahinungód/Oblation Corps Brochure

together by a commitment to the empowerment of people and selfless service to the nation."

Program objectives

The UP/OC aims to optimize the multifarious resources of the University – skills, talents, expertise and intellectual capacity of its constituents – through volunteer service. The University engages in voluntarism:
(a) to share with society what U.P. has analyzed and discovered;
(b) to enrich teaching and research with knowledge culled from the people themselves about the conditions and needs of the nation;
(c) to promote the study of voluntarism and related topics as a subject of scholarship and instruction;
(d) as a means of propagating actions and values most honored in society – human dignity, social justice, love of country, and respect for all beings; and
(e) as a means of building character and promoting values education.

Program administration

The UP/OC is being implemented in all the autonomous units of the University (except in the Open University), including the regional unit in Baguio City.

A Director working with a full-time staff heads each UP/OC unit. The Directors and the staff meet annually to plan, trouble-shoot, coordinate and assess the direction of the volunteer program at the system-wide level.

The University allots annual funding for the program which is, in turn, shared by all the UP/OC units.

Volunteer programs

Each UP/OC unit defines its own programs, based on its expertise and on the needs of the community where it is situated. The following list shows the breadth of volunteer service provided by the different UP/OC units.

(a) UP/OC System

These are programs common to all the UP/OC units and which are coordinated at the system-wide level.

(i) Affirmative Action Program

Conducts Summer Bridge Programs for high-school students in provinces under-represented in U.P. to democratize access to the University.

(ii) Teachers' Training Program

Conducts training workshops in English, Mathematics, Science and History for public high-school teachers, with U.P. faculty members serving as volunteers.

(iii) Gurong Pahinungód (Pahinungód Teachers)

Deploys new U.P. graduates for one year, under a Memorandum of Agreement with the Department of Education, Culture and Sports, to teach Science, Mathematics, English and History in public schools in underserved areas.

(iv) Service Learning

Enables students to engage in public service as part of their coursework. It integrates classroom learning with social service.

(b) UP/OC Diliman

(i) Ecology Camp

Promotes environmental consciousness through the organization of ecology-related activities in communities.

(ii) Disaster Response

Provides medical/psychosocial services and temporary relief.

(iii) Social Welfare

Assists social welfare agencies and institutions. Services include help in the training of social workers and direct counseling of women and children in especially difficult circumstances.

(iv) Tutorials

Allow U.P. students and faculty volunteers to share their knowledge with young people living in welfare institutions and in underserved communities.

(v) Quezon City Jail Project

Addresses the needs of Quezon City Jail inmates and their families by providing paralegal, psychosocial and livelihood services.

(vi) E-ROTC Program
Engages in civic welfare service as part of the curriculum of the Reserve Officers Training Corps (ROTC).

(vii) Community Service
Deploys volunteers for long-term commitment to serve pre-identified agencies and communities.

(c) UP/OC Manila

(i) Health Missions
Send volunteer doctors, dentists, nurses, pharmacists and students to poor and underserved communities that have requested free medical services.

(ii) Health Training Program
Works side by side with other health-related Pahinungód programs in sharing modern medical skills and practices with local health practitioners and volunteer health workers.

(iii) Summer Immersion
Immerses students in selected underserved or indigent communities in urban and rural areas.

(iv) Tutorial Services Program
Sends volunteers, under a Memorandum of Agreement with the City of Manila, to assist slow learners in identified public elementary schools.

(v) Disaster Management Program
Responds directly to disaster emergencies by sending multi-disciplinary teams for pre- and post-disaster activities.

(vi) Hospice Care
Aims to give palliative care to terminally ill patients in the hospital or home setting.

(vii) ER Volunteers Program
Provides quality care for patients who seek treatment in the emergency room.

(viii) Program for Street Children
Promotes the interest and welfare of street children in coordination with various institutions of similar thrust.

(ix) Earth Camp
Promotes environmental consciousness and behavior within various institutions of similar thrust.

(x) Sports Science Wellness and Consultancy
Conducts multi-disciplinary training on sports science and medicine to medical and paramedical professionals, athletes, coaches, trainers, physical education teachers and school physicians.

(d) UP/OC Los Banos

(i) Technical Assistance to Agrarian Reform Communities
Assists Agrarian Communities in cooperative development, use of new rice varieties, control of locusts, seminars on foot-and-mouth disease, and similar activities.

(ii) Farmer-Scientist Training Program
Aims to equip hilly-land farmers with adequate knowledge and technologies in contour farming in a corn-based cropping system; also aims to strengthen the research and extension capabilities of state colleges and local government units.

(iii) Cooperative Development Support
Supports developing cooperatives of Agrarian Reform Communities with training.

(iv) Summer Immersion Program
Exposes student volunteers to rural community life.

(v) Literacy and Numeracy and Tutorials Program
Enriches education for students and indigenous folk in rural communities.

(vi) Youth Development Program
Harnesses and promotes the potential of young people in a community through leadership training.

(e) UP/OC Visayas

(i) Advocacy Work for Conservation and Management of Fisheries and Aquatic Resources

Includes mangrove reforestation project, fisherfolk-organizing and environmental education.

(ii) Community-based Health Program

Fields volunteer doctors, dentists, nurses and students to program sites to render free medical and dental services.

(iii) Community Empowerment

Enhances the knowledge and skills of municipal development workers to promote community-based and people-oriented interventions.

(iv) Training and Technical Assistance

Assists communities, cooperatives, non-governmental organizations and government organizations through training and workshops geared to their specific needs.

(v) Student Health Workers Program

Equips student volunteers with the necessary know-how in first aid treatment as well as in what to do in case of urgent and non-urgent illnesses on campus.

(vi) Children and Youth Welfare Program

Provides tutorial services as well as training, assistance in home life supervision and psychosocial counseling.

(f) UP/OC Mindanao

(i) Mount Diwata Restoration Program

Assists residents situated in the periphery of Mt. Diwata in meeting their medical and education needs.

(ii) Affirmative Action Program for Indigenous Communities

Conducts an academic bridge program for the Bilaan and T'boli youth.

(iii) Youth Welfare Program

Serves pre-identified agencies, namely the Regional Rehabilitation Center for the Youth and the Home for Sexually Abused Children.

(iv) Environmental Awareness Program

Pursues projects that aim to protect and preserve the environment in partnership with the Philippine Eagle Foundation.

(v) Semestral Break Immersion

Exposes volunteers to societal realities by allowing them to live in rural communities for a period of time.

Program personnel

The UP/OC involves several individuals in the University responsible for their respective tasks and obligations in pursuing the objectives of the program. Aside from the Director and staff who directly manage the program, the UP/OC also relies on the following personnel in the implementation of activities:

(a) Agency Supervisor

Supervises, guides and assists the volunteers and their team to help implement volunteer programs in their areas of involvement.

(b) UP/OC Supervisor

Monitors and supervises the volunteers who are assigned to specific partner agencies and institutions. He/she is usually a member of the faculty involved in Pahinungód endeavors.

(c) Pahinungód

Directly involved with program implementation of the agencies/institutions, local government units and non-governmental organizations in which he/she is fielded on site in on-the-job training as the community organizer, researcher, extension worker or development worker.

Volunteer involvement

Pahinungód volunteers are drawn from among the faculty, students, alumni, non-teaching staff and retirees of the University, including the units and organizations they represent. Volunteers are fielded in areas of need after appropriate orientation and preparation, taking into consideration their schedules and the needs of the community.

The duration of volunteer work is one year on a part-time or full-time basis. Volunteers are expected to share their expertise with and learn from the community they choose and, upon their return, share their insights and lessons from their experience.

The UP/OC ensures that a relevant government agency or non-governmental organization (NGO) will lend support to the volunteer during his/her stay in the community. Each volunteer will be visited and monitored on a regular basis. The volunteer may expect the program to provide all possible support necessary for the success of his/her community work.

A volunteer is assured of insurance coverage, medical assistance depending on the area of assignment, and training in community work and in the social development perspective.

There are two required outputs from the Pahinungód upon completion of his/her volunteer work. The first is the fieldwork diary that includes reflection papers. It summarizes the day-to-day activities or involvement for the whole duration of volunteer service. It also includes the volunteer's reflections on understanding of the community/agency/institution structures and processes. It is an account of the psychosocial and psychospiritual processes experienced by the volunteer. It includes the documentation of personal realizations, turning points, apprehensions or resolutions.

The second output is an integrated paper that summarizes the entire volunteer-service experience of the Pahinungód. It can be used for academic purposes like for teaching materials or case studies. The paper must present a thorough analysis and reflection of the Pahinungód on the entire issue of volunteer service activities. Here, the Pahinungód must be able to put himself/herself in a context wherein he/she takes part in the development process. He/she must then be made to delve into his/her role, contribution and higher aspirations in the pursuit of the elusive goal of change and social transformation.

Partners

Considered as partners are government line agencies, local government units, non-governmental organizations and people's organizations with programs in underserved communities. Partners are expected to provide accommodation for the volunteers, ensure their safety and provide all the necessary support to ensure the success of the volunteer programs being implemented in the area. A Memorandum of Understanding between the partner and the University is forged to formalize the partnership.

The principle of partnership is adhered to so that the tendency toward or temptation for dole-out service is discouraged.

4. DESCRIPTION OF THE INSTITUTION RESPONSIBLE AND ITS ORGANIZATIONAL ASPECTS

The University of the Philippines is an institution of higher learning. It is a center of the arts and sciences, the professions and health sciences, agriculture and forestry, fisheries and aquaculture. As the premier State University, U.P. offers a wide range of degree programs, conducts basic and applied research, and performs many public service functions. Founded in 1908, it now has five autonomous units strategically located all over the country. These autonomous units are U.P. Diliman, U.P. Manila, U.P. Los Banos, U.P. Visayas and U.P. Mindanao. The sixth autonomous unit is the U.P. Open University. There are five regional campuses, namely Baguio, Cebu, Davao, San Fernando in Pampanga and Tacloban. As of 1998, it has a total of 4,383 faculty members and about 48,090 students in the 11 campuses, in addition to the 27 learning centers of the U.P. Open University all over the country. A Chancellor heads all the U.P. autonomous units. The highest official is the U.P. President.

5. PROBLEMS OR OBSTACLES ENCOUNTERED AND HOW THEY WERE OVERCOME

Just like in any pioneering activity, the institutionalization of the volunteer service program of the University at the system-wide level had its share of problems that had to be immediately addressed.

Aside from the huge financial resources that this program obviously entailed, there were other more fundamental concerns that were raised during the initial stages of institutionalization. Some of these concerns included the following.

Nature of volunteer work and programs

Initially, there were different ideas on the nature of volunteer work and programs. There were those who proposed that the kind of volunteer programs that the University should go into had to be community-based and instituted on a long-term basis as opposed to one-shot volunteer work. These programs would then require volunteers to immerse themselves in the community, to live with the people for a minimum of one year.

This had implications on whom to consider as volunteers. The University recognized that many of its constituents were willing to engage in volunteer work but could not possibly do so on a full-time basis. This was especially true for the faculty.

In the end, the University recognized that there was a whole range of volunteer work, from one-shot volunteer work like the health missions of UP/OC-Manila to long-term community-based programs like the Community Service Program of UP/OC-Diliman. Volunteers were then classified as either part-time or full-time, depending on the length of time for which they were available to serve.

All agreed, though, that the volunteer service program of the University should attempt to inculcate self-reliance among and work toward the empowerment of the people. This called for the active involvement of the people in the volunteer work; whenever necessary, volunteers should help establish or strengthen existing local or people's groups that will initiate or sustain social actions to address their priority community problems.

Volunteer incentives

It was clear from the start that people volunteered not for remuneration but for rendering service. It was agreed, nevertheless, that volunteers, especially those deployed in far-flung areas, had to enjoy some incentives like insurance coverage and medical assistance. Another consensus was that full-time volunteers who rendered service for at least one year should be entitled to monthly allowances which, though minimal, would cover some of their personal needs while in the area.

In the case of faculty and staff members who did volunteer work, it was asked whether their voluntary involvement should be recognized for promotion purposes. It was agreed that even though volunteers from the ranks of faculty and non-teaching staff did not expect anything in return, it was incumbent of the University to recognize their involvement by giving them points for promotion.

Selection of partner communities/agencies/institutions

Questions were raised on the manner of selecting partners. Assessment of UP/OC involvement in the initial stages of implementation raised some questions as to whether the University was reaching those that were truly in need of volunteer service. To answer these doubts, basic principles in doing volunteer work were reiterated. One of these was the principle of felt needs, where the people themselves were the ones who expressed their problems and issues. These problems and issues were different from those needs which outside agencies have determined based on their perceptions.

In selecting partner communities, some guiding criteria were formulated, namely:

(a) A request has been made for external help.
(b) The area is relatively depressed but not necessarily the most depressed.
(c) Local leaders and other key informants are receptive to development-oriented projects.
(d) Area can serve as a radiation point for development to other areas.
(e) No serious peace-and-order problems.
(f) There are chances of success for a community project.

In overcoming these initial problems in relation to the institutionalization and implementation of the volunteer service program of the University, the importance of regular assessment and planning activities must be emphasized. These dialogues encouraged the open discussion of issues and allowed for reaching consensus among the people involved in the program.

6. EFFECTS OF THE PRACTICE/INNOVATIVE EXPERIENCE

In the last four years of implementation, the volunteer service program of the University has reached around 40,000 individuals all over the country. Pahinungód volunteers, numbering around 4,500, have been involved in the different volunteer programs, including Affirmative Action, Disaster Relief and Rehabilitation, Peer Counseling, EcoCamp, Coastal Resource Management, Cooperative and Livelihood projects, Agrarian Reform Communities and Farmer-Scientist Training. Many volunteers have been involved in short-term, relief-type work that included distribution of donations during calamities, providing psychosocial processing and stress debriefing, and medical missions. Others have opted for longer-term service through community organizing, formation of cooperatives, resettlement of disaster victims and similar undertakings.

To give an idea of the concrete involvement of the University, two volunteer projects of UP/OC-Diliman are hereby presented.

(a) Assistance to urban poor families in Metro Manila

A Memorandum of Understanding was forged in November 1995 between the University and the Clean and Green Foundation to assist urban poor families from the metropolis who have resettled at the Family Village Resource, Gen. Mariano Alvarez, Cavite.

Two full-time Pahinungód volunteers have been fielded to conduct a needs assessment and a survey on the economic profile of the community. A skills inventory was similarly produced to determine how potential labor can avail themselves of the job opportunities in the area. A major task of the volunteers is to help facilitate the capability-building and socio-economic endeavors of the 45 families. The relocatees have formed an organization called THUMBS. The partnership has created an integrated livelihood program to assist family members in developing alternative sources of income, aside from widening networks and facilitating several medical and dental missions in the resettlement area.

(b) Assistance in lahar rehabilitation

Food relief, food for work, supplemental provisions, networking, advocacy and resettlement assistance have preoccupied Pahinungód volunteers since the devastating October 1995 *lahar* upsurge (due to the 1991 Mt. Pinatubo eruption). Volunteers assisted in psychosocial processes, procurement of relief donations, rummage sales, solicitation of both cash and goods, capability training programs, actual community work and construction work.

Over 150 families belonging to an adopted community organization from Palawe, San Juan and San Fernando, Pampanga have been the motivators and inspiration of the volunteers. About 30 of them are reconstructing their community in San Isidro, Isabela, where a land grant has been acquired through the San Isidro Municipal Government and the PAMANA La Sallete Foundation. The remaining families, totaling around 120, are still spread out among the different evacuation centers in Pampanga. The University has forged a partnership with the Habitat for Humanity and the Provincial Government of Tarlac for the construction of resettlement units in Camp O'Donnell Resettlement Area. Volunteers and affected families have been involved in the actual construction of the resettlement houses.

The various volunteer programs that have been implemented so far have involved different sectors and institutions. Partners included some student organizations which have done their own volunteer work in pre-identified communities. With this, the objective of offering these student organizations avenues for service and worthwhile activities has been met.

Certain volunteer programs also entailed collaboration with other state colleges and universities in the country, thereby increasing the number of volunteers, who are no longer limited to U.P. constituents.

Many of the volunteers have expressed dissatisfaction with the inability of the government to provide services to the people. Their exposure to the harsh realities of life in the communities has strengthened their social commitment. Volunteers have expressed these sentiments in the debriefing activities and sharing sessions that were held to process their experiences.

The University has similarly benefited from the four-year experience in relation to its functions as an academic institution. Already, important documents have been written, including training modules, scholarly papers and journals, that contained the lessons and insights the volunteers gained in their involvement. A curriculum for a Diploma and a Masters program in Public Administration, Major in Voluntary Sector Management has already been developed, while the University has actively participated in international and national conferences on voluntarism.

In sum, the first three years of the volunteer service program of the University were a period of unprecedented commitment to serving the people. The program has reached out to different communities and sectors all over the country, each with varying problems and concerns. The success of these programs was due primarily to the unquestionable dedication of the volunteers, who came from the ranks of faculty, students, alumni and non-teaching staff.

7. SUITABILITY AND POSSIBILITY FOR UPSCALING

Though the volunteer service program of the University has served many individuals nationwide, there are still areas that have not been served, and many possible volunteers that have not been tapped.

However, experience shows that it is not hard to tap volunteers from the different sectors in the University. All that is needed is to provide the appropriate programs and projects that these people can involve themselves with.

The University is optimistic that by the year 2000 each faculty member, student and non-teaching staff member would have done volunteer work of some form. The sustainability of the volunteer service program is assured with its institutionalization. However, there is an increasing need for financial and material support for the services rendered by the volunteers. This calls for the generation of funds aside from the regular budget received from U.P. and outside sources. The Kaibigan ng Pahinungód (Friends of Pahinungód) was formed for this purpose. Kaibigan is a network of individuals and organizations who are willing to support the program financially. Its creation means that more and more individuals and groups outside of the University are being tapped to support the efforts of voluntarism in the country.

Another possibility for upscaling beyond U.P. is the involvement of other state colleges and universities that are located across the archipelago. The experience of the UP/OC could encourage these colleges and universities to also institutionalize their own volunteer service programs. If this happens, academic institutions in the country can become real conduits of the people and the government in the pursuit of development.

8. SIGNIFICANCE FOR (AND IMPACT ON) POLICY-MAKING

The experience of U.P. in making voluntarism an integral part of its mission as an academic institution shows what it can do for social change. Voluntarism may help address some of the varied and complex problems being faced by the people.

Voluntarism can be adopted by other government institutions as part of their mission. The goal is to make voluntarism a way of life, a mass movement that involves different institutions with the means of helping the people overcome their problems. However, as shown by the U.P. experience, institutionalization becomes effective only if supported by policy. At the same time, the government may be encouraged to give more support to institutions that have made a commitment to voluntarism.

9. POSSIBILITY AND SCOPE OF TRANSFERRING TO OTHER COMMUNITIES OR COUNTRIES

The institutionalization of voluntarism at U.P. is a practice worth emulating. As shown by the experience, voluntarism benefits the University for it enhances its functions as an academic institution. In view of the U.P. experience, universities in other countries may tap their vast resources to get involved directly in development issues of their people.

10. OTHER COMMENTS

In adopting voluntarism as an integral part of their mission, institutions must likewise advance the very same ideals that promote the spirit of voluntarism. The management of the volunteer service program must in itself be consultative and democratic. Finally, voluntarism has to be viewed within the context of people's empowerment and the pursuit of social transformation. Voluntarism must help people help themselves because in the final analysis, it is they who will determine their future.

References

1. *Brochure*. Ugnayan ng Pahinungód/Oblation Coprs: The Volunteer Service Program of the University of the Philippines, University of the Philippines, Diliman, Quezon City, 1998.

2. Javier, Emil Q. Freedom in the Context of the New Millenium. Speech delivered at the U.P. Alumni Association Grand Alumni Homecoming, June 10, 1998, U.P. Diliman.
3. *Annual Report.* Ugnayan ng Pahinungód/ Oblation Corps, University of the Philippines, Diliman, Quezon City, 1997.
4. Carino, Ledivina. Pahinungód Towards Institutionalization. *Pahinungód: A Quarterly Newsletter of the Oblation Corps.* Vol. 4, Issue No. 1, January-March 1997.
5. *Preparing the Seeds: Training Module of Volunteer Preparation.* Ugnayan ng Pahinungód/Oblation Corps-Diliman, University of the Philippines, Diliman, Quezon City, 1996.
6. *Annual Report.* Ugnayan ng Pahinungód/ Oblation Corps-Diliman, University of the Philippines, Diliman, Quezon City, 1996.
7. Flores, Ramona, ed. *Pahinungód, Annual 1995.* Ugnayan ng Pahinungód/Oblation Corps, University of the Philippines, Diliman, Quezon City, 1995.

Part II
Education and Information

8.

Databanking and research for popular education

1. GENERAL INFORMATION

1.1 Title of practice or experience

IBON: Databanking and research for popular education

1.2 Category of practice/experience and brief description

Documented here is the experience of IBON, a private institution in the Philippines which has established innovative methods of making use of data and information to help empower people. The institution's databank and incisive analyses have helped serve the information needs of grassroots organizations, teachers, students and professionals, including policy-makers such as legislators.

1.3 Name of person or institution responsible for the practice or experience

IBON Foundation, Inc., Databank and Research Center

1.4 Name and position of key or relevant persons or officials involved

Antonio Tujan, Executive Director
Rosario Bella Guzman, Head, Research Department

1.5 Details of institution

- (a) Address: Third Floor, SCC Building, 4427 Interior Old Sta. Mesa, Manila P.O. Box SM 447, Philippines
- (b) Telephone: ++ (63) (2) 713 2737
- (c) Fax: ++ (63) (2) 716 0108
- (d) E-Mail: ibon@info.com.ph

1.6 Name of person and/or institution conducting the research

Tebtebba Foundation, Inc. (Indigenous Peoples' International Center for Policy Research and Education)

1.7 Details of research person/institution

(a) Address: Rm. 3B Agpaoa Compound, 111 Upper General Luna Road, 2600 Baguio City, Philippines
(b) Telephone: ++(63) (74) 444 7703
(c) Fax: ++(63) (74) 443 9459
(d) E-Mail: tebtebba@skyinet.net

2. THE PROBLEM OR SITUATION BEING ADDRESSED BY THE PRACTICE/INNOVATIVE EXPERIENCE

The idea of establishing a databank was born out of necessity. The databank was set up because of the dearth of information under the late ex-president Ferdinand Marcos' martial law regime (September 1972 to February 1986). During that period, information flow had been controlled by the regime and the public felt the need for more objective data and information on what was really happening and what the social and economic trends were in the country.

Throughout the martial law period, people's organizations, religious groups, workers, farmers, students, professionals and other sectors were seeking ways to understand and help ease the prevailing social conditions. But they needed informed judgment on issues such as the rising foreign debt, widespread poverty, heavy military spending, how much of the national budget was going to social services, unemployment and the like. They needed data and information to help educate, organize and mobilize people in relation to the excesses of martial rule. They needed a databank or a research group. This urgency led to the birth of IBON Foundation, which was known then as IBON Databank. (Note: In the succeeding parts of this research, the Foundation is referred to as "IBON" for short.)

From a borrowed space in a counseling office of a Catholic Sisters' convent, IBON Databank's pioneer staff labored. They pored over and thumbed through government data from government agencies and from the government-controlled newspapers. Using a borrowed typewriter and a borrowed mimeographing machine, IBON came out with its first published issue called *IBON Facts & Figures* in August 1978.

The publication, at first, was a mere collage of data. But it later evolved into an alternative way of presenting issues, from what the IBON founders call the "people's perspective". IBON Databank did not only present issues from another angle; it also presented alternatives or some way out of the problems martial rule created.

IBON Facts & Figures became a hit among "cause-oriented groups" (as the various people's and sectoral organizations opposing martial law were called then). Focusing on socio-economic issues, the publication became the basis and reference for group discussions on the country's economic status, labor and farmers' concerns, foreign debt and the like. Its main purpose, therefore, was to service the information needs of people's organizations.

If these people's organizations used the information to help arouse, mobilize and organize people, then this was so because, as IBON had envisioned it, information can be a tool for enlightenment and social transformation. The martial law regime tried to curtail the public's right to be informed. IBON Databank was among those institutions which tried their best to help people from being kept in the dark.

From its early days, IBON established its distinctive competence. *IBON Facts & Figures* became known as a concise and handy twice-monthly, eight-page fact sheet which made economic concepts and developments understandable to non-economists. A few months after its first publication, *IBON Facts & Figures* was succeeded by two local-language editions. This was followed by *IBON Industry Primers* on mining, garments, fishing, oil, industrial estates, commercial banks, footwear, beverages and drugs, among others.

These publications had a common goal: to help empower the grassroots by disseminating in popular terms information on and analyses of socio-economic realities.

Having established its reputation in interpreting and analyzing economic trends and developments, IBON in summer 1980 launched its Seminars Project. Coordinated with the Education Forum, another non-governmental organization (NGO) servicing the academe, the project involved two main programs – IBON's Socio-economic Seminar and Philippine History Seminar. The *IBON Socio-Economics Workbook* and the *IBON Teachers' Manual on Philippine History* first served as seminar aids. But teachers later adopted these as supplementary material for their social-science classes. Getting the teachers involved in popular socio-economics under IBON's guidance was crucial as they could reach out to the student population.

From a simple databank with a twice-a-month publication, IBON has expanded its services in the field of popularizing socio-economics. These services and the needs served are further discussed below.

3. DESCRIPTION OF THE PRACTICE/INNOVATIVE EXPERIENCE AND ITS MAIN FEATURES

IBON Databank started off simply. It employed a simple documentation and filing technique or system called OASIS. Under the system, each file was labeled under a key code or key word. These files were then categorized by subjects or themes such as "agrarian", "labor", "debt", "economy" and so on. Sub-themes were also provided if necessary. Under each category, the files were alphabetically arranged in shelves or boxes. Corresponding labels and codes and abstracts were also entered in index cards for easy accessing.

The system employed the basic techniques of a library. The only difference was that IBON's files mainly comprised current newspaper clippings, journals, and documents from agencies such as the government's National Statistics Office, National Economic Development Authority, and others.

Going hand in hand with the documentation and filing system was IBON's publication. Through *IBON Facts & Figures*, now published twice a month, accumulated data and information were processed. The eight-page, 8.5-inch-by-11-inch publication had a fixed format. The first spread stated the basic facts and figures; the second, the nature of the problem; and the third, analysis and alternatives. The publication states, explains and discusses in layperson's terms socio-economic issues and developments.

In the late 1980s, IBON went high-tech. It computerized its systems. It innovated a filing and indexing system which it called IDEA or IBON Index Data Easy Access. A bit more complex than OASIS but user-friendly, IDEA employs "cross-indexing" where an article or document does not only fall under one index. For instance, a key code or entry on "Farmers and GATT" is also indexed under other key codes such as "Poverty" and "Trade". Thus, a user or researcher can trace the relation, for example, of farmers' problems, such as landlessness, to poverty. The key code on "Trade" can also have information on how GATT affects farmers.

For easy access, each key code is assigned a number. So, in accessing data, a user can just type the key code number, and all he/she needs appears on the computer screen. The computerized key code numbers are also the same index numbers of the manually-filed hard copies of newspaper clippings, manuals, documents and other literature. Thus, the user or researcher can easily retrieve the hard copies if he/she so wishes to get further details.

Copyrighted by IBON, IDEA has five major features: retrieval, maintenance, subscription list, thesaurus and data sources. Its retrieval system is multi-coded, employing "cross-indexing" as explained above. To maintain its bank of data, all incoming materials are listed in indices. All subscriptions to outside publications, including their expirations, are also properly listed. Its thesaurus of properly-coded key words is an important guide to users. Through a key word and its code, a user can easily retrieve his/her needed data or information. Data sources are also properly inventoried. IBON has to employ ten "thinking" regular staff to maintain the databank on a daily basis. Once the databank is neglected, if even for a week, the whole set-up collapses.

Side by side with the computerized system is the use of Master Cards. Under each Master Card, all important indicators are arranged chronologically. The chronological arrangement is most helpful to the paper chaser who wishes to establish the historical development of an issue.

Aside from its *IBON Facts & Figures*, IBON has also devised other services through which utilization of its wealth of data and information can be maximized. It experimented with a telephone service called "Dial a Data". This service enables users to request for data over the phone for a fee. IBON later evolved what it calls a Datasavers program which provides institutions, organizations and offices immediate access to information by telephone, fax or modem. The program includes regular monitoring of issues according to what datasavers specify.

The main clients of IBON Foundation are from the grassroots, such as organized farmers, fisherfolk, laborers, indigenous peoples, women and church workers. Its clientele expanded later to include students, professionals and even policy-makers such as legislators. A senator, for example, requested for IBON's data and analysis on the issue of oil deregulation. Several congressmen and some cabinet officials also subscribe to *IBON Facts & Figures*.

Because of its rich information warehouse, IBON has gone into publishing English and Filipino editions of *IBON Facts & Figures* for gradeschoolers and secondary school students. These magazines are used for social-science and economics subjects. It also publishes what is called *Econokomiks*, which explains complex economic trends and issues in simple, comic form. Written in the vernacular, this comic-type publication is intended for grassroots folk. Both the school magazines and *Econokomiks* are aimed at popularizing or simplifying economic facts and figures.

IBON also comes out from time to time with a *Special Release*, which dissects and analyzes current issues such as globalized free trade, oil deregulation, privatization of government-controlled corporations and the like. Aside from popularizing economic terms and trends, the *Special Release* clarifies issues and presents or explores alternative options.

IBON has come a long way. It also now publishes journals, primers, textbooks and supplementary publications such as *Maya Komiks, Sibikomiks, Philippine Currents, Asian Currents, World Currents* and *Education for Development Quarterly*.

Published occasionally, IBON's *IPE* (Institute of Political Economy) *Primer Series* is a simplified but comprehensive analysis of socio-political issues. Published as the need arises, the 20-page *Primer Series* helps give a theoretical framework to political activists, community leaders and advocacy groups.

The 40-page *IPE Journals* extensively look into the impact of development policies and programs at the national and global levels. The 24-page *Education for Development Quarterly* caters to faculty members and school administrators. It analyzes issues and trends pertaining to the educational system.

IBON's textbooks for gradeschoolers are mostly on social studies and culture. It also has an *IBON Environment Workbook Level 1*, also for grade school.

For high school, IBON has textbooks on Philippine history, Asian civilization, world history, economics and also an environment workbook.

Through its databank and various publications, IBON has blazed the trail in the field of popular education, popularizing socio-economic issues and making economics easy to grasp even for non-economists.

4. DESCRIPTION OF THE INSTITUTION RESPONSIBLE AND ITS ORGANIZATIONAL ASPECTS

IBON Foundation is a research-education development institution. It studies socio-economic issues confronting contemporary Philippine society and seeks to bring this knowledge and information to the greatest number of Filipinos. In this way, according to IBON's Mission Statement, more Filipinos will be able to effectively participate in building "a self-reliant, progressive, sovereign and democratic Philippines".

From its simple beginnings in 1978, IBON has developed into a multi-program institution now strongly present in the formal education sector. Besides its original databanking, research and publications program, it now provides non-formal education and training to people's organizations, conducts in-depth research for and offers information services to all sectors of society, and services the mainstream mass media via its weekly news and features dispatches.

In recent years, IBON has expanded its reach through branch offices in the Visayan islands in central Philippines and in Mindanao island in southern Philippines.

Its main programs are:
(a) IBON Databank and Research Center

(b) IBON Partnership in Education for Development
(c) IBON Popular Education Program
(d) IBON Media Services Program
(e) IBON Environment Desk
(f) Institute of Political Economy

(a) IBON Databank and Research Center

One of the original programs of IBON, the Databank and Research Center, as discussed above, provides up-to-date information on various socio-economic issues for advocacy, education, policy-making, development planning and implementation for non-governmental organizations, people's organizations, academic institutions, government agencies, media practitioners, business enterprises and individuals.

Through its databank, IBON maintains a large, specialized library that allows quick and easy computerized retrieval and is open to the public. The databank gives quick access to data inquiries. A Datasavers program for institutions, organizations and offices provides immediate access to information by telephone, fax or modem, and regular monitoring of issues according to the specification of the datasaver, among other services. IBON also has a continuing research program which provides the base for its information systems and publications. The Research Center accepts commissioned researches and surveys on various relevant issues specific to industries, sectors, regions, etc.

As stated earlier, the Databank and Research Center's final fruit of its labor is its publications. Under the Databank and Research Center program, IBON also provides databanking and library training and consultancy. It also trains interested individuals in research, writing and desktop publishing skills.

Still another sub-program is the Sectoral Research Desks. Sectoral desks have been set up to give focused, specialized services. The Workers' Desk conducts researches on labor and industry issues and gives research consultancy for financial statement analysis for CBA (collective bargaining agreement) negotiations.

The Peasant and Women's Desks also conduct specialized researches.

(b) IBON Partnership in Education for Development

The IBON Partnership in Education for Development (IPED) consolidates IBON's long-standing program support for the formal education sector. After IPED was formed, IBON publications have been well-received by the schools. These publications have become much-sought-after references for students and teachers. Through IPED, teachers have also sought out IBON's seminars. IPED is a full program that includes the development of textbooks, supplementary publications, teacher training, and several other services needed by schools in realizing what IBON calls "transformative education". Transformative education is oriented towards helping transform or change society for the good of the greatest number of people.

Other related services include educators' fora, audio-visual-aid development and library enrichment. IPED conducts fora on various issues to help update teachers and educators on current developments. IBON is on call to its partner schools, when they wish to hold symposia and other fora. It also offers specialized seminars for staff and institutional development.

Part of the IPED program is the *Education for Development Quarterly*, a journal that dissects various urgent issues in the formal education sector.

IPED also develops various kinds of audio-visual aids for classroom and other use for subject areas such as social studies, environment, economics and history. These materials include videos, slide shows, acetate folios and flip charts.

For its library enrichment program, IPED coordinates with schools in coming out with reference books and publications for school libraries. It also offers school library staff training in computerization, databanking and electronic hook-up.

(c) IBON Popular Education Program

IBON's Popular Education Program or PEP develops education modules for people's organizations and NGOs on socio-economic topics. Regular Seminar Modules provide popular but substantial discussion on topics such as the Philippine economy and globalization, among others. Special Seminar Modules tackle specific issues like oil deregulation, devaluation, liberalization and privatization.

PEP also provides audio-visual aids for popular education like videos and acetate folios on the environment, the economic history of the Philippines, the national situation and globalization. It also offers consultancy services and specific sectoral seminars which help in the popular education of trade unions and people's organizations.

(d) IBON Media Services Program

The IBON Media Services Program has three main services. It services mainstream and alternative media (note: alternative media, as differentiated from its mainstream counterpart, refers to those independent media outfits which are free from the control of big business interests) through databank and research support. It also has a news and features service which publishes a weekly dispatch for the mainstream newspapers, as well as a broadcast features service particularly designed for radio listeners.

(e) IBON Environment Desk

The IBON Environment Desk is a full program that includes a specialized environment databank with a separate database from IBON Databank. It acts as the secretariat of the Philippine Environment Databank Network. It undertakes researches on environment issues and has an active education program that includes the publication of workbooks, primers and video programs on the environment.

(f) The Institute of Political Economy

The Institute of Political Economy was established to respond to the clamor for more in-depth studies and education modules about the national and global economy, and economic theory. IPE studies are published in monographs and books and through the *IPE Journals* distributed through a mailing list and through bookshops and book sales. IPE also responds to the need to arm social activists in clarifying urgent issues to grassroots folk via the *IPE Praymer*, a primer distributed free to grassroots users.

IBON Foundation Inc. has a Board of Directors as its policy-making body. The Board is composed of a chairperson, a vice-chairperson, a secretary, a treasurer and eight directors. Its programs are implemented by committed staffers assigned to the Foundation's six major programs. An Executive Director oversees the whole implementation of the various programs.

In its campaign to help clarify the issues behind globalized free trade, IBON has established networks overseas. Among these overseas networks are IFAG or International Forum Against Globalization and some international alliances of groups against globalization.

5. PROBLEMS OR OBSTACLES ENCOUNTERED AND HOW THEY WERE OVERCOME

Like many other NGOs, IBON had relied on foreign funds for its operations. So, when major funders in 1995 – 1996 stopped their support, the Foundation faced a crisis. As a remedial measure, IBON downscaled its staff. The hardest part was when IBON had to downscale even its committed staff. But

IBON did its best to redeploy the terminated staff to other NGOs and people's organizations. At the same time, it pushed its self-reliance program by aggressively marketing its publications in various schools across the country. The goal for at least 70% self-reliance was achieved.

As a result of staff reduction, IBON faced some backlogs in its databanking as at the time of writing of this report. However, it has taken the crisis as a challenge. IBON is determined to be fully self-reliant in the few years ahead through a marketing strategy that can support the Foundation's operations while remaining committed to achieving its mission and role.

This episode has shown that the most valuable asset of the organization is the high quality and public commitment of IBON's staffers. Those who remained through the crisis period were determined to keep IBON going and moreover to see it progress in new activities under more self-reliant conditions.

6. EFFECTS OF THE PRACTICE/INNOVATIVE EXPERIENCE

IBON's databank and publications have served and continue to serve the educational needs of grassroots and sectoral organizations as well as the public. Various organizations and the academe often refer to IBON's publications during forums on socio-economic issues. IBON continues to provide timely information and analysis to illuminate public debates on controversial issues such as oil price hikes or long-standing problems such as the country's agrarian question, foreign and domestic debt, and the impact of globalization.

Workers' organizations also use IBON's data on consumers' average daily food basket and poverty thresholds as bases for demanding wage increases from their employers. Through the use of data based on official and independent studies, IBON can compute the average daily food consumption of the average Filipino family and the current poverty threshold based on the current inflation rate and the buying power of the Philippine currency.

7. SUITABILITY AND POSSIBILITY FOR UPSCALING

IBON continues to diversify its initiatives. It continues to publish not only *IBON Facts & Figures*, but also books on socio-economics which schools, from gradeschool to college level, can use as reference material. Through its news agency, IBON Features, IBON's wealth of information and analyses of socio-economic trends and issues are disseminated to the public via the mainstream media.

8. SIGNIFICANCE FOR (AND IMPACT ON) POLICY-MAKING

That legislator-subscribers refer to IBON for their legislation is one way by which IBON helps influence policies. IBON's well-researched publications on certain issues also help form public opinion, thus helping to indirectly shape policies.

In 1997, a senator who subscribes to IBON, for example, used IBON's data in filing a Senate resolution urging the Supreme Court to probe the legality of the proposed oil price hike the oil companies were seeking. The Supreme Court responded favorably, issuing a restraining order on the companies' petition for a price increase. In its study, IBON showed how the oil companies had profited from an earlier increase the companies sought while the price of oil in the world market dipped, and showed why the proposed new round of oil price hikes was unnecessary.

9. POSSIBILITY AND SCOPE OF TRANSFERRING TO OTHER COMMUNITIES OR COUNTRIES

Any institution or non-governmental group that has an interest in improving its databanking, research and publication can easily adopt IBON's technology, which makes use of a wealth of information and data, which can help influence policies or in conceptualizing programs based on concrete needs.

Basic baseline data on rural outmigration, for example, can give both government agencies and non-governmental development organizations some inputs on how to approach rural development. Basic data on major agricultural or agro-business landholdings can also help in instituting policies on how to address agrarian issues such as landlessness, unfair crop-sharing patterns, or low farm wages.

The possibilities inherent in deciding on what data to study, process and analyze are endless. Given an enormous amount of data, a community databank outfit can be overwhelmed with information. But as IBON has shown, any databank center can succeed if it knows how to organize the data and information in selective ways and to focus on the topic studied.

10. OTHER COMMENTS

IBON has shown how to use data for advocacy, for helping shape or change policies, and for popular education of grassroots organizations. It has also shown that socio-economics need not be the exclusive domain of economic technical experts. Through IBON, seemingly complex economic concepts are explained in a way which ordinary peasants, laborers and laypeople can easily grasp. This enables ordinary people and their organizations to better articulate and assert their economic rights such as the right to just wages, the right to government social services, the right to earn a living, and the right to fair access of the country's wealth and resources.

References

1. IBON Foundation, Inc., *Annual Report 1988*.
2. IBON Foundation, Inc., Brochure, 1998
3. Interview with Rosario Bella Guzman, Research Department Head, IBON Foundation, Inc., February 1997.

9.

Pioneering gender awareness in the academe

1. GENERAL INFORMATION

1.1 Title of practice or experience

St Scholastica's College Institute of Women's Studies: Pioneering gender awareness in the academe

1.2 Category of practice or experience and brief description

The integration of women's studies in the course offerings in the academe is now a common initiative of educational institutions. In the Philippines, the pioneer in this respect has been the St. Scholastica's College Institute of Women's Studies. This effort would have come to naught, however, if not for the vision of the College President and concurrently the Institute's Director, Sister Mary John Mananzan. Nursia, the home of the Institute, has come to mean home to the many scholars of the courses offered by the Institute, notably its Intercultural Course on Women and Society.

The establishment of the Institute was inspired by the growing women's movement in the Philippines in the 80s. The personal involvement of Sister Mary John in the movement at the very start showed her the need to mainstream women's studies in the academe as she saw that this sector was lagging behind in gender-awareness efforts. Through a thoroughly participative process that lasted for almost four years, the Institute was established in 1988. Its main programs are:
    (a) Seminar and Training Program
    (b) Research and Publications Program
    (c) Resource Center Development Program
    (d) Radio Program
    (e) Women, Ecology and Wholeness Farm

One of its direct contributions to women's empowerment in Asia and the Pacific is the scholarships it provides women from these regions to undertake the three-month Intercultural Course on Women and Society.

At the outset, the Institute ventured into publishing because of its realization that there is a dearth of material on women by Filipinos and on women by women. Its resource center has now become a haven for students, especially in Metro Manila, who want to study women's issues.

1.3 Name of person or institution responsible for the practice or experience

St. Scholastica's College Institute of Women's Studies

1.4 Name and position of key or relevant persons or officials involved

Sr. Mary John Mananzan, President, St. Scholastica's College and Director, Institute of Women's Studies

1.5 Details of institution

- (a) Address: Institute of Women's Studies, 931 Estrada Street, Malate Manila, Philippines
- (b) Telephone: ++ (63) (2) 522 3551
- (c) E-Mail: nursia@snap.portalinc.com

1.6 Name of person and/or institution conducting the research

Ms Victoria T. Corpuz, Executive Director, Tebtebba Foundation, Inc. (Indigenous Peoples' International Center for Policy Research and Education)

1.7 Details of research person/institution

- (a) Address: Rm. 3B Agpaoa Compound, 111 Upper General Luna Road, 2600 Baguio City, Philippines
- (b) Telephone: ++ (63) (74) 444 7703
- (c) Fax: ++ (63) (74) 443 9459
- (d) E-Mail: tebtebba@skyinet.net

2. THE PROBLEM OR SITUATION BEING ADDRESSED BY THE PRACTICE/INNOVATIVE EXPERIENCE

The increasingly vigorous people's movement in the Philippines in the 70s saw the effort of women activists to find their space in the movement.

MAKIBAKA (Malayang Kilusan ng Kababaihang Makabayan) was founded in 1970. Because of the declaration of Martial Law in 1972, it went underground, like other progressive organizations. As activists regained ground in the latter part of the decade, many women's organizations either emerged for the first time, like the SAMAKANA, Center for Women's Resources (CWR) and PILIPINA, or re-emerged, like KaBaPa. The Aquino assassination in 1983 spurred further the women's movement opposed to the Marcos regime and saw WOMB (Women for the Ouster of Marcos and Boycott), WATCH and others marching in the streets representing the women's voice.

Filipino women, especially those involved simultaneously in the movement opposed to the Marcos regime and in the broader people's movement for social transformation, were now looking for a Third World perspective on women's liberation.

The CWR took the initiative in 1984 to convene a consultation among women's organizations, women's desks of NGOs and women activists to discuss a common women's orientation in the Third World. An important resolution of that consultation was the founding of a nationwide federation of women's organizations which became known as GABRIELA.

Sr. Mary John Mananzan had been involved in the foundation of PILIPINA and Center for Women's Resources and eventually became the chairperson of GABRIELA. She was at the same time Dean of College of St. Scholastica's College. Since she had been conducting women's awareness seminars in the different organizations she was involved in, she felt that the academe was definitely lagging behind, including St. Scholastica's College which, ironically, is a women's college. She found it urgent that the 400 women that graduated annually from the college should be given the opportunity of a basic women's orientation.

In the first semester of 1985, she invited members of GABRIELA and PILIPINA, as well as some of the women faculty members of St. Scholastica's College, to a weekend seminar to create a syllabus for an Introductory Course for Women's Studies. After three days of enthusiastic and intensive discussion, the group came up with a syllabus and each one committed herself to study a topic she was assigned to lecture on. A dry run was conducted the following month where each lecturer presented her paper to the group for critique and suggestions.

In the second semester of 1985, a pilot class of juniors majoring in psychology was chosen. Since the lecturers wanted to listen to each other, each session had 18 teachers and 16 students! At the end of the semester an evaluation was made among the students and teachers. The evaluation was overwhelmingly positive although some recommendations were made regarding the content and methodology of the course.

According to a student, the content was not only a content course, but a perspective course, that is, it gave the students another perspective in looking at reality. Other students found the course needed an organizational component and this paved the way for a women's organization in campus called S-KAIBA.

Such a positive evaluation of the course eventually led to the decision to make it a requirement for graduation from St. Scholastica's College.

The course developed into a Women's Studies Program that later on became the Institute of Women's Studies, founded on the following goals:

(a) to awaken a consciousness to and provide an understanding of the woman question through a strategy of formal (institutional) and non-institutional alternative education;
(b) to engage in research and study on gender issues, and projects that uphold the cause of women; and
(c) to conduct outreach programs that serve women outside the formal educational institution.

(*Women's Studies in the Philippines: An Assessment of the Impact of WSAP in Promoting the Gender Perspective,* Sylvia H. Guerrero, *et al.,* UCWS UP and WSAP, Quezon City, 1996)

3. DESCRIPTION OF THE PRACTICE/INNOVATIVE EXPERIENCE AND ITS MAIN FEATURES

Designing/initiating the project

Organizational location

The success of the Introductory Course for Women's Studies launched the Women's Studies Program of the College Department of St. Scholastica's College. The College Department was the logical locus of the project because a certain maturity is essential for undertaking Women's Studies. Besides, the originator of the idea was the Dean of College. The Women's Studies Program was at first directly under this office. Since the methodology of the introductory course was mainly team teaching, faculty members were "borrowed" from the different departments, namely the Theology, Sociology and History Departments.

After two years, the Women's Studies Program offered a cognate course on Women's Studies. It consisted of more specific courses such as Women in Politics, Women in Literature, Gender Issues in Development, etc., and anyone who finished 18 units (six courses) was given a minor or cognate certificate in Women's Studies.

Interestingly, the first recipients of the cognate certificate were the initial lecturers of the pilot class. It should be noted that at this time there were no doctoral, masters or bachelor's programs in Women's Studies in the country, which proved to be a blessing in disguise, because the first teachers of Women's Studies had to be the women activists themselves. This is important because in many First World countries, there is a dichotomy and sometimes even conflict between the women academics in Women's Studies programs in universities and the women activists. In the Philippines, those who teach Women's Studies in schools also happen to be women activists directly involved in the women's movement.

When the Women's Studies Program started to branch out into outreach programs for women in the communities, it became necessary to create a separate entity. In 1988, the St. Scholastica's Institute of Women's Studies Foundation was registered with the Securities and Exchange Commission. In 1990, it obtained its own physical center, the Nursia building, and became administratively and financially autonomous, although as an institute, it still falls under the jurisdiction of the President of St. Scholastica's College, who is a member of its Board of Trustees.

Description of the courses

At present, the courses offered by the Institute may be classified into credit and non-credit courses. There is a common pool of resources for both programs and a cognate certificate is granted by the College to the participants of one particular program, the three-month Intercultural Women's Studies Course given by the Institute.

Credit courses

The credit courses are the following:
(a) Introduction to Women's Studies (3 units)
The Introductory Course for Women's Studies attempts to give the students a fairly comprehensive view of women's issues. It evokes in the students an interest in gender issues in the context of the socioeconomic, political and cultural conditions of Philippine society. It uses a combination of creative and participative methodologies which includes lectures, workshops, exposure programs, research papers, case studies, role-playing, film book, article analysis, etc.

(b) Cognate Course on Women's Studies (18 units) (Please refer to Annex A for details of subjects)

This consists of four core subjects and two electives that are credited three units each. A Certificate in Women's Studies is awarded on completion of the course.

These are core subjects:
(i) The Development of Women's Thoughts and Feminism
(ii) Gender Issues in Development
(iii) Women and Religion
(iv) Current Issues on Women

Two electives are chosen from the following:
(i) Women and Literature
(ii) Women in Philippine History
(iii) Women in the Arts
(iv) Feminist Research
(v) Women and Politics

(c) M.A. in Religious Studies, Major in Feminist Theology (Please refer to Annex B for description of subjects)

In consortium with the Institute of Formation and Religious Studies, the Institute of Women's Studies has launched a three-year MA program on Feminist Theology. Fourteen participants enrolled in this course would have graduated in 1996.

(d) M.A. in Humanities, Major in Women's Studies

This course was first offered in 1997. It requires 36 units of the academic subject, 200 practical hours, a written comprehensive and a thesis defense.

Non-credit courses

(a) Intercultural Course on Women and Society (International participants, 3 months (Please refer to Annex C for description of subjects)

The Intercultural Course on Women and Society is a three-month study program that aims to assemble multicultural groups of women who will share ideas and experiences regarding the issues and concerns of women in their society. Fifteen to eighteen women from the Third World are given full or partial scholarships for airfare, board and lodging and tuition fees.

The course consists of the following modules:
(i) Current Issues of Women in Different Countries
(ii) Feminist Theories and Analysis of the Woman Question
(iii) Gender Issues in Development
(iv) Women and Religion
(v) Women and Culture
(vi) Feminist Education and Creative Pedagogy
(vii) Feminist Research
(viii) Violence Against Women and Feminist Counseling
(ix) Women and Organizing
(x) Feminist Agenda and Action Planning

(b) Trainers' Training

This one-month intensive course for facilitators of seminars on women offers content courses on the different aspects of Women's Studies as well as pedagogical and facilitative skills in imparting knowledge in the context of an alternative education for women. A minimum of fifteen Filipino trainers are given full scholarships which cover travel, tuition fees, and board and lodging. The modules are similar to the Intercultural Course's but are presented in a shorter form and are focused on the Philippine situation.

(c) Towards a Gender-Fair Education

This is a three-day course which caters especially for teachers and students to help them analyze sexism in education with regard to the system as a whole, structures, policies, educational materials, medium of instruction and practices. It also provides strategies for ensuring that education is gender-fair.

(d) Basic Women's Orientation

This is a two-and-a-half-day course for women in the basic sectors, such as women peasants, workers and urban poor. It is a conscientization course geared toward awakening the participants' awareness of their situation, understanding the socializing forces that form their consciousness and helping them to strive towards self- and mutual-empowerment.

The resource persons for the courses are drawn from among the faculty of the school, women activists and professionals, as well as representatives of women from the basic sectors. Team teaching is often employed. For longer courses such as the three-month Intercultural Course and the one-month Trainers' Training, a process facilitator coordinates the modules and sees to the continuity of the process. The seminar grid is usually prepared by the training coordinator and the Director of the Institute. Whenever feasible, the resource persons are invited to a preliminary meeting to show the flow of the course and how their particular modules fit into the logic of the program.

Curricular mainstreaming strategies

The focus on gender is actually the outcome of a process of social orientation which the College had been undergoing since 1975. At that time, the school was undergoing a re-orientation toward social awareness and social responsibility. Conscientization seminars were given to faculty, students, staff and administration. The curriculum was revised according to the newly formulated vision-mission.

Innovative methodologies were created and co- and extra-curricular activities were re-focused. In 1985, there was no strong opposition to the introduction of the gender issue since the whole academic community was already geared toward innovation and social transformation. It was simply necessary to show how this issue is a constitutive dimension of social transformation, since one cannot talk of total human liberation or social transformation if half of the population remains oppressed and discriminated against. Minor opposition from some individual faculty members was not a real obstacle to the project. Gender-sensitivity seminars were given to interested faculty members while the S-KAIBA provided the students opportunities for consciousness-raising as well as concrete actions in coordination with women's groups outside the school.

Obtaining institutional commitment and financial support

Initial institutional support

At the start, when the project was merely a Women's Studies Program, the item for the program was included in the budget of the College Department. The Dean of College negotiated with the President of the College to the effect that this item would remain in the budget for 10 years or until the Institute of Women's Studies could get its own funding, whichever came first. During this time, office space, facilities and office materials as well as equipment were borrowed from the school, even for outreach seminars.

Outside funding was obtained for outreach programs like the basic women's orientation for women peasants, urban poor and workers. The Inter-Institutional Consortium (IIC) to which St. Scholastica's College belonged also included in its budget gender-fair training seminars as well as women teachers' exposure programs for the five member schools.

Financial and administrative autonomy

After three years, the Institute obtained funding for some of its projects from a foreign funding agency based in the Philippines. As agreed upon, the item for Women's Studies in the budget of the College Department was removed.

In 1989, the Institute began its three-month Intercultural Course. This brought up the need for the Institute's own seminar house, because it was quite difficult to reserve seminar houses for three months every year. The President of the College made an agreement with the Director of the Institute of Women's Studies, who was simultaneously the Dean of College, that the school would provide for half of the funding of a seminar building if the Director could come up with the other half. At this time, the Director was sending out quarterly circular letters to friends of the Institute. One of these letters reached a funding agency in Austria. The head of this agency wrote to the Institute Director expressing interest in its projects and requested her to give the details of the building plan.

This funding agency eventually contributed half of the building cost for the construction of the home of the Institute of Women's Studies, Nursia, in December 1990. The building has offices and a library on the first story; a kitchen, dining room and conference room on the second story, and dormitories on the third story.

A representative of a funding agency in Germany came to visit the Institute in 1991, just at the time when the Intercultural Course was going on. He was quite impressed with the course and suggested to the Director of the Institute that a three-year comprehensive project proposal for the Institute be made. This was subsequently approved and at present, the Institute is in the last year of the second triennial subsidy provided by this agency.

Ensuring financial viability

The Director of the Institute is aware that although funding for projects can be sourced on a continuous basis, there is a possibility that funding for staff salaries may dry up. So, an endowment fund was created right from the foundation of the Institute where all unspecified donations to the Institute were placed and put in the care of a portfolio manager. The purpose of this endowment fund is to give a sense of security to the Institute staff that their salaries are assured. At present, just the interest earned on the fund is enough to provide for the salaries of the staff.

To ensure a healthy financial portfolio, the Institute has a diversified scheme. It undertakes short-term projects outside its comprehensive project proposal and funds are sourced elsewhere. Meanwhile, the Institute is also earning from the board and lodging fees that it receives for the duration of the courses as well as from the sale of its books. All these proceeds augment the endowment fund and will guarantee financial viability in the future, independent of funding agencies.

Current status of the Institute of Women's Studies

Current programs
The Institute of Women's Studies at present offers the following programs:

(a) Curricular Program
It consists of the credited courses: Introduction to Women's Studies and Course in Feminist Theology offered by the Institute in consortium with the Institute of Formation and Religious Studies. It also recently (1997) launched an M.A. in Humanities Major in Women's Studies.

(b) Seminar and Training Program
Provides for alternative education on a wide range of topics for women both locally and internationally. The main courses offered are the Intercultural Course on Women and Society, two five-week Trainers' Training in Feminism and EducationWork with Women Courses, four short-term Gender-Fair Education Seminars, six Basic Women's Orientation for Grassroots Women, four short-term courses on various topics and special courses like Ecofeminism.

(c) Research and Publications Program
It provides information and materials on women's issues in the Philippines and the Asia-Pacific region through the publication of books, research, and other printed materials like references, literary works and critiques, and monograms on women and by women. It has also been a venue for feminist expression by being an alternative publishing house for women writers and artists. The Babaylan Women's Collective, set up in 1990 after a group of women writers and artists shared experiences on the difficulties of getting women's works published, serves as a resource and talent pool for women's writings. Undergraduate theses, masteral and doctoral dissertations, and joint research ventures with other women's organizations are also undertaken (*IWS Publications Brochure*). To date, it has published 17 books which are locally and internationally marketed, one of which won the National Book Award for 1992. It also publishes a semi-annual *Asia-Pacific Women's Studies Journal*, and has put out a packet of printed cards featuring Filipino feminist artists.

(d) Resource Center Development Program
The IWS Resource Center boasts of a wide collection of women's books, vertical files on women's issues, and audio-visual materials. It provides the public access to these resources. Its current special features are a collection of documents on women and Philippine history and its special collection on women and world religions.

(e) Center for Women's Wholeness – Women and Ecology Wholeness Farm

This new program aims at an integrated approach to women's spiritual corporeality. Its main features are monthly women's celebrations, alternative retreats for different groups of women, courses in Zen, yoga, Qi Gong and paneurythmic dance, lectures on spirituality, etc. Recently it acquired 1.2 hectares of land in Mendez, Cavite which has a seminar house and a bio-diverse farm featuring organic farming and alternative sources of energy: biogas, windmill and solar lighting. Its main activity is holding Women and Ecology seminars.

(f) Women's Radio Program – *Tinig ng Nursia*, Women's Studies on the air

A weekly one-hour program on Women's Studies is aired from 9am to 12pm every Sunday on DWSS-K-Love. It aims to reach women who cannot come to the Institute or to St. Scholastica's College. It follows a course syllabus and has four anchorpersons who take turns to host the program. Visitors are also invited for live interviews.

(g) Nursia Seminar House

It not only houses the staff of the Institute and accommodates the courses offered by the Institute but also serves as an accessible venue for seminars of other women's groups, consultations, meetings, symposia, panel discussions, book launchings and exhibits.

(h) IWS Scholarship Program

This is an outreach program for needy and deserving women students. It provides for tuition fees and, in some cases, living allowances for women who cannot otherwise afford to go to college. At present, the program is supporting 23 college students.

4. DESCRIPTION OF THE INSTITUTION RESPONSIBLE AND ITS ORGANIZATIONAL ASPECTS

The Institute is governed by a Board of Trustees composed of 10 women, all well-respected in their fields of specialization. Its Director is Sr. Mary John Mananzan, OSB, who is also the President of St. Scholastica's College. The Institute maintains nine full-time staff members and a number of consultants.

It is a founding member of the Women's Studies Association of the Philippines (WSAP), "currently the only national network of teachers promoting the gender perspective in the Philippine education system".

5. PROBLEMS OR OBSTACLES ENCOUNTERED AND HOW THEY WERE OVERCOME

In the Institute's experience, there has not been any serious obstacle to the mainstreaming of Women's Studies. However, in another setting, obstacles would be very likely to occur. The main obstacle is the lack of gender sensitivity on the part of the administrators who are the decision-makers in any institution. It is good if ideas originate from below, but when one is working in an institution, unless one can convince the policy-makers and those who have the final say of the importance of Women's Studies, mainstreaming will be difficult.

Funding is, of course, important in order to have a rich, varied and significant program. However, this is not an insurmountable obstacle. Funding agencies are on the lookout for worthwhile projects and as long as one has creative projects in mind, and is committed to accurate reporting, this should not be a problem.

Another issue in mainstreaming is the question of whether to have an autonomous Women's Department or to develop the women's perspective for all the subjects. Sr. Mary John Mananzan always held the position that there is no need to choose between the two approaches. One should have a Women's Studies Program as well as develop the women's perspective in all the other subjects. The latter, of course, necessitates that the department heads be gender-sensitive and convinced of the necessity of developing the women's perspective in their respective subjects.

6. EFFECTS OF THE PRACTICE/INNOVATIVE EXPERIENCE

The experience of the Institute of Women's Studies has shown that the educational strategy is one of the most crucial and most indispensable aspects of the women's movement. Unless the majority of women become aware of their disadvantaged situation, unless they are empowered to assert their rights and to struggle together for societal change, no amount of legislation or affirmative action can bring about a lasting transformation.

The Institute's experience has also shown how consciousness-raising can bring about a great change in the lives of women and how these women can influence many others in turn. In its 10 years of existence, 4,000 students have graduated from the College Department who have experienced a change in consciousness. Some of these graduates have become mothers and hopefully are rearing and will rear their children in a non-sexist way. The Trainers' Training has about 150 graduates and the Intercultural Course about 90 graduates. These are women who are themselves involved in training, and their sharing (in a special reunion-evaluation conference held in 1994, for representatives of the first four batches of graduates) revealed the extensiveness of their reach, which encompassed not only the Philippines but other different countries of the Asia-Pacific region as well. For example, when Sr. Mary John Mananzan visited a graduate in Madras, India, she found out that the graduate had translated all the Institute's modules into Tamil. Moreover, the graduate introduced Sr. Mary John to the 20 women whom she had trained to give basic women's orientation in the villages of Madras.

7. SUITABILITY AND POSSIBILITY FOR UPSCALING

The Institute has embarked on an enrichment program. It submitted its Comprehensive Project Proposal for the three-year period 1996-1999 to continue with its main programs, namely the Center for Women's Wholeness and the radio program. It likewise submitted a proposal for another subsidized Course on MS in Feminist Theology which was scheduled to run from April 1997 to October 1998.

It has received funding for Women and Ecology seminars, seven of which were held in 1999 and six were planned for the year 2000. A project proposal for a twenty-day Woman and Ecology Seminar from Asian Women has been submitted to the Japan Foundation.

A new program was submitted at the request of the National Economic and Development Authority (NEDA) which was a five-week Women's Studies and Exposure Cruise that was scheduled to run for three years from 1997-1999. From 1996-1999, the Institute hoped to develop another program that it has already initiated, namely Gender Issues for Men.

Upscaling may also be in terms of increasing enrolment, facilities and faculty. This can be done as long as resources are available. At the moment, the Institute is concentrating on program enrichment.

8. SIGNIFICANCE FOR (AND IMPACT ON) POLICY-MAKING

In the light of its experience, the Institute would like to offer the following suggestions for the development of Women and Gender Studies in Philippine schools:
   (a) Target top school officials, presidents and deans for gender-sensitivity seminars.

(b) Initiate regular and systematic training of Women's Studies teachers.
(c) Create a core group of committed faculty members in each educational institution that will pursue the mainstreaming of Women's Studies.
(d) Produce interesting instructional materials for all levels: elementary, high school, college.
(e) Create a high profile through national and regional (Asian) Women's Studies conferences.

9. POSSIBILITY AND SCOPE OF TRANSFERRING TO OTHER COMMUNITIES OR COUNTRIES

Replication of the program may be more feasible for those in the education sector who have a degree of influence in the formulation of the education programs and policies of institutions and governments. In the Philippines, a number of colleges and universities have developed their own gender or women's programs. The adaptation of the education modules at the grassroots level has been shown by the Madras women to be possible.

References

1. Guerrero, Sylvia H., *et al.*, (1996) *Women's Studies in the Philippines: An Assessment of the Impact of WSAP in Promoting the Gender Perspective*, UCWS UP and WSAP, Quezon City.
2. Institute of Women's Studies, *Intercultural Course on Women and Society* brochure.
3. Institute of Women's Studies, *The Institute of Women's Studies Publications* brochure.

ANNEX A

Description of course offerings in Certificate in Women's Studies

Cognate Course on Women's Studies (18 units)

This consists of four core subjects and two electives that are credited with three units each. A Certificate in Women's Studies is awarded on completion of the course.

The core subjects are the following:

(a) The Development of Women's Thoughts and Feminism

Historical development of the woman question and the women's movement (local and global). Discussion of sexism and patriarchy as well as the socializing forces that form women's consciousness.

(b) Gender Issues in Development

Women's role in different economic systems. Critique of development models. The effect of changing technology on women. Decision-making and appropriate technology from women's viewpoint.

(c) Women and Religion

Liberating and oppressive aspects of religious concepts, structures and practice, particularly in Christianity. Alternative agenda in the Church and feminist theology.

(d) Current Issues on Women

In-depth analysis of women's issues in the Philippines such as discrimination and inequality, violence against women, different forms of trafficking of women, as well as the specific sectoral problems of women workers, peasants, urban poor and professionals.

Two electives are chosen from the following:

(i) Women and Literature

Survey and analysis of the images of women as presented by prominent authors in literature.

(ii) Women in Philippine History

Role of women during the different periods of Philippine history starting from pre-colonial society.

(iii) Women in the Arts
Critique of the objectification and commodification of women in the arts and media, i.e., advertisements, pornographic movies, etc. Discussion of alternative gender-sensitive arts and media.

(iv) Feminist Research
Principles and methods of research from a feminist perspective.

(v) Women and Politics
Discussion of the involvement of women in politics, beginning from the efforts of the suffragettes to the participation of women in the legal and the underground struggles in the Philippines.

ANNEX B

Description of course offerings for Masters of Arts in Religious Studies, Major in Feminist Theology

The curriculum for the MA in Religious Studies, Major in Feminist Theology includes the following subjects:

(a) PH 201– Feminist Theories (3 units)
An analysis of women's reality. The origins of gender oppression as part of the overarching social system called patriarchy. The woman question seen from different theoretical standpoints: liberational, traditional Marxist, radical, socialist, Third World and ecological feminism.

(b) PH 205 – Women in Asian Religious/Philosophical Traditions (3 units)
An exploration into the role, status and image of women in Islam, Buddhism, Hinduism and Confucianism. An examination of contemporary efforts and movements to overcome the negative impact of these religious and cultural traditions on women.

(c) SC 201 – Biblical Research and Feminist Hermeneutics (3 units)
Mastery of the basic tools and methods of Biblical research from the feminist perspective. Basic overview of various methodologies of Biblical interpretation being employed today.

(d) SC 203 – Women in the Bible I (Old Testament) (3 units)
Rereading of familiar stories of women in the Old Testament to uncover aspects which reinforce women's inferior status in Church and society, and to discover hidden historical contributions of these women.

(e) TH 201 – Methods of Theological Research – Women Doing Theology (3 units)
Theological reflection based on women's reality and experience of oppression and discrimination. A survey and critique of major theological themes and their reformulation from the women's perspective.

(f) TH 227 – Women in Church History (3 units)
Tracing patriarchal elements in the history of Western Christianity from the Patristic times to the present. A study of the forms of resistance in the lives of outstanding women in Church history.

(g) TH 215 – Christology and Women (3 units)
Overview of main Christological dogmas. Contemporary challenges to these dogmas arising from the women's movements, the impact of other world religions and the growing ecological consciousness in the Third World.

(h) TH 21 – Feminist Ethics (3 units)
Study of the ethical dilemmas facing Church and society in relation to women. Presentation of other solutions proposed by leading feminist ethicists. Discussion of their applicability to local contexts.

(i) SC 203 – Women in the Bible II (New Testament) (3 units)
Rereading of familiar stories of women in the New Testament to uncover aspects which reinforce women's inferior status in Church and society and to discover hidden historical contributions of these women.

(j) TH 202 – Foundations of Religious Education (3 units)
Study and critique of the prevailing theories and practice of religious education. Presentation of gender-fair religious pedagogy. Training in module-making, creative facilitation and alternative modes of communication of the Gospel.

(k) TH 236 – Feminist Spirituality: Agenda for Renewal (3 units)
Delineating the characteristics of the emerging feminist spirituality. Implications of this spirituality in the renewal of religious institutions of the Church and of society.

(l) TH 299 – Thesis Presentation
Each participant chooses a thesis topic when she enrolls for Methods of Biblical Research. She works on this under the guidance of a mentor of her choice approved by the dean. In this course, each participant presents and defends her thesis before a panel of faculty members and all the other students.

The course also includes a written comprehensive.

ANNEX C

Description of course offerings for Intercultural Course on Women and Society

The Intercultural Course consists of the following modules:

(a) Current Issues of Women in Different Countries
A presentation of the national political, economic and sociocultural situation as well as the women's conditions, initiatives and issues in the different countries where the participants come from.

(b) Feminist Theories
Theoretical analyses of the woman question and critiques of these. Includes an open discussion about female and male sexuality as related to the social, political and cultural dimensions of society.

(c) Gender Issues in Economic Development
A review of different economic models, the role of women in their societies' development efforts and a critique of prevailing development strategies and programs as they affect women. Also covers the attempts of women to participate in their countries' policy- and decision-making and in planning appropriate technology.

(d) Women and Religion
An analysis of the oppressive as well as liberating aspects of world religions concerning the woman question. Includes a survey of the agenda of renewal in Church structures, teachings and practices toward women's equality and empowerment.

(e) Women and Culture
A study of the different ways women are portrayed in the arts, literature and media, and how other cultural norms and traditions contribute to or counter the problem of women's oppression. Includes the impact of the dynamics of language on the women's situation.

(f) Feminist Education and Creative Pedagogy
A critique of mainstream education philosophies and content, and a presentation of women's alternatives. Includes concepts of gender-fair education and feminist popular education, as well as the use of theater arts for creative facilitation.

(g) Feminist Research

A discussion on the principles and methods of research, with special attention given to the ethics of feminist research and to participatory or action research methods.

(h) Violence Against Women and Feminist Counseling

A discussion on the different types of violence experienced by women. Includes theories and myths surrounding violence against women to enhance participants' own counseling abilities and self-defense training.

(i) Women and Organizing

An examination of principles and methods of organizing women toward their empowerment. Includes lessons on more effective organizing and mobilization through the sharing of programs and campaigns of various women's groups and collectives.

(j) Feminist Agenda and Action Planning

The drafting of a feminist agenda and concrete plans by the participants based on lessons learnt from the previous input.

10.

The Other India Bookstore and Press

1. GENERAL INFORMATION

1.1 Title of practice or experience

The Other India Bookstore and Press

1.2 Category of practice/experience and brief description

The Other India Bookstore (OIB) is a unique social institution set up ten years ago by a group of Indian intellectuals to put serious effort into South-South interaction in the areas of book publishing and distribution.

Despite years of political independence, citizens from India can rarely procure books from Africa, South America or even other countries in South (including Pakistan and Sri Lanka) and Southeast Asia. Neither can the citizens of those countries procure titles easily from India.

All countries, North and South, however, continue to be flooded with the output of the publishing and distribution houses based in a few centres in the Western world. It is certainly not the case that all the intellectuals of the planet are only to be located in London and New York, but this is in effect what the North's publishing industry implies when one is faced with its prolific output. OIB was set up to undermine this dominance and control of Western publishing houses over the intellectual life of the people of the South.

In the process of building bridges between publishing houses in the South, the Bookstore has not only survived, but found new niches to explore as well. One of these is the successful distribution of the vast quantities of non-governmental organisation (NGO) literature unavailable in commercial bookstores. Another is the publication of the entire range of alternative literature from the continent of India.

1.3 Name of person or institution responsible for the practice or experience

Other India Bookstore

1.4 Name and position of key or relevant persons or officials involved

Jerry Rodrigues, Manager, Other India Bookstore
Claude Alvares, Editor, Other India Press

1.5 Details of institution

    (a) Address: Above Mapusa Clinic, Mapusa 403 507, Goa, India
    (b) Telephone: ++ (91) (832) 263306, 256479
    (c) Fax: ++ (91) (832) 263305
    (d) E-Mail: oibs@goatelecom.com

1.6 Name of person and/or institution conducting the research

Claude Alvares, Editor, Other India Press

1.7 Details of research person/institution

As in 1.5 above

2. THE PROBLEM OR SITUATION BEING ADDRESSED BY THE PRACTICE/INNOVATIVE EXPERIENCE

When the Other India Bookstore (OIB) was set up by the Third World Bookstore Society in 1988, it set itself the limited objective of establishing interactive links between the book trades of India and those of Africa, South America and Southeast Asia. The Society was set up by committed Indian intellectuals who felt it a scandal that nearly 50 years after independence, one still could not access books from Africa, South America or Asia. All the books one could get in the Indian market from publishers outside India were restricted to titles from publishing houses based in the UK or the USA.

The dominance of the Western book trade naturally implied the domination of intellectual culture as well and the continued influence of Western ideas – whether such ideas were appropriate or not – over activities carried out in different regions of the South. Either in various syllabi prescribed by the universities or through conditioned response, there remains even today a near-total dependency on the foreign, specifically English and North American, written word. Even academic scholarship focused on or around the so-called "Third World" is dominated by the word as proclaimed from the West.

The result of this dominance is that an author feels his/her work is recognised only if it is published in Europe or America, since those are the places where it gets recognition and from where its importance slowly filters down to other countries. When a book is published in the West, the so-called leading intellectual journals might review it, some colleges might prescribe it as recommended reading for students, quotes from the book might appear in other publications and the author thus feels he is recognised as an intellectual, poet, novelist, scientist, etc. by those who matter.

The dominance extends to marketing practices as well. More than 30 to 40 years after political independence, all the ex-colonies are still flooded with books, magazines, and journals from powerful Western publishers and their outlets. Ask in an Indian bookshop for books published in Sri Lanka, Pakistan, Nigeria or Kenya and you will draw a blank.

Ask in those countries for a book published in India and you will receive a similar negative response. But ask for a book published by Harper and Collins, USA or Oxford University Press, UK, and chances are that the title is readily available for sale.

The domination of the book trade by Western publishing houses is so powerful that literature generated in countries of the South eventually find their way to other countries in the South only through the North. A good example is the African Book Collective in London which dominates and controls the flow of literature from Africa to the rest of the world. To read, for instance, the Kenyan writer, Ngugi wa Thiong'o's outburst against his former rulers, in *Decolonising the Mind*, Indians had to first obtain it courtesy of a publishing house in London. Due to the stranglehold exercised by Western centres, African writers are unable to trade their work directly with their counterparts in other parts of the South. The same situation holds true for hundreds of other writers from the South.

Efforts to change this wholly undesirable scenario have not borne much fruit, despite the emergence of "South-South" political institutions like the Non-Aligned Movement (NAM) and the South Asian Association for Regional Cooperation (SAARC), or, for that matter, a greater awareness than ever before that the "world information order" is highly distorted as it tilts in favour of the countries of the West.

3. DESCRIPTION OF THE PRACTICE/INNOVATIVE EXPERIENCE AND ITS MAIN FEATURES

OIB was formally set up in October 1988 by a registered Trust called the Third World Bookstore Society. Prior to that, for a period of nearly two years, there was only an informal arrangement for the distribution of books in order to gauge the Indian book market and ascertain the viability of such an operation. These two years (1986-88) saw a limited distribution of books and monographs from well-known and significant institutes and NGOs sympathetic to the idea and which, fortunately, also had several publications for sale. Chief among these were the Consumers' Association of Penang, Malaysia, and the International Organisation of Consumer Unions, Malaysia, both of which had a voluminous amount of consumer literature unknown and therefore unavailable in India at the time, even though these are extremely important and well-known organisations in Southeast Asia. Another institute which readily sent its monograph series to India for distribution was the Third World Studies Centre, based in the University of Manila, Philippines.

The groups named were even prepared to sell at a loss to start with, provided they could develop a market and an audience in India. But to everyone's amazement, there were plenty of takers for the Malaysian titles in this country, particularly among the NGOs, who were pleased to find other like-minded Asians. The prices were also affordable despite their being "foreign" books and this enhanced their attractiveness. Thus, confident that the idea was not merely feasible but that it also made good business sense, the Society was registered and plans laid out for implementing the objectives.

In 1988, after wrangling a travel grant, Bookstore staff visited bookstores and publishing houses in Southeast Asia, including Thailand, the Philippines, Hong Kong, Singapore and Malaysia. Titles selected from these countries were then featured in an annotated printed catalogue sent out by mail to about a thousand addresses within India. These included NGOs and libraries as well as individuals. The response was tremendous.

A similar exercise was tried out with Africa. Here, Bookstore staff visited West Africa: Tanzania, Uganda and Kenya and later, the Zimbabwe Book Fair at Harare. The result of these reconnaissance tours was that a large inventory base of bookshops and publishers in these countries became available to the Bookstore in India, for purposes of importing attractive titles produced by such publishers for sale in the Indian market. The face-to-face contact with Southeast Asian and African publishers created the trust necessary for such operations.

The sale of books from Africa and Southeast Asia in the Indian market was a fairly successful operation and the Bookstore found itself repeatedly making fresh orders for titles it had promoted through its mail-order catalogues.

The Bookstore also took a policy decision not to market each and every book available in the South. It set up selection criteria. First and foremost, for a book to be marketed by OIB, it had to be written and published in some country of the South. Books on the South written by intellectuals and academics living in the South but published in the North were not eligible for distribution through the Bookstore's network of mail-order or direct sales. The subject matter of a book must naturally be of some interest to a book buyer in India. And in addition, every book that OIB selects for distribution must be well printed and produced.

Today, the present stock of OIB's books includes 1,200 titles: none of these titles comes from the UK or from the USA. Instead, OIB has much to offer on what Asia thinks, Africa feels or Latin America writes. It markets a wide range of titles, which runs the gamut from literature from Kenya and children's tales from Bhutan to a Malaysian lawyer's analysis of Trade-Related Aspects of Intellectual Property Rights (TRIPS).

OIB soon found that bringing other regions into contact with NGOs, research centres, activists and other interested individuals was not enough. Indian NGOs themselves were strangers to each other. An environment organisation in Gorakhpur did not know what a group with similar interests had done in Kerala, because nobody was marketing their publications. OIB confidently stepped into this new niche. Having a vast array of potential buyers easily available on its computerised mailing list, OIB now proceeded to tap the vast market in NGO literature within the country.

It wrote to NGOs offering its services to help market their publications. A deluge of publications followed. Applying its own criteria for good publishing, OIB now selected relevant titles and placed these also within its printed catalogues.

Perhaps the most important feature of OIB today is that it is the only outlet in the country marketing the entire volume of publications brought out by voluntary groups, NGOs and environmentalists – the ultimate "one-stop shop" for whatever is produced in India by non-commercial publishers, activist groups and alternative thinkers.

The titles marketed fall under a broad range of categories, like environment, women's issues, natural and traditional resources, human rights, alternative children's stories, health, tribals and dalits, development: the list is endless. Environmental titles include subjects like water management, Himalayan earthquakes and a hundred practical ways to lead a greener lifestyle. Consumer literature is always popular, as are practical how-to-do-it books on health, alternative medicine or cooking.

OIB helps act as a clearing house for books presenting the reality of the "other", disempowered and much neglected India and its aspirations for a better life. In its ten years of operation, OIB has managed to position itself as a leading outlet for books on just about any "alternative" subject on India. It is even good business, simply because people are seriously looking out for alternatives and are willing to pay to be guided along this path. Books on subjects like the environment and alternative-health options are at an absolute premium today and OIB sells its books without having to push them too much. In fact, very often, people come a long way searching for OIB.

The Bookstore today operates from a tiny office in the small commercial town of Mapusa, Goa, best known for its colourful Friday market which is a great tourist attraction. It operates chiefly as a mail-order bookshop although it has adequate facilities for the book buyer to browse through the shelves as well. Each day, the postman and office staff shuffle in and out with piles of letters, papers and neat packages. Letters and orders for books come from different parts of India, several from small towns, like Dhulia in Maharashtra, Hazaribagh in Bihar or Assam and occasionally even from the Andamans.

Anyone who writes to OIB for a book automatically gets on to OIB's mailing list, which ensures that he/she receives OIB's annual catalogue regularly.

People from small towns are in fact the main reason why the mail-order service works and continues to bring in business. But orders also come from abroad, especially now that OIB's catalogue is also on the Internet. There are also school and college teachers, librarians, tourists and visitors to Goa who make it a point to visit OIB and place orders for books they can use back home. The fact that OIB operates as a mail-order service and guarantees that the parcel will reach its destination in mint condition is a great help for it saves the visitors the burden of carrying the parcel themselves.

Initially, OIB's clientele was restricted to NGOs. Later, OIB found a market in universities and colleges. Facing a dearth of material for contemporary studies, the academic network turned to NGO publications, which were small, up-to-date and offered useful insights. Booksellers too started to examine the commercial viability of such publications and began to place orders. A fairly substantial percentage of OIB sales is now routed through the book trade, though the largest chunk still comes from its mail-order service.

In many ways, the OIB style of functioning has also remained unconventional. Contrary to normal business practice, this outlet does not necessarily demand advance payment from its distant and unknown clients. In its experience, people always pay. OIB trusts its customers and has rarely been cheated out of its dues.

Conscious that books must be cheap if they are to be read widely, the Bookstore decided fairly early on to see to it that its books were priced at reasonable rates. In importing its books from other countries of the South, OIB also makes sure it is able to purchase books from the exporting country at local rates and not the rates charged for dollar exports. That way, OIB does not fall into the export-price circuit and is able to keep its prices down.

But this does not mean that OIB is run like a charitable outfit. Far from it; OIB's operations are fully professional and commercially viable. In fact, unlike several other successful initiatives from the South, the Bookstore decided to operate on a professional and commercial basis from its very inception and without depending on grants. OIB does not put a book in the catalogue unless it gets a commission, however small. It is the profits from the minimal commissions charged which enable OIB to survive and function as a fairly well-established business activity, operating within its means.

In 1990, the Bookstore added a publishing wing to its operations. There are far greater profits to be made in publishing when compared to distribution and retail. The Bookstore continued to develop its distribution arrangements, but its publishing house also became a runaway success. The titles published reflected the major strands of alternative thinking within India, for which there was an eager and steady market.

Today, the publishing wing of the Bookstore, the Other India Press (OIP) is already India's largest publisher of alternative titles covering topics ranging from animal rights to environment, organic farming and alternative schooling. Books published by OIP are professionally produced and no compromise is made with regard to any element of book design. The Press operates to international standards of printing, binding and publishing. OIP comes out with 10-12 publications a year and expects soon to increase this tally to 20 books a year.

OIB's unusual methods have also brought in cheap capital. Under a unique scheme called the Social Investment Fund (SIF), supporters voluntarily loan their money to OIB to enable it to undertake its publishing programme without having to resort to loans from commercial banks. Individuals loan money to the Bookstore for periods ranging from one to five years at rates of interest set by the donor, subject to a maximum of 10% per annum, with simple interest. Some opt to take no interest returns at all. This is also acceptable but the principal amount contributed is always returned.

Sticking to its green concerns, the Trust has recently begun to levy an environment tax on all books produced through OIP. The environment tax, collected from OIP and the buyer of the book, is handed over to organisations involved in the successful regeneration of forests.

OIB, launched a decade ago to promote the availability of literature from other countries of the South, alternative ideas and publications of non-profit organisations, has proved that there is a formidable niche for titles that do not originate from the well-established publishers of the West. It has also established that grassroots ideas sell. The strength of the organisation can be gauged from the fact that it has been able to make a concept like this work without the infusion of funds from aid agencies or grants.

4. DESCRIPTION OF THE INSTITUTION RESPONSIBLE AND ITS ORGANISATIONAL ASPECTS

The Third World Bookstore Society which was formed in 1986 under the Indian Societies Registration Act 1860, has approximately 15 trustees.

They come from different parts of the country. The Trust oversees the work of the Bookstore, the SIF, the OIP and other related activities.

Though the Trust carries out commercial activities through its bookstore operations, income from the activities cannot be allotted as dividends to any individual trustee, but is placed instead at the disposal of the Trust for improving and enhancing the range of activities.

5. PROBLEMS OR OBSTACLES ENCOUNTERED AND HOW THEY WERE OVERCOME

The principal obstacle to its operations the Bookstore has faced is the continuing inferiorised mentality of many intellectual centres in Asia, Africa and South America. In several African countries, the book trade is still controlled either by whites within the country or by publishing and distribution circles based in the UK. Such centres will brook no opposition or competition. It is hard to persuade book publishers in Africa to sell their books directly to OIB because they are fearful of violating their contracts with their distribution house in the UK which may be purchasing their books in bulk.

Many people, particularly intellectuals and academics, are still firmly hooked on the belief that good ideas can only emanate from books imported from the West. Many writers in the South feel it is far better to publish in the North than in the South, thus reinforcing existing habits of intellectual dependence on the North.

Pricing policy is another area of concern. To keep prices low, books from abroad have to be received by seamail. However, it can take several months before the books arrive and sometimes these are held up at customs in Mumbai on some pretext or the other. This has meant that OIB staff have had to sometimes even visit Mumbai to clear the packages. Fortunately, this does not happen too often.

There is also the problem of currency conversion rates fluctuating quite drastically, necessitating major price revisions which are naturally not seen favourably by customers who have placed orders based on prices quoted in the printed catalogue. To surmount this problem, OIB usually tries to buy in bulk and also make immediate payment so that the price stays fixed even if the currency value fluctuates.

The initial OIB policy was to charge the same price for a book to any customer, whether an individual, a library or an institution. Special reduced rates were, however, given to students, activists and those who genuinely appeared to be financially in need. For all the others, whether they were from India or abroad, the same rate applied.

However, when a reputable university in the USA which had sent in an order for books not only insisted on paying according to strict currency conversion (which meant that several publications had to be billed in decimal points) but also wanted a refund of one US dollar since the title could not be supplied, OIB decided to revise its policy of uniform prices. It now has an export rate (in US dollars) for books sold to customers in the Western world only. The export prices, however, are marginally higher than the equivalent rupee rates and constitute a more satisfactory arrangement.

Even though OIB provides an efficient distribution service for NGOs, dealing with them is not always easy. Most NGOs know next to nothing about invoicing, billing discounts etc. and they are very casual about such matters. They also have very little idea about packaging their books and care little about using cheaper forms of transport to save costs. Very often, the books arrive at OIB frayed and dishevelled, with their spines damaged, pages dog-eared and so on. No self-respecting customer would purchase such copies.

Sometimes, an NGO would despatch its consignment of books by courier or letter post, which is frightfully expensive, and OIB would be expected to reimburse the NGO its forwarding costs.

In its own interests, therefore, OIB set about educating the NGOs it dealt with on matters like packaging, postal rates for despatch, discount structures, invoicing, and book-trade terms like "Consignment Basis", "Sale or Return", "Approval Memos" etc. OIB printed a detailed information circular which it now routinely mails to all its NGO suppliers. Most of those who have received this circular have expressed their thanks for the service.

Often, NGOs would insist that the selling price of their books was as per costs incurred and there was no room for giving discounts. Once again, it was left to OIB to explain to them why it is necessary to have a proper pricing policy, particularly if one wants to enter the mainstream commercial bookshops which, unlike the NGOs, do not get free spending money from donor agencies but have to watch their balance sheets all the time if they are to survive. Similarly too, OIB would survive only if it received its commissions. The message was not only understood but implemented by NGOs when they brought out and priced their new publications.

In fact, commissions have been one of the reasons why regular bookshops initially expressed reluctance to stock NGO publications. NGO publications are generally low-priced and their discount margins are minimal. This results in very small earnings for the bookseller when he does make a sale. This is a genuine problem, especially for booksellers, for which there are no easy solutions since OIB, like other NGOs, aims at reasonable prices for books. However, OIB has persuaded booksellers to stock these titles too by agreeing in turn to list the bookshop in its catalogue and promote it among buyers from that region.

University librarians, OIB discovered, sometimes expect personal commissions in return for placing orders. When OIB did its first mailout to libraries, the response was a poor 5% as compared with the rather high 40 to 45% response it was generally receiving from its regular mailing list. That was when OIB became aware of the kickback system that was in operation. OIB refused to pay personal commissions to anyone and this meant losing a large chunk of the library market.

Fortunately, however, OIB discovered an ingenious way of overcoming this problem. It sought out interested lecturers and professors who would place their requests for OIB's titles with their librarians who then could not refuse to buy the books even though personal commissions were not paid.

This has not wholly taken care of the problem and there are still several professors, teachers and students who do not have access to OIB titles simply because the librarian does not circulate OIB's catalogue as well as the others.

Finally, keeping abreast with the new publications produced abroad (i.e. in the countries of the South) has been difficult since it is expensive to mail brochures. Moreover, due to staff changes, the new staff have to be briefed all over again on OIB's philosophy and ideology especially since it is not the standard way of doing business. This can be time-consuming and quite frustrating too at times.

Even within the NGO community in India, activists sometimes fail to inform OIB of new publications or whether the earlier ones are out of print. Such errors invariably come to light only after, say, 5,000 copies of the new catalogues have been printed and mailed out. However, OIB continues to try out new ways of overcoming these hurdles. Since the Bookstore's work represents a new thinking within countries in the South which many people empathise with, there is always adequate support and sympathy from the people across the counter, making it all that easier.

6. EFFECTS OF THE PRACTICE/INNOVATIVE EXPERIENCE

OIB can trace its origins to an idea floated in 1986. Today, as a result of its operations, books from Africa, South America and South and Southeast Asia are now available within the Indian subcontinent. This is the Bookstore's unique contribution. One of the most profound consequences of the Bookstore's operations is thus making available hundreds of books and titles from Africa and Southeast Asia in India and vice versa.

The fact that the Bookstore can operate a major commercial outlet with not a single book on the shelves originating from the UK or the USA is an eye-opener to most people who hitherto never raised such questions. Lonely Planet, the guidebook for alternative international travellers, recently labelled OIB as "the best book-shop" in Goa. It specifically noted that all the books in the store were published in Asia, Africa or Latin America.

For serious readers of fiction in English and for the small but growing number of scholars interested in fresh and different view-points and perspectives in the humanities and social sciences, OIB is a much-valued bookstore, since it provides access to what has been written, printed and published in English in many countries of the South.

OIB has also persuaded other bookshops to emulate its example. Less than a decade after the inception of OIB, Indian mainstream bookstores are stocking and selling books and periodicals published in English from Southeast Asian countries and Africa. They also now stock the publications of several NGOs on their shelves, something that was thought impossible just a few years ago.

Today, OIB has built up a network of outlets that stock its books. Together with its partners, it also organises exhibitions coinciding with any alternative seminar and participates routinely in several of the book fairs organised within the country and abroad. A couple of years ago, OIB was invited to take part in the international fair at Frankfurt. Booksellers there were surprised at the quality that alternative publishers in India were capable of achieving.

In August 1997, just under a decade from the date it was founded, OIB was awarded a Distinguished Bookseller's Award by the Federation of Indian Publishers, India's apex federation of book publishers. The award was given in the category, "Unique Bookshop for Specialised Books". The award was instituted for the first time to coincide with the occasion of the 50th year of

India's independence. It carries a citation which states that the award was given to OIB "for dedicated and distinguished services to the book-reading society".

7. SUITABILITY AND POSSIBILITY FOR UPSCALING

Not applicable.

8. SIGNIFICANCE FOR (AND IMPACT ON) POLICY-MAKING

The impact of the Bookstore's work on policy-making has yet to be felt. Though there is a great deal of talk about South-South cooperation, the government's commitment to the actual movement of books and other products of the mind across the South has been fairly minimal despite the fact that much would change if a country as large as India could take some sensible initiatives.

9. POSSIBILITY AND SCOPE OF TRANSFERRING TO OTHER COMMUNITIES OR COUNTRIES

There is no reason why the organisation of the Bookstore and of its publishing house with its present emphasis cannot be replicated in other parts of the world. No great skills, funds or even support is required.

What is essential in ample measure is dedication to the idea of intellectual freedom and to the idea of decolonising the mind, combined with a firm decision to work hard and produce quality work. If these qualities are available, OIBs can sprout anywhere.

The Other India Bookstore is a fiercely principled idea put into practice which proves that a new "information order" is not only desirable, but also possible.

11.

Theater for education and liberation

1. GENERAL INFORMATION

1.1 Title of practice or experience

PETA: Theater for education and liberation

1.2 Category of practice/experience and brief description

The Philippine Educational Theater Association, one of the most outstanding cultural groups in the Philippines, believes theater is not just an art form and is not just for entertainment. Theater can be used as a very effective medium for education and for liberation.

From the time of its inception, and especially during the Marcos administration, PETA spearheaded a cultural resurgence in the Philippines with the aim of developing a national theater movement that would reflect the people's condition, history and experiences of struggle, their hopes and their aspirations. A people's theater for empowerment and development, especially of the most disadvantaged sectors of society. A theater movement that would contribute to the individual's need for personal actualization and the people's need for societal transformation.

1.3 Name of person or institution responsible for the practice or experience

Philippine Educational Theater Association (PETA)

1.4 Name and position of key or relevant persons or officials involved

Cecilia Reyes Guidote, Founder
Ma. Gloriosa Santos-Cabangon, Executive Director
Ernesto Cloma, Program Director, School of People's Theater

1.5 Details of institution

(a) Address: No. 61, Lantana Street, Cubao, Quezon City, Philippines
(b) Telephone: ++ (63) (2) 410 0819, 410 0820, 410 0821, 410 0822
(c) Fax: ++ (63) (2) 410 0820

1.6 Name of person and/or institution conducting the research

Gigi Sarfati, Researcher-Writer, Tebtebba Foundation, Inc. (Indigenous Peoples' International Center for Policy Research and Education)

1.7 Details of research person/institution

(a) Address: Rm. 3B Agpaoa Compound, 111 Upper General Luna Road, 2600 Baguio City, Philippines
(b) Telephone: ++ (63) (74) 444 7703
(c) Fax: ++ (63) (74) 443 9459
(d) E-Mail: tebtebba@skyinet.net

2. THE PROBLEM OR SITUATION BEING ADDRESSED BY THE PRACTICE/INNOVATIVE EXPERIENCE

The Philippines' long colonial history has to some extent contributed to the distancing of Filipinos from their indigenous value-systems, traditions, rituals, songs and dances. The prevalance of a highly-Westernised modern culture has prevented the development of a Filipino cultural identity based on the country's rich indigenous heritage.

The colonial period saw the development of theatre traditions which reinforced existing hierarchies of social and political power. From religious dramas to popular variety shows, theatrical productions tended to reproduce dominant colonial stereotypes of Filipino identity.

After independence, the country's political and economic stability gradually worsened into crisis. The Philippines was faced with huge foreign debt, rising inflation, widespread unemployment and the challenges of meeting the social development of a large and poor population. In this context, the need for a viable medium of articulation and expression, as an alternative to the mainstream media, grew stronger. Both art and information, however, were subject to strict scrutiny and censorship during the Marcos regime.

Since the fall of the Marcos government in 1986, there has been an easing of restrictions on the media. It remains however, that the cultural scene continues to be dominated by a Westernized and commercialized culture that is not reflective of the Filipino people's history, experiences, values and realities.

The people's issues and concerns, their hopes, dreams and their aspirations need expression and a medium of expression. The Philippine Educational Theater Association (PETA) addresses this need through the People's Theater and the School for People's Theater, which strives to educate the Filipino people about the richness of their heritage, and liberate them from the forces that threaten to erode that cultural wealth.

3. DESCRIPTION OF THE PRACTICE/INNOVATIVE EXPERIENCE AND ITS MAIN FEATURES

PETA, like other nationalist organizations in the country, took form in the middle of the political and social unrest of the late sixties. The realities that existed in the country during the late seventies and early eighties further contributed to its development. But it grew strong mainly because it was nurtured by the heightening political and social consciousness of a people whose long search for national identity and sovereignty was slowly taking shape.

Cecilia Reyes Guidote founded PETA in April of 1967. She came from an upper-middle-class Filipino family and was then a fresh graduate of a masteral course in drama from the Trinity University of the United States of America.

The concept

Unlike many Filipinos who had studied in the US, Guidote was deeply cognizant of existing social realities in her country. She was proud of her own Filipino heritage. And she wanted to change, not her Filipino culture, but practices and programs which led the masses of Filipinos away from their national identity.

She strongly believed the depiction of art, in theater as well as in other forms, could find meaning only within the context of Filipinos' lives. She envisioned a national theater movement that would make the arts accessible to the masses of Filipinos, not only to those born to the higher echelons of society. The young woman was determined to use the theater and the skills and knowledge she had acquired, as a weapon to counteract the forces which subjugated the Filipino people's spirit.

In its Preamble, PETA declared: "The theater plays a tremendously significant part in the growth, development and propagation of a country's culture and arts. Particularly in these distressing times of 'mass culture' (a culture propagated by the mass media) which tends to confuse instead of edify minds, corrupt instead of purify taste, there is an almost compelling need for theater to be at the vanguard of a movement to lift man's spirit ..."

This grandiose mission was guided by the need to clarify the people's identity as Filipinos toward the formation of a national culture and eventually liberate them from an alienating culture. It thus required PETA to initiate and nurture a national theater movement for the promotion of a national culture, and, as such, develop groups of socially committed artists-teachers-leaders that would spearhead and bring to the fore such a movement in various parts of the country.

There also remained the need to raise the level of national and social consciousness among artists and audiences, which pushed PETA to create a Filipino people-based theater aesthetics, one that reflects what they now call the "aesthetics of poverty".

In essence, theater as an art form, and PETA as the vanguard of the national theater movement, were called upon to awaken the people and act as a catalyst for social transformation.

The People's Theater

At first, Guidote managed to recruit only four more associates into PETA. There were others, but many stayed only as guest actors/actresses or directors. The four worked on their own, most of the time draining their own personal, financial and logistical resources to get their productions through. Later, Guidote encouraged several students in her drama class at a local college to become members of PETA. And with a dedicated workforce and a vision, PETA strove "to embrace the capital, the cities, the towns and the barrios of the Philippine islands." (van Erven, 1989)

After a few years, the Kalinangan Ensemble, PETA's professional performing arm, was formed. It branched out to poverty-stricken communities, to schools, to trade unions and to remote peasant communities. In addition to its performances, PETA was also able to lay the groundwork for an experimental theater, an international exchange program, a touring company, a television and cinema unit and a performing arts academy. But in 1972, Martial Law was declared.

Before the declaration of martial rule in 1972, many considered theater "a secondary activity, a useful means to attract and entertain an audience between speeches at political rallies, but not a political weapon in its own right". But after the declaration of Martial Law, theater was recognized as a potent and practical tool for political expression and PETA took "its first hesitant steps on the slippery surface of political culture with several socially critical plays". (van Erven, 1989)

Most of these plays were staged at the "Dulaang Rajah Sulayman" (the Rajah Sulayman Theater)[1], characterized by what was conceptualized by Guidote as an "open" theater. The structure, which is an open-air theater, has been described by Grefalda, in an article entitled "Life at the Ruins", as "sculptural, three-dimensional, easily restricted, easily enlarged. Light and sound form an integral part of its space and its basic feeling is that of size and strength".

Aside from these inherent qualities the Rajah Sulayman Theater renders to each PETA play, creative sounds and original musical scores also enhance each production. PETA conducts research and studies on ethnic and tribal music and sounds, always to provide itself with an understanding on the context and significance of each art form so that choices of production design and musical arrangement suit each particular play, especially if the story concerns indigenous people. It uses a lot of materials and resources on Philippine traditional theater and indigenous art, sculptures, installation art, masks and puppetry. Several forms are combined, not only to enhance the play with ornaments but to be a medium in itself, to bring their message to the fore. Ernesto Cloma, PETA's present Program Director for Curriculum Development, says, "A PETA artist-teacher must be proficient in integrating various arts toward developing an issue or theme."

The use of the audience's language (mainly Filipino) is almost always stressed. As Ernesto Cloma puts it, "theater should tell the people's stories in the language of the people."

Creative movements used by the participants are confusingly of different origins but are beautifully combined. Western influences are noticeable in the form of ballet and modern jazz movements. But gestures identifiably Eastern, specifically those originating from the martial arts (Korean, Chinese, kung-fu and *arnis*[2]), are more commonly used to enhance stage presence and projection. Many plays also make use of movements and dances from Filipino ethnic groups, especially those of the Muslim Filipinos in the southern part of the country and the indigenous people of the Cordillera in the northern hinterlands. In each adaptation, there is always an element of improvisation and experimentation. And this is where the strength of PETA's performances lies: in their ability to experiment and improvise in order to always create something new, something distinct and yet familiar. The training of each performer in creative movements and its precise execution is a part of PETA's inventive program.

With the Dulaang Rajah Sulayman, PETA's experiments with movement, and the use of creative sounds and original musical scoring, PETA "stormed out of the mirrored, self-conscious palace of the conventional theater and started the big movement to render the theater accessible to all." (Almazan, 1983)

The principle of propagating what PETA calls a "mass-oriented culture" is also very evident in the group's production designs. Many stage props and backdrops are strikingly common but purposively and creatively designed. "Artistically, a typical PETA style was beginning to emerge in the productions. This style came to be known as the 'aesthetics of poverty', the fruits of artistic inventiveness forced upon the company by a chronic lack of finances." (van Erven, 1989)

Brenda Fajardo, PETA designer in 1985, had explained, "How can an artist claim to be socially responsible when he mounts high-cost productions during times of deprivation? But what is initially a by-product of material poverty becomes an expression which results from his sensitivity to the world around him. The artist begins deliberately to choose particular nuances and tones of color and texture that would express the qualities that he perceives around him – economic deprivation, cultural pollution, and violence. He evolves a new art which is authentic because it expresses life which happens to be poor; thus, the 'aesthetics of poverty'.... it implies that there is a sense of beauty which belongs to people who live in a condition of material deprivation." (van Erven, 1989)

The production entitled *Juan Tamban* is one of the best examples of PETA's application of the principles of the "aesthetics of poverty". The set was conceptualized and created by a designer's pool through a deliberate collective process. The group first went on a fact-finding mission to several of the metropolis' shanty towns, or what is locally called "the squatters' area"[3]. There, they chose pieces for the play's set based on each material's capacity to evoke meaningful and functional images, not for ornamentation nor for local color. For instance, empty plastic pails were lined up in rows and formed part of the set to suggest the lack of water supply, a basic government service being neglected in many urban poor communities (van Erven, 1989).

Up to the present, the concept of the aesthetics of poverty makes PETA stand out. It struggles to get by with little or no funding at all, and, as a result, is forced to work with found materials and junk which it employs so creatively.

At the back of PETA's strengths, however, was a very striking irony: from 1967 to 1974, "PETA's repertory consisted mainly of adaptations, imitations and translations of predominantly western plays". (van Erven, 1989) In the same grain, PETA had to invite foreign directors for many of its plays, among them, Brook Jones of the Cincinnati Playhouse, and Ladislav Smoceck, a guest theater director from Czechoslovakia.

This seemed to contradict its beliefs. But closer scrutiny helps us understand that this occurrence was a by-product of social and cultural realities existing during that same period. Cultural work was financially fulfilling only if the cultural worker catered to the elite. And the taste of the Filipino elite was not Filipino- but foreign-oriented. Cultural programs, projects and scholarships that aim to develop Filipino playwrights and directors with a nationalist orientation were virtually non-existent. As such, at that time, PETA had very little material and human resources to work with.

In spite of this problem, PETA did not lose sight of its strategic objectives.

In staging these translations and adaptations, PETA had made careful and intelligent choices. Lutgardo Labad, one of PETA's artistic directors, admits, "PETA also drew lessons from the heritage of Western Theatre as one form of stimulus for the development of a national dramatic literature." These adaptations, he claimed, proved to be stepping stones to "unveil and clarify existing social contradictions" in Philippine society. Among them were the likes of Bertolt Brecht's[4] *Mother Courage and Her Children* and *The Good Woman of Setzuan*, which were translated into Filipino and adapted to Filipino conditions (Labad, 1983).

Nevertheless, PETA was quite aware of the limitations of these adaptations and in 1975 began to stimulate potential playwrights by including a scriptwriting course in the arts academy it had established. The course is a compact, comprehensive training program that it holds for six weeks every summer (van Erven, 1989). This training program proved to be the quantum leap that brought PETA where it is right now.

In 1975 alone, eight outstanding original Filipino plays were created. From then on, PETA made a conscious effort to develop excellence in the art of playwrighting. A writer's pool and a laboratory production scheme for new dramas were created. This strategy had mined gold in the form of several moving plays, among them, *Si Tatang at ang Iba Pang mga Tauhan ng aming Dula (The Old Man and the Other Characters of Our Play,* 1979), *Juan Tamban* (1979), *Panunuluyan (The Search for an Inn*, 1979), *Pilipinas Circa 1907 (The Philippines During the 1900s*, 1982), *Buwan at Baril sa Eb Major (Moon and Gun in E Flat Major,* 1984), and *Oratoryo ng Bayan (The People's Oratorio,* 1983). *The People's Oratorio* was striking, in particular because it dramatized, in song, dance and dialogue, very essential articles of the United Nations Declaration of Human Rights. Using 11 cantos, it exposed the systematic violations of the Marcos regime of provisions to a universal declaration it was a signatory to (van Erven, 1989).

"*Si Tatang at ang Iba Pang mga Tauhan ng aming Dula* [which dramatizes the life and times of Valentin de los Santos, founder of the Lapinga Malaya or Freedom Party] is a historical documentary play that uses slides, newspaper clippings, and radio excerpts to convey its information." (van Erven, 1989).

Since April 1967, PETA has mounted more than 200 productions and performances of socially relevant plays, most of which are original. It has helped much in enriching Philippine contemporary theater through the study and use of various theatrical forms to ventilate local, national and international issues. It has also disseminated studies, reports of experiences and products of its own and those of the network's cultural and theater work and administration through its research, documentation and publication program.

Through its different productions, PETA made theater function as an effective tool for re-educating a people whose long colonial past had confused its national identity.

But PETA refused to exist simply as a cultural group. It carried upon its shoulders the more challenging task of propagating a national theater movement. This it achieved, not only by staging socially relevant plays, but also by developing a training program and by using workshops as a mechanism for organizing different sectors of the population.

The School of People's Theater

The School of People's Theater is PETA's training and teaching arm. It was once called the Central Institute of Theater Arts in the Philippines (CITAP) which, in 1971, was renamed the Central Institute of Theater Arts in Southeast Asia (CITASA) after PETA received a grant from the United Nations Educational, Scientific and Cultural Organization (UNESCO) to expand CITAP and serve the entire Southeast Asian region.

Through the years, PETA was able to develop what it now calls the People's Theater Pedagogy. It is a creative, participatory and collective process which encourages not only the transfer of skills and the development of aesthetic excellence, but more so, the awakening, organizing and further development of a national and international people's theater movement.

It is creative because together with the people they teach, a lot of improvisation in drama, writing, visual art, music and storytelling is used. It is participatory because the content of the training, its objectives and results are drawn out of the people they serve, who come from various sectors of society (school youth, students, doctors and health practitioners, engineers, peasants, urban poor, trade unions, women groups, etc.).

PETA believes they are not omniscient teachers and trainers. They also learn from the group they teach while they teach. It is a collective process because everyone works together toward the attainment of common goals. Through the workshop and this training program, theater becomes a vehicle for development work, for the ventilation of issues, for organizing, for campaigns, for education, but most of all, for personal and social liberation.

Eugene van Erven, who did extensive and in-depth research on PETA in 1989, describes the process as follows:[5]

Typically, PETA gets invited to do its outreach work by local people's organizations. "The dynamics, strategies and exercises of the people's theater workshop have evolved considerably over the years, but the basic structure remains the same. The workshop process can be divided into three phases: the pre-workshop period; the workshop proper and the post-workshop period."(van Erven, 1989)

In the pre-workshop period, the PETA actors-teachers-researchers[6] who are tasked to facilitate the workshop first conduct an extensive investigation into the social, political, economic and cultural situation of their target group (i.e. the group, sector or organization who invited them). This they do even before going to a specific area or community. Local organizers or officials of the organization/group furnish them with the necessary data in written or oral form during several consultations.

Later, the actors-trainers-researchers visit the area to get acquainted with the people and their environment. This also gives them a chance to conduct informal interviews to enrich whatever data they already have.

According to van Erven, and PETA actors-trainers-researchers themselves, the best workshop results can be obtained if they, along with other participants of the workshop, can live and work together for several days at a stretch. Thus, the workshops are usually scheduled during strikes, holidays, or off-season periods for fishermen, plantation workers and farmers. It is also very important, they said, for them to live and eat with their target group and adapt themselves to the local conditions existing in the area. This practice becomes more important for workshops held in rural peasant communities. The rural population tends to look up to the educated middle class from the cities and this sometimes becomes an obstacle to achieving a creative liberation process in the workshop.

The workshop proper follows and can be further subdivided into three stages, namely:
(a) integration with the community, group dynamics and get-to-know-you games;
(b) basics of acting and drawing-out of people's stories through structural analysis of the community; and
(c) production of a collectively created original script.

The workshop proper begins with the getting-to-know-you phase wherein games and exercises are used to break the ice between the participants and between the participants and PETA facilitators (of the workshop) in order to establish rapport, mutual trust and sensitivity.

After the getting-to-know-you phase, the facilitators try to find out exactly what each individual participant expects to learn or gain from the workshop through another exercise. The cartoon-drawing exercise is most commonly used. At this stage, the participants get an initial exposure to acting because they are encouraged to imitate sounds, gestures, intonations and other characteristics of the other participants of the workshop.

In his research, van Erven observed that new participants are not encouraged to enter the group late (i.e. on the second or third day of the workshop proper). This, according to PETA members, is because the workshops are structured cumulatively. Relationships and collective working attitudes would have already begun to gel to such a degree that the introduction of a newcomer would only disrupt the process. For the same reason, the effectiveness of the second process depends on the success of the first. If inhibitions have not been sufficiently broken down and healthy cooperative group dynamics not been established, then the people's stories to be drawn out in the second phase will be proportionally meager.

One of the aims of the people's theater workshop is to be non-threatening and transparent. Upon completion of a certain phase or after major exercises, the whole group sits down at a round table for feedback. In addition to this, the facilitators also conduct a separate evaluation at the end of each day and make adjustments whenever necessary.

The second phase opens with a creative version of structural social analysis of the community. The participants are requested to make a "social map" where they indicate what they consider to be the most prominent landmarks in their community by means of symbols they can either draw, cut from a magazine or paint. They select, for instance, visual symbols of people or institutions that hold the reins of political or economic power in their community. The result of these is a collage that the participants exhibit in an improvised gallery and discuss. They come up with a unified view and analysis of their community and finally present their collective map in a short skit or in songs.

This structural analysis is always followed by a round-table discussion where participants tell stories of their lives or of others in their community. These stories, which are often moving, form the basis for the drama pieces that will evolve later on in the workshop. At this stage, the facilitators may opt to introduce basic acting techniques, or exercises in story construction and storytelling. Alternatively, they may introduce some more exercises that enhance imagination, creativity and spontaneity or activities that enhance trust and sensitivity between participants. Also during these exercises, the participants are able to explore the musical and rhythmical possibilities of common objects in their surroundings like cans and pieces of wood or bamboo. At the same time, while performing together, they realize how none of them should dominate the group with his or her instrument, for it disturbs harmony.

In the last phase of the workshop proper, one or more original people's plays are created and produced by the participants themselves, who by now would have virtually taken full control of the workshop process. Divided into groups of five or six, they work out scenarios based on the stories they have shared with each other. The participants are encouraged to utilize art forms indigenous to their culture. They also compose songs, rehearse and finally stage their plays. They perform either for the whole community or for the rest of the workshop group.

After the final showcase performance, the facilitators and participants get together once more for a final evaluation of the entire workshop. Results are matched with expectations shared in the beginning of the workshop and future possibilities are discussed. An effort is made to convince the participants that with a minimum of training and practice, they themselves can conduct workshops with other members of their community or in neighboring villages and towns. Often, the participants spontaneously decide to form their own community theater group.

4. DESCRIPTION OF THE INSTITUTION RESPONSIBLE AND ITS ORGANIZATIONAL ASPECTS[7]

PETA members describe themselves as "a community of theater artists dedicated to the development of a People's Theater that mirrors Philippine social realities, a theater that serves as a potent agent and instrument toward personal, social and societal transformation".

They envision the "full actualization of the human person. They envision a liberating people's culture, and a free society, a sovereign nation."

Their mission: to be a people's theater for empowerment; to develop and transfer skills using theater and related arts as a medium; to provide, most especially to the disadvantaged members and sectors of society, the necessary tools and instruments for personal actualization and societal transformation.

With these in mind, they aim to:
(a) develop a theater that reflects the people's condition, history and experiences of struggle, their hopes and aspirations;
(b) evolve People's Theater aesthetics and pedagogy, based on the people's actual condition, simultaneously raising standards of artistry in creative work and performance, enhancing competence and excellence in teaching and communication, and popularizing the creative use of theater for people's expression, education and organization;
(c) promote and forge partnerships and linkages with theater groups at the sectoral, regional, national and international levels, as well as with non-

theater people's organizations sharing PETA's vision of man, culture and society; and

(d) define, develop and operationalize the Dramatic Arts Center as a main synergizing mechanism for the development of resources, skills and facilities for People's Theater by the year 2000.

PETA has four main implementing units: the Dramatic Arts Center; the Partnership and Liaison Office; the Program Support Services; and the PETA Broadcast and Film, Inc.

(a) The Dramatic Arts Center (DAC) builds the infrastructure for the Institute of People's Theater. Under the DAC are:

(i) The Kalinangan Ensemble. The Kalinangan Ensemble is the production and performance unit of PETA. It develops People's Theater Aesthetics.

(ii) School for People's Theater. This is the training and teaching unit of PETA. It develops the People's Theater Pedagogy.

(iii) People's Theater Resource Center. This is PETA's research, documentation and publication unit. It develops and makes accessible resources and facilities in the resource center.

(iv) Theater Collectives. These are specialized production-performance-training-research and documentation units. Among the theater collectives are the Dance Theater Collective which develops a people's dance theater; and the Children's Theater Collective which develops People's Theater for children.

(v) Playwrights Circle. This is a special study and training unit that develops People's Theater plays and playwrights.

(b) The Partnership and Liaison Office (PAL) develops People's Theater partnerships and linkages. At the national level, it coordinates and manages projects and programs with sectoral, regional and national networks. At the international level, it identifies, develops and coordinates cultural programs and projects with groups abroad supportive of PETA and the national cultural network's vision and goals. Under the PAL is the Marketing and Promotions unit which is in charge of public relations, marketing and sales for PETA's productions, workshops, conferences, publications and other activities.

(c) The Program Support Services (PSS) handles specialized administrative and managerial services and tasks. It takes care of Human Resource Management and Development, Financial Management and Office Administration.

(d) The PETA Broadcast and Film, Inc. (PETA-BFI) is a spin-off production-training-research unit with a very special concern: alternative mass media for people's empowerment. At present, it concentrates on alternative television programming. The unit intends to develop radio broadcasting and film as instruments for people's empowerment.

5. PROBLEMS OR OBSTACLES ENCOUNTERED AND HOW THEY WERE OVERCOME

Since the time of its inception, PETA has always had two perennial problems: money and ideology. The two are very closely related.

Funding has always been a problem because theater is widely seen only as a form of entertainment, something one indulges in after a hard week of work to relax and unwind. The theater's potential and capacity to be a medium of education and liberation is not recognized by many. Very few are willing to fund a theater production. The moneyed elite of the country, whom PETA attacks through its socially relevant plays, definitely do not want to fund a production that exposes their weaknesses. And the poor majority, who do recognize the theater's capacity to be a medium for social change, do not have the financial nor logistical capacity to sponsor expensive productions.

The ideological direction of PETA's productions has always been a problem because theater is seen mainly as a form of entertainment. And in entertainment, the aesthetic content of each production is a number one priority. In entertainment, the objective is to provide recreation, not the vexation of the mind and spirit through socially critical and sometimes dramatic and disquieting plays. In seeking entertainment, the objective is to escape from realities, not bring them to the fore of human consciousness; the objective is to trap one into a state of inaction, not induce action. The elite of the country benefit from and strongly favor the former objectives. The basic sectors of society benefit from and favor the latter. Through its more than 30 years of existence, PETA has been vexed by both problems. Its membership determines its direction and the methods the organization employs in order to handle both problems. And the bulk of PETA members come from the middle class of Philippine society, a class torn apart by its sympathies for the poor majority and its need to belong to the financially, politically and socially secure "cultured" elite.

Since most of PETA's members are young students who come from the middle-income group, the lack of financial returns for the time, energy and talent they invest in PETA does not become an issue – at first. However, when most of these students graduate, or marry and raise their own families, their perspectives change. Many branch out into the movies or into television productions where they earn a lot, leaving PETA with a diminished workforce and a need to recruit and train a new set of members.

In recruiting and training new members, PETA always puts the stress on the value of each member's commitment. A commitment to serving the poor, a commitment to mirroring reality, a commitment to becoming sensitive and socially responsible artists and teachers, and a commitment to practicing the principles of the aesthetics of poverty.

But this commitment is not easily developed. It is developed through a long process of internal and external struggles. Time and again, PETA members find themselves locked in a quiet rift. There are those who want to use theater as a liberating medium and those who are only after the artistic rewards of theater performance. In 1986, Labad, one of the most artistic directors PETA has ever produced, said, "PETA became more socially relevant through a historical process. In 1975, most of our writers came from the student movement and carried over the concerns that lived in the universities (which, at that time, were very critical of the Marcos dictatorship). But we had to be protective; that's why we were doing mostly psychological plays and artistic experiments. It was the workshop programs that really politicized our people (i.e. members) ..."

As such, PETA consciously launches training programs that would expose its members to social realities. They are encouraged to go to the slums, to the countryside, to the picket lines. They are encouraged to learn and feel the sentiments, hopes, dreams, experiences of exploitation and struggles of the people they serve. They are encouraged to be a part of the lives of the poor and the marginalized – if only for a short while. Only in this way can they depict the people's lives, can they understand the context of the "aesthetics of poverty", and can they carry out PETA's mission to be a medium of liberation.

At times, when the financial side of the problem dominates the scene, PETA exerts more effort to increase ticket sales and to find more sponsors for its productions. There are church groups, non-governmental bodies and even government agencies, schools and universities that support PETA.

It also enters into mutually beneficial partnerships with other organizations and institutions. In these schemes, it shares its skills and expertise in exchange for the logistical and financial resources of its partners.

PETA is acutely aware of its financial limitations and thus, always keeps production costs at a minimum. When production costs threaten to exceed the specified budget, substitutes (i.e. of materials and designs) are used, also in congruence with its principle, the "aesthetics of poverty".

It must be noted, at this point, that the "aesthetics of poverty" initially emerged as a solution to the organization's financial and logistical limitations. But it later developed into one of PETA's trademarks, an essential component of its practice. By practicing the principle, PETA has developed a resourceful and creative workforce, able to survive in dire conditions.

More than this, PETA has developed, over the years, a network of cultural groups from the basic sectors, from urban poor communities and rural peasant communities, from indigenous peoples' communities and trade unions. And these people's organizations remain PETA's strength. Their experience of deprivation has accustomed them to living a hard life, to utilizing whatever resources are available, to making do with only whatever it is they have. For most of these groups, the constant lack of finances is not a problem. What they need is to develop a keener aesthetic eye in order to see what is beautiful around them and maximize its use. In most of these groups, such rifts as exist between PETA members are virtually non-existent. Among these groups PETA had helped develop, there is no question about the theater's role. It is their medium for education and for liberation.

6. EFFECTS OF THE PRACTICE/ INNOVATIVE EXPERIENCE

The particular effects of each PETA play can be gauged from the audience's reactions. A standing ovation is not uncommon after each PETA play. Spontaneous discussions and debates among peer groups who have just finished watching a play happen every time.

Whether PETA has just finished performing for a specific sector in a community or for the general public, its performances invariably result in an open forum of sorts in which the issues raised in the plays are discussed. In this sense, the people's theater can be regarded as a grassroots exercise in people's democracy. On a different level, people's theater can be a powerful instrument for communal therapy. It can assist a community in creatively expressing its defeats or in celebrating its victories.

It is not uncommon to find people being awakened and moved into action because of the social realism evident in PETA's plays. There were individuals, for instance, who became interested in the problems encountered by prostituted women in the vicinity of the former US Military Bases in Clark and Subic after watching a PETA play depicting the plight of these women. There were others who, after watching a play, became more open to discussions about national issues and would later be seen in rallies or demonstrations of nationalist organizations. Other forces (i.e. militant organizations actively recruiting and organizing individuals in a particular sector) are at play here but one cannot discount the fact that PETA's socially relevant plays served as an eye-opener for many.

PETA's workshops and training programs are even more effective. For the PETA facilitators, the workshop experience is infinitely more rewarding than a ten-minute standing ovation from a middle-class audience in Manila. For the workshop participants, they gain in courage and self-respect from discovering a voice and a creativity they never knew they possessed.

This increased confidence of community members in their own abilities and in the effectiveness of collective cultural action often results in direct social action.

Meanwhile, picket-line workshops organized in collaboration with the Kilusang Mayo Uno (First of May Movement)[8] have had similar effects. In many ways, strikes are perfect occasions for such activities because the participants have time to spare. They are also in desperate need of a voice to express their grievances.

The most common result of workshops, however, is the formation of a new cultural group within the community or sector they have serviced. As such, PETA has helped give birth to hundreds of drama groups in schools, parishes, peasant communities, trade unions and other disadvantaged sectors in Philippine society.

In sum, PETA has succeeded in contributing to the development of a national theater movement, of which it is a part. This movement continuously contributes to the advancement of a national culture and a national identity. It is a movement that truly reflects the Filipino people's history, traditions, present conditions, struggles, dreams and aspirations.

7. SUITABILITY AND POSSIBILITY FOR UPSCALING

There is no question as to the suitability and possibility of upscaling the PETA practice. In fact, it is necessary, considering PETA's mission to further develop a national theater movement in the country and later, an international theater movement catering to the marginalized peoples of the world.

During the past decade, upscaling became its focus. As a result, PETA has formed different theater and dance collectives, in addition to playwrights' circles and other similar groups. Moreover, it has now expanded its operations to include broadcasting, and television and film production. TV and film productions, however, require large amounts of manpower, finance and logistical resources, which is a difficulty it is finding hard to overcome.

Similarly, its training program, which was expanded in the early seventies to reach out to other Southeast Asian countries, has been difficult to sustain. This is primarily because of the lack of finances and logistics.

Nevertheless, what is more important right now is to maintain and sustain its operations and the large network it has created. Meanwhile, it should further develop its capacity for resource mobilization in order to successfully implement projects related to broadcasting, and television and film production. The organization must also sustain and enhance its liaison work at the international level in order to be able to reach out to more marginalized peoples in other Third World countries.

As a fulfillment of many of its long-term goals, PETA plans to construct a Theater Center to enable it to pursue its vision of a Philippine Theater that is truly integrated and vital to the development of people and society. The infrastructure shall provide the necessary venue that would ensure the company's sustainability. It shall be used as the physical base for all programs of PETA in community theater outreach as well as professional theater repertory performances. Apart from performances, the center will also serve as a learning space, where courses dealing with theater arts, educational theater, community theater, people's aesthetics and children and youth will be developed and taught. The Theater Center will also serve as a juncture for cultural exchange in the Asia Pacific region, facilitating the realization of an Asian-Pacific cultural awareness within a global multicultural space. At the same time, the center will function as a specialized resource center, where the expanding datatbase of PETA's artistic and pedagogical experience shall be accessible to its constituents. And lastly, the Theater Center shall be the enduring symbol of PETA's significant role in Philippine Theater. It shall present the pioneering work PETA has done in influencing theater and education for the past thirty years. PETA sees the Theater Center as a fruition, a celebration of its decades-long commitment that has made possible the lasting achievements it has had in the past. The Theater Center sets a new beginning, a gate to the next millenium.

8. SIGNIFICANCE FOR (AND IMPACT ON) POLICY-MAKING

Much of PETA's impact on policy-making was indirect. PETA helped awaken the disadvantaged sectors who later moved to change policies and programs affecting their specific sector. Their performances, especially those staged in front of the Congress or Senate, added strength to the impact already created by militant organizations demanding changes from the government, especially during the time of the late President Marcos.

In the area of national culture, PETA, through its artist-members, moved for the formation of a Ministry of Culture, way back during the Marcos administration. This led to the establishment of the President's Committee on Culture and the Arts during the Aquino administration that later created the Cultural Bill or Republic Act No. 7356. This Republic Act provided for the creation of the National Commission for Culture and the Arts.

In spite of this, an elitist culture patterned after foreign tastes remains dominant. But the weakness here, it seems, lies not with PETA but with the dominance of foreign media and cultures.

9. POSSIBILITY AND SCOPE OF TRANSFERRING TO OTHER COMMUNITIES OR COUNTRIES

The community theater group PETA assists can best be regarded as a micro-media unit. As a product of PETA's Basic Integrated Theater Arts Workshops, its first activities consist of repeating the showcase performance in its own or neighboring communities.

Secondly, it organizes and echoes the workshop to other interested members of the community. From the start, the activities of the community theater group are split (like PETA was, before it expanded its programs) into training and performing, pedagogy and aesthetics. As a performing unit, the group develops original plays that are performed during important political or religious occasions. As a training unit, the group develops its own trainers who are capable of conducting outreach workshops. Thus, a snowball effect is created of one community theater group founding another and so forth.

In short, the practice of PETA is easily transferred to other communities within the country. Likewise, it is also possible for other countries to adapt the methods that are suitable to their particular situation and culture. The key is to unlock an individual's or group's creativity and resourcefulness. Another key is an in-depth understanding and appreciation of one's own culture and life.

Today, after more than 10 years of its systematic outreach training program, PETA can pride itself on some extraordinary sociopolitical and artistic results (van Erven, 1989).

In sum, it has given training and developed a curriculum in People's Theater through about a thousand workshops throughout the Philippine archipelago. It has initiated theater organizing and networking, helping give birth to hundreds of drama groups based in schools, parishes, communities, sectors, regions and even overseas. It has been to all corners of the Philippines, and has organized a network in the three major islands, Luzon, Visayas and Mindanao. It has successfully created independent bodies that replicate PETA's work, whom it treats as partners and deals with on an equal footing.

It has also gone to Pakistan, Thailand, Indonesia, New Zealand, Australia and several Third World countries. There, it shared its skills, pedagogy and experiences for replication. Some of the countries it went to had their own existing theater groups. In such cases, PETA helped enrich both its own and the host countries' experience, knowledge and skills. It considers the International Drama Educational Association in Holland, the Asia-Pacific Adult Education, the World Council of Churches, the Asian Christian Communicators and a few cultural groups abroad, some of which comprise overseas Filipino workers, as associates and partners in its unending cultural work.

Endnotes

1. The Rajah Sulayman Theater, which was designed and conceptualized by Guidote, was christened Rajah Sulayman in honor of the leader of the Mohammedan Malays who first inhabited the area (Almazan, 1983).
2. *Arnis* was a once popular Filipino martial arts technique for self-defense.
3. A "squatters' area" is a cluster of shanties built by the city's landless urban poor in a small vacant lot (which may be either public or privately owned land).
4. Bertolt Brecht was a German playwright who advocated what many call a "theater of liberation".
5. This section has been lifted from Eugene van Erven's research entitled Stages of People Power: The Philippine Educational Theater Association, The Hague, 1989.
6. PETA calls its pool of trainers actors-teachers-researchers because they perform all three functions at once, especially while facilitating workshops.
7. Lifted from *The PETA Brochure*, 1991.
8. The Kilusang Mayo Uno is an organization of militant labor unions in the Philippines. In the Philippines, Labor Day is celebrated on the first of May, hence its name.

References

1. Almazan, Elizabeth Cecile, (1983) *A Case Study of the Philippine Educational Theater Association: Towards the Realization of a National Culture,* Metro Manila.
2. Labad, Lutgardo L., (1983) *PETA and Brecht: A Story of Friendship,* Weimar, German Democratic Republic.
3. Philippine Educational Theater Association, (1991) *The PETA Brochure,* Metro Manila.
4. van Erven, Eugene, (1989) *Stages of People Power: The Philippine Educational Theater Association,* The Hague.
5. Interview with PETA members, Metro Manila, 1998.

12.

Alternative news agency as an instrument of social change

1. GENERAL INFORMATION

1.1 Title of practice or experience

Philippine News and Features: Alternative news agency as an instrument of social change

1.2 Category of practice/experience and brief description

The experience documented here tells how an independent news agency continues to help achieve little victories for society's small people – landless farmers, underpaid workers, indigenous folk, women and children. It also tells how this news agency has developed a kind of journalism that adheres to the core values of balance, fairness and accuracy, even as it ensures that those on the margins – who compose the majority – are heard clearly.

This news agency has helped set a trend in issue-oriented, rather than simply personality-based, news- and feature-writing as well as analysis and commentaries. Mainstream newspapers, for instance, generally play up the arrival of a Hollywood star or some foreign dignitary. But this alternative news agency gives more importance to the likes of farmers fasting in front of the agrarian reform office to protest the conversion of their land into a golf course.

This news agency also covers government bureaucracies such as the National Congress, the various cabinet agencies, and even the presidential palace. It emphasizes, however, issues and matters of public interest.

It also examines government policies and programs, as well as "development projects" of the private sector, that further marginalize lowly folk. So-called "development projects" include big dams and big open-pit or open-cast mines that displace indigenous folk, conversion of productive farmlands into real estate enclaves, and other ventures that threaten both people and the environment.

With 12 years as an alternative news agency under its belt, the independent Manila-based Philippine News and Features (PNF) has shown that journalism can also be oriented toward helping develop and raise social consciousness for social change.

1.3 Name of person or institution responsible for the practice or experience

Philippine News and Features (PNF)

1.4 Name and position of key or relevant persons or officials involved

Maria Cristina Rodriguez, Editor

1.5 Details of institution

   (a) Address: First Floor Lola Taya Building, 1165 Quezon Avenue, Quezon City, Philippines
   (b) Telephone: ++ (63) (2) 927 4454
   (c) Fax: ++ (63) (2) 927 4455
   (d) E-Mail: PNF@Phil.gn.apc.org

1.6 Name of person and/or institution conducting the research

Tebtebba Foundation, Inc. (Indigenous Peoples' International Center for Policy Research and Education)

1.7 Details of research person/institution

   (a) Address: Rm. 3B Agpaoa Compound, 111 Upper General Luna Road, 2600 Baguio City, Philippines
   (b) Telephone: ++ (63) (74) 444 7703
   (c) Fax: ++ (63) (74) 443 9459
   (d) E-Mail: tebtebba@skyinet.net

2. THE PROBLEM OR SITUATION BEING ADDRESSED BY THE PRACTICE/INNOVATIVE EXPERIENCE

The *Philippine Signs,* a bi-weekly newspaper and forerunner of Philippine News and Features (PNF), came out in 1984, during the time of the late Ferdinand Marcos' martial law regime.

The *Philippine Signs* contained news, features, analyses and commentaries about issues such as human rights violations, economic issues such as the country's rising foreign debt to the World Bank and the International Monetary Fund, farmers' demand for real agrarian reform, labor strikes, and coverage of the various levels of sectoral protests against Marcos' rule.

In a political climate which was not exactly conducive to press freedom, the *Philippine Signs* and a number of other "alternative" newspapers, alongside underground publications called the "mosquito press", found readership among a public hungry for an alternative perspective to what emanated from the mainstream media.

The alternative newspapers under Marcos went mainstream under the presidency of Corazon Aquino, who took over the reins of power following the former's ouster in 1986. During Aquino's presidency, other newspapers also emerged. At this point, the *Philippine Signs,* which was being published by a group led by socially critical church people, could not compete with the business-backed mainstream newspapers. The men and women behind the *Philippine Signs* thought of an alternative: set up a news agency which would come out with a regular dispatch of news, features, analyses and commentaries. The mainstream newspapers would be the news agency's outlets.

The news agency became known as Philippine News and Features or PNF, originally the pseudonym of a correspondent of the now defunct *Philippine Signs.*

PNF immediately set itself a special mission: to help articulate, interpret, analyze and comment on the basic issues the mainstream media tend to gloss over. These issues include the continuing clamor for no-nonsense agrarian reform, environmental woes, and the various issues and advocacies marginalized sectors have since taken up. These sectors include landless peasants, laborers, indigenous peoples, women and children. While PNF recognizes that all these issues have existed since the time of the Marcos regime, it also acknowledges that the world situation has changed since 1986.

PNF thus sees a new challenge: the eclipse of the bipolarized world. 1986 onwards saw the emergence of the current trend of "globalization", rapidly integrating national economies into a world economy. States are under pressure to "reform" their political institutions and social and economic policies to accord with globalization. However, citing worldwide evidence, PNF has seen that globalization, despite its claims of creating new wealth, is further driving a wedge between the few haves and the many have-nots among the world's family of nations. The result: a rising economic imbalance among nations and within them. This spurs social tension. PNF warns that the human rights of peoples, communities and individuals might be trampled on, and their social and cultural values undermined, once these hamper globalization's drive toward "market efficiency" and "maximized profits".

The Philippines is not exempt from the harsh impacts of neo-liberal globalization. In this light, PNF sees its tasks ("to develop and raise social awareness and to foster change, human dignity and genuine development") to have become more challenging than ever. PNF has to be attentive, for example, in monitoring new government policies embracing globalization designs.

For instance, a mining law approved in 1995, has practically liberalized and opened up the country's mining industry to foreign mining prospectors. The law has courted conflict. Many villagers in indigenous communities, where gold, copper, silver and other minerals are found, either have been displaced or are under threat of being forced out of their ancestral land. The liberalization of mining, bioprospecting and biopiracy, massive conversion of food-producing lands into real and industrial estates, the contractualization of labor, and the social conflicts spurred by these phenomena are among the impacts of globalization which PNF seeks to help address.

3. DESCRIPTION OF THE PRACTICE/INNOVATIVE EXPERIENCE AND ITS MAIN FEATURES

PNF comes out with a regular packet of news, features, analyses and commentaries. In its earlier stage, PNF's dispatch was distributed weekly (every Saturday) to its subscribers, which include almost all of Manila's over a dozen newspapers. Its writers and correspondents in Manila and in the provinces therefore had to send in their stories by 12:00 noon Friday or even as early as Thursday to give time for editing and packaging.

As PNF's capacity (writers' skills and proficiency) improved, it later came out with a twice-a-week dispatch. Aside from the Saturday edition, another midweek dispatch was added. The deadline for submitting articles for this midweek edition was 12:00 noon Wednesday or even earlier. Distribution was early morning Thursday.

A dispatch usually carries an average of eight to ten articles. These are mostly features, news features and investigative reports. From time to time, the dispatch also includes an analysis and a commentary.

The average length per article is two pages, single space, and double space after every paragraph on short bond. A simple news feature can be a page or a page and a half long. Special features and investigative reports, however, can go as far as three pages. Other lengthy special reports are cut into two, three or even four parts, and these are expected to be reprinted in installments.

Unless in exceptional circumstances, PNF's story lengths are kept to a minimum for practical reasons. Shorter stories have better chances of getting reprinted than longer ones. There are some newspapers, however, which have special sections for lengthier pieces. But based on PNF's experience, it is often best to keep an article as brief and concise as possible.

In its early stages, PNF's articles were edited by a veteran editor who had been in the journalism profession even before Marcos imposed martial law. Another equally competent and excellent woman editor-writer soon took over for a time. The job was soon delegated to a senior staff member who eventually got trained in editing. Assisting the editor is a managing editor who also helps rewrite or edit manuscripts, aside from making sure that writers and correspondents on the field submit their stories.

From time to time, the editor or managing editor sends memos to province-based writers and correspondents. These memos usually contain suggested story ideas or subjects which writers and correspondents can pursue.

For a well-planned and synchronized coverage of both old and emerging issues and events, province-based writers and correspondents periodically meet with their editors in Manila. Planning and strategizing help writers focus. Writers and editors would have to meet on how to cover, for example, a national election. Such meetings are necessary to help writers do stories that have a cutting edge over other media outfits. A PNF story angle, for instance, would delve into how and where politicians get money for their political campaigns. This entails some effort like chasing the politicians' money trail, research, interviews and other investigative requirements.

Beats

PNF's Manila-based writers are assigned beats or special areas of coverage. Somebody is assigned, for example, to cover the "popular movements" (labor, urban poor, women, etc.) beat; another, the government beat (which includes the presidential palace, Congress, education and health departments, etc.); and there are other beats such as the business sector.

Province-based writers and correspondents have a general beat. But they are encouraged to focus on major issues which affect the marginalized sectors in their areas. A writer based in the Cordillera upland region in northern Philippines, for example, can set his eyes more on issues and problems affecting the region's indigenous communities. Specifically, he can look into the impact of a current rush of foreign mining prospectors lured by the new government policy of liberalizing the mining industry.

This issue alone has many key players, such as the mining companies and government officials on one hand, and the affected people on the other. By applying journalism's core values of balance, fairness and accuracy, the PNF writer can present, interpret and analyze a variety of voices and viewpoints on the mining issue. But he also ensures that the powerless and even voiceless victims of big commercial mining are heard clearly.

Writing style and guidelines

PNF employs practically the same standard journalism techniques and values in writing news, features, news features, analyses and commentaries. If there is any difference, it is in the angling of stories. As cited earlier, PNF strives to present opposing views and voices, but ensures that the voiceless and powerless are also heard.

PNF's seven-point writing principles are the key to further understanding journalism as PNF practices it. Thus:

"1. We shall adhere to journalism's core values of balance, fairness and accuracy, even as we declare our bias for the poor, marginalized sectors of society. We shall endeavor to present the variety of voices and viewpoints on vital national concerns and issues, but ensure that those on the margins – who compose the majority – are heard clearly.
2. In writing on an issue where competing cause-oriented (advocacy) groups put forward differing viewpoints and calls to action, we shall apply balance, fairness and accuracy in such a way as to enable the public to discern which viewpoint and call to action best responds to the issue. We shall continue to give priority coverage to organizations with a proven track record of credibility and leadership.
3. We shall illuminate issues by digging into the underlying tensions of seemingly surface conflicts and help the people make sense of what goes on around them. We shall challenge the people to confront issues adversely affecting them. We shall endeavor to show them the possibilities that exist, or that they can create, for moving forward.
4. We shall maintain and enhance the authenticity, depth and credibility that PNF dispatches have earned through the years. We shall try harder always to get correct facts to provide background, context and perspective to our news stories, features, analyses and commentaries.
5. We shall foster change that will enhance human dignity and enable the Filipino people to develop along the path of their choosing, and shall oppose and expose 'change' that seeks to achieve the opposite effects.
6. We shall examine and challenge government policies and programs, as well as 'development projects' of the private sector, that are inimical to the people's interests to expose the ill intents underlying the hype. We shall endeavor to detail their harmful impacts (actual or potential), and critique the aspects that such policies, programs and projects may miss, gloss over or inadequately deal with.

7. We shall develop reportorial 'niches' that PNF writers and contributors are most competent to handle in a sustained way, and which the media outlets may not be covering adequately." (PNF *Statement of Principles*, as revised in August 1997)

Featurized stories

PNF minimizes, if not does away with, spot or straight news reporting. Although it sometimes includes straight news, PNF prefers to featurize its stories, adding more background and context to a current event. This is because PNF cannot compete with wire agencies which give spot news stories almost every minute.

In being able to featurize, PNF is helping not only to inform readers about an event or issue, but also to clarify the various underpinnings of and emerging trends from an issue. A PNF story therefore stresses the whys and wherefores of an issue.

Let us take a look at how PNF covered, for example, an issue involving the use by some vegetable farmers of cyanide as a pest antidote. The usual straight news reporting would simply state that some farmers are using cyanide, which is hazardous to consumers. More often than not, the farmers would get the blame for the whole mess.

PNF, on the other hand, dug deeper into the issue and found out that farmers' use of cyanide was just the tip of the iceberg. It found out that farmers had resorted to using cyanide because of their helplessness against certain pests, which had become resistant to even the most potent pesticide.

PNF also discovered that the farmers experimented with various possible ways to control pests. Farmers, for example, had experimented with "cocktailing" or mixing two or more brands of pesticides, which they thought would be more effective, but to no avail. They experimented with cyanide, and it snuffed out the most resistant cabbage pest, the diamondback moth. PNF thus concluded that lack of government intervention coupled with the farmers' desperation and helplessness caused the cyanide fiasco.

In the process of unearthing the surrounding issues of the cyanide fiasco, PNF also exposed a parallel issue: multinational agrochemical firms' profiting from the farmers' helplessness and desperation. As farmers "cocktailed" or mixed two or more pesticide brands, which is unadvisable, this meant more profits for the companies. PNF cited hard facts and data from annual sales reports of and interviews with distributors.

PNF's presentation of the cyanide issue was critical of the government's role and responsibility. From then on, the government's agriculture department began to give importance to an alternative pest-control method organic-farming advocates had earlier been pushing – the use of an insect predator called diadegma, which preys on the larvae of the diamondback moth.

Also as a result of PNF's in-depth reporting, the government was able to get financial support from the Food and Agriculture Organization (FAO) for biologically safe pest-control methods. The government also organized what it called Farmers' Field Schools where farmers are oriented and trained in the use of safe alternative pest-control and management methods.

In this case, the finger of blame on the cyanide mess was not directed at the farmer. In fact, through the PNF report, it was found that the farmer himself was a victim. After the PNF report, the government responded accordingly, stressing on a better pest-control approach other than relying on destructive pesticides.

Other writing approaches

Other PNF feature-writing forms and approaches include profile, backgrounder, wrap-up or trend analysis, and others such as a-day-in-the-life feature of a farmer, urban poor, worker or working mother.

Profile

A profile can apply to a village or a person. Profiling a village can be descriptive. Description of a village or community includes hard data such as on annual crop production, health and medical facilities and health and medical woes, and transportation and communication access, and, of course, selected quotes from people in the community. A PNF article that came out on July 5, 1995, for example, had this heading, "Western Visayas: Rich Land With A Sick People".

The article tells about a region in central Philippines which boasts of being a food basket but manifests "a curious anomaly" – the region's population "lives constantly without proper food and nourishment". The story's central idea or theme is "hunger and malnutrition amid abundance". It was around this theme that the writer focused his data and information gathering. The writer took data and information from the agriculture department and nutrition council, interviewed officials of these agencies, and cited specific cases of malnourished mothers and children. Quoting an expert, the writer was able to point out somewhere in the story that the root of the problem was not lack of food but poor families' "not having access to food".

Persons that PNF profile include ordinary farmers, tribal elders, laborers, women leaders and other people on the margins who are often overshadowed by big personalities. In Western-oriented journalism, one value in news- and feature-writing is "prominence", which suggests that big personalities in politics, showbusiness and business can command interest from readers. But PNF has turned this "prominence" value upside down.

PNF, for example, featured a village medicine man in northern Philippines who, although illiterate, was able to discover herbal antidotes to intestinal diseases and scabies, among others. The article showed how the man first tested his herbal concoctions on "laboratory animals" – his pet dogs and pigs, which suffered from diarrhea. After his animals got well, the man tried his concoction on his grandchildren. They got well. Many of the villagers, who hardly had any access to government clinics or hospitals, sought the knowledge of their own medicine man. Therefore, in a way, the profile of the man also gave readers an idea of the village (i.e., that the village had no health facilities, which also says something about government neglect).

Backgrounder

A backgrounder aims to give some historical context to a long-standing issue or problem. A backgrounder about the Philippines' 32-year-old armed conflict, for example, can relate how the conflict evolved from peasants' landlessness and from the unfair deals they experienced under landlords and usurers.

Wrap-up and trend analysis

Under this technique, PNF seeks to see the interconnection of seemingly unrelated events, analyze them and draw conclusions. Of course, other research and investigative work is needed to strengthen and validate whatever conclusions that have been drawn.

A-day-in-the-life ... feature

If one wants, for example, to tell about the difficulty faced by a family living in a cramped four-square-meter room in a mining company's bunkhouse, one can employ this technique. Perhaps one could focus on a miner's wife, from how she starts her day until the time she puts the children to sleep. In the process, the writer discovers how the wife is harassed when the toilet needs flushing and there is not a drop of water from the faucet. This entails some effort because it requires the writer to live in the bunkhouse himself. A probing interview might suffice, but actually immersing oneself in the goings-on in a bunkhouse helps the writer to be more effective in communicating what it is really like to live in such an abode.

PNF has other approaches in writing the feature piece. But much depends on the individual creativity, gift of observation, data and information gathering ability, ability to find and develop the right sources, and other skills of the writer.

PNF's commentaries and analyses also focus on issues affecting the public, particularly the majority on the fringes of society. Commentaries and analyses, which are more often written by PNF's editors and senior writers, can cover subjects such as the impact of a new government policy or an official's pronouncement, and a current event or issue such as an election.

Continuing training and assessments

PNF always strives for professionalism. To help achieve this, writers are encouraged to participate in journalism workshops offered by credible sponsors. From time to time, PNF's staff writers and editors, along with an invited resource person, also discuss and share what needs to be improved on.

PNF would also schedule meetings during which the agency's performance is evaluated. PNF usually holds quarterly, mid-year and year-end assessments and evaluation. Through these, "strengths, weaknesses, opportunities and threats" or SWOTs are pinpointed, the main aim of which is to draw vital lessons.

During these assessments, the staff analyze contents of articles which have been reprinted many times and those not reprinted at all. Again, the purpose is to draw lessons.

4. DESCRIPTION OF THE INSTITUTION RESPONSIBLE AND ITS ORGANIZATIONAL ASPECTS

PNF is a major program of Crossroads Publications, Inc. or CPI, a non-stock, non-profit outfit. A Board of Directors comprising a mix of church people, veteran journalists and two rank-and-file staff representatives sets CPI's policy directions.

At its height from 1987 until 1997, PNF maintained a staff of 11, who included an editor, a managing editor, seven writers strategically posted nationwide, an editorial assistant and a messenger. Three staff writers were based in Manila, covering the government, the business sector and popular movements. The other staff writers were province-based. One covered the northern provinces of Luzon island; another, southern Luzon; and two others, central Philippines. For a time, PNF maintained a writer in Mindanao island in southern Philippines. There were also correspondents and contributors to cover areas out of reach of regular staff writers.

PNF also is linked with region- or province-based independent news agencies, which contribute exclusive articles. In fact, PNF helped found what was called the Federated Independent News Services or FINS, a national federation of independent news agencies which includes southern Philippines' Media Mindanao News Service (MMNS), Negros island's COBRA-ANS (Correspondents and Broadcasters Association News Service), and northern Philippines' Northern Dispatch or Nordis.

As a major program, PNF has been entrusted to carry out CPI's mission to help in the overall national endeavor for social change. PNF's weapon is communication and its battlefield, the major newspapers and, if possible, the broadcast media.

Aside from PNF, there are special projects and other program desks designed to help strengthen and reinforce PNF. PNF, for example, has a sister publication called *Philippine Agenda,* a magazine which high school students use in their social science subjects. Like PNF's dispatch, *Philippine Agenda* also churns out features and analyses about issues affecting farmers, laborers, indigenous peoples, women, children, consumers and other marginalized sectors.

CPI's other program desks are pro-print and marketing. The pro-print desk accepts layout and printing jobs. This desk was intended to generate income and help in meeting CPI's "self-reliance" goals.

The marketing desk takes charge of "selling" PNF to prospective subscribers. It also promotes and sells CPI's other products and services such as *Philippine Agenda* and pro-print's services, both of which were targeted to help in realizing CPI's self-reliance goals.

Of CPI's three major programs, PNF bears CPI's mission and vision – which is to help in the national endeavor for social change. To an equal extent, *Philippine Agenda,* which caters to students, is also geared toward this end.

5. PROBLEMS OR OBSTACLES ENCOUNTERED AND HOW THEY WERE OVERCOME

One problem PNF encountered was the "leftist" label some sectors used to hurl at the independent news agency. This is because PNF usually features issues and advocacies also being raised by groups perceived to be "left-leaning". But PNF was able to overcome this by its professionalism.

The mainstream media has come to patronize PNF because it adheres to the core values of accuracy, balance and fairness. Hunger, landlessness, environmental destruction, unfair labor practices and the like may be "left" issues. But these are also issues of public concern and interest, and PNF has written about them in a style and approach acceptable to the mainstream media.

Another major problem that PNF and the whole CPI have been wrestling with since mid-1997 was the sudden halt in funding from a foreign donor. The funding halt came at a time when CPI had not yet achieved even its 50 percent self-reliance targets. The halt was so sudden and drastic that CPI was forced to reduce its staff numbers.

Despite what happened, PNF was determined to pursue its mission. The services of PNF's staff writers were practically terminated. But PNF continues to come out with a weekly dispatch, written by former staff writers who still contribute articles and edited by editors who now work part-time.

As at the time of writing of this research, PNF and the whole CPI are still in the process of finding ways by which to revitalize the once-vibrant PNF. PNF at this point is down but not out. One possibility that the CPI board and former staff are looking into is a cooperative-run PNF. Under this set-up, PNF and the whole CPI may not have to rely on external support for their operations.

6. EFFECTS OF THE PRACTICE/INNOVATIVE EXPERIENCE

PNF has helped articulate the voice of those on the fringes of society. It has also helped form public opinion on crucial issues such as the hazards of highly potent pesticides, which were banned in developed countries but were being sold in the Philippines. It has likewise brought to the attention of concerned authorities problems of farmers and villagers such as a neglected bridge, and lack of schools and health facilities.

PNF also helped set a trend in issue-based reporting and feature-writing and investigative journalism. Other media outfits have followed suit, also venturing into more in-depth journalism.

7. SUITABILITY AND POSSIBILITY FOR UPSCALING

PNF since mid-1997 has downscaled its operations because of funding woes. But it intends to resume and possibly expand its reach. PNF before had intended to expand its market to encompass the broadcast media.

PNF had also come out with a monthly magazine which high school students could use in their social studies classes. Employing PNF's issue-based and investigative journalism, the magazine had helped explain and clarify in simple, easy-to-understand language the complex issues of the day. With the funding problem, this magazine has been temporarily halted. The magazine is one of those programs which PNF intends to revive once it reestablishes itself. But despite the funding crisis, PNF has shown that a news agency can diversify its services, if only to reach a wider readership.

8. SIGNIFICANCE FOR (AND IMPACT ON) POLICY-MAKING

PNF's significance for and impact on policy-making cannot be underestimated. At one time in 1995, PNF came out with an article exposing the dangers and health hazards of a pesticide intended to snuff out golden apple snails, which had been wreaking damage in the country's rice fields.

The PNF writer who did the story cited an upland woman farmer exposed to the pesticide, quoted medical experts and cited studies supporting the conclusion that the pesticide against golden apple snails was doing more harm than good to both people and the environment. The woman farmer the writer interviewed complained of rotting fingernails and toenails and itchy and dry skin. The medical expert and other studies said that the pesticide had been banned in developed countries because it causes cancer.

After the PNF report came out in Manila's major papers, the German manufacturer of the snail pesticide filed a P20 million (US$500,000) libel suit against the writer, PNF's editors, the medical doctor quoted in the story, and the editors of the papers which reprinted the article. The case dragged on for almost two years but was later dismissed. The case also became moot and academic after the government declared that the snail pesticide should be banned because of its hazards to public health and the environment. PNF would like to believe that its investigative report about the whole fiasco helped influence the government's decision.

There are other examples of PNF articles that had, in one way or another, helped draw government action. These include an article about a neglected vital road bridge connecting two islands in central Philippines. Soon after the article came out, the government's public works and highways department repaired the bridge. To PNF, the repair of the bridge was a victory for the small farmers who use the bridge to transport their products.

Another example was how legislators made use of PNF's articles as sources of data for their legislation. Data from PNF's articles about the problems of potato farmers, for example, were incorporated in the rationale for a draft bill on a Magna Carta for farmers. This was so because some members of the Lower House of Congress also subscribe to PNF's regular dispatch. Of course, this was also on top of public opinion generated by PNF's published articles.

9. POSSIBILITY AND SCOPE OF TRANSFERRING TO OTHER COMMUNITIES OR COUNTRIES

Every Third World country needs information for empowerment, and an independent news agency, free from the dictates of vested interests and big business, is an appropriate weapon. An independent news agency can help articulate the voice of the powerless and the neglected.

In the Philippines alone, some committed journalists in southern Philippines' Mindanao island put up a similar news agency called the Media Mindanao News Service (MMNS). MMNS also helped set the trend in issue-based and investigative journalism in the island, which the Manila-centered mass media failed to sufficiently cover.

As long as the mainstream media has some space for issue-based journalism pieces, an independent news agency is a feasible proposal. All it needs is professionalism and a large dose of commitment. Professionalism includes mastering the craft and ethics of journalism. Commitment, on the other hand, involves advocacy of socially relevant issues.

10. OTHER COMMENTS

Many non-governmental organizations (NGOs) come out with their own publications. Unfortunately, these publications end up gathering dust in some corner without being read. Tapping the mainstream media through an independent news agency is thus a better alternative. NGOs, therefore, could pool their resources and start a news agency.

References

1. PNF, *Statement of Principles*, as revised in August 1997.
2. Reprinted PNF articles.

13.

The Education Forum experience in alternative education

1. GENERAL INFORMATION

1.1 Title of experience

The Education Forum experience in alternative education: A post-mortem appraisal

1.2 Category of practice/experience and brief description

This paper presents the case of Education Forum's unique experience in alternative education, in both the formal and informal/non-formal systems. EF was re-established at the height of the Marcos administration and was thus a response to the concrete conditions then.

Guided by a liberative and transformative philosophy of education (i.e., education as a tool for social justice), EF undoubtedly contributed to a new breed of teachers and their charges, their students who are nationalists, critical and appreciative of the ideals of democracy and equality for all. EF also made the learning and teaching process relevant and creative, without losing sight of its ultimate purpose to develop skills and form values. These are ideals and values that remain in the hearts and minds of thousands of teachers and students who were reached by EF.

Although EF (i.e., national office) no longer exists, its experience stands as one of the best practices in the Philippines and in the Third World, because of its enduring impact on the education sector and the society as a whole.

1.3 Name of person or institution responsible for the practice or experience

Education Forum (EF) – the task force on education of the Association of Major Religious Superiors of the Philippines (AMRSP), the organization of the heads of different Catholic religious orders or congregations in the Philippines.

1.4 Name and position of key or relevant persons or officials involved

Prof. Diego Quejada III, Executive Director
Sr. Ching Bravo, Executive Director
Ma. Luisa Doronilla, Ph.D., General Consultant
Sr. Ma. Luz Mijares, OSA, Chairperson of the Board
The Association of Major Religious Superiors of the Philippines (AMRSP)

1.5 Details of institution

Not applicable since Education Forum has already closed down

1.6 Name of person and/or institution conducting the research

Raymundo D. Rovillos, Assistant Professor of History, University of the Philippines College in Baguio, for Tebtebba Foundation, Inc. (Indigenous People's International Center for Policy Research and Education)

Raymundo D. Rovillos was a volunteer facilitator/resource person of EF from 1986-88. In 1989-1990, he became the Executive Secretary of EF-Baguio. Many of the insights in this paper, unless citations are made, are based on the author's personal experience working with EF.

1.7 Details of research person/institution

Tebtebba Foundation, Inc.:
   (a) Address: Rm 3B Agpaoa Compound, 111 Upper General Luna Road, 2600 Baguio City, Philippines
   (b) Telephone: ++ (63) (74) 444 7703
   (c) Fax: ++ (63) (74) 443 9459
   (d) E-Mail: tebtebba@skyinet.net

2. THE PROBLEM OR SITUATION BEING ADDRESSED BY THE PRACTICE/INNOVATIVE EXPERIENCE

In terms of budgetary allocation, education is given a low priority. From the 1980s through the early 1990s for instance, education received only 7.2% (or lower) of the total national budget. This allocation was not sufficient to cover the needs of the sector. This explains the chronic problems of lack of teachers, classrooms and other facilities throughout the country. The quality of education is also not satisfactory. In 1977, 97% of the students in the public elementary school grades were unable to develop sufficient skills in reading, writing and arithmetic. For every elementary graduate, it has been found that only two-thirds of what should be learned was actually comprehended and absorbed by the student (see Ministry of Education, Culture and Sports Report, 1977). These trends continue to manifest themselves up until today.

The government also has a policy of privatization of secondary and tertiary education resulted in its policy of privatization of these sectors. "As monetary gains motivate private education, its principle of social service is lost in the effort to minimize the cost of production in order to maximize profits" (Quejada, 1986:34). In 1972 for instance, the summed-up profit of eight big schools (Arellano, Centro Escolar University, Far Eastern University, FEATI, Manila Central University, MLQU, University of Manila and University of the East) was P8.28 million. In 1975, their profits increased to P14.66 million. This means that between 1972 and 1975, the profits of these institutions increased by 77%.

As government involvement and subsidies progressively decreased and education for profit dominated the higher levels, many students were economically "selected off" as they progressed up the ladder of educational attainment. In a study published by the Presidential Committee to Survey Philippine Education (PCSPE) in 1970, it was found that out of 100 students entering grade one, 60 usually would be able to finish grade six; 40 would graduate in high school; and only 4 would finish college. In other words, the educational system posted a mere 4% finishing rate. This trend persists today.

3. DESCRIPTION OF THE PRACTICE/INNOVATIVE EXPERIENCE AND ITS MAIN FEATURES

This section is lifted from Prof. Diego G. Quejada III and Ma. Luisa c. Doronilla, Ph.D., "Alternative Education: The Education Forum (EF) Experience", in *Towards Relevant Education: A General Sourcebook for Teachers* (Quezon City: Education Forum) 1986. The article was revised and edited by the author for this paper.

Nature and objectives

EF was the task force on education of the Association of Major Religious Superiors of the Philippines (AMRSP), the organization of the heads of the different Catholic religious orders or congregations in the Philippines. Established in 1968 and revitalized in 1974 as a direct response of the Catholic religious in the country to the conditions brought about by the imposition of martial law in 1972, the AMRSP now has eight task forces which look into and undertake remedial steps and long-term programs in the areas of its apostolate in the Philippines, such as health, urban and rural missionary work, justice and peace, and education.

As a service institution, EF was organized to provide assistance to public and private educational institutions at all levels, as well as to groups and individuals engaged in the reorientation of Philippine education for social transformation. Specifically, it sought to
(a) define and clarify the theological basis of education for the transformation of Philippine society for the promotion of justice and peace in this world;
(b) create an awareness of the state of Philippine education and of the need to promote an inter-faith, nationalist and people-oriented education as the Filipino educators' contribution to social transformation;
(c) undertake programs to assist educators in carrying out the reorientation of Philippine education;
(d) assist educational institutions in designing, preparing and implementing their particular social orientation programs; and
(e) establish solidarity and working relationships with other institutions, and with other groups and individuals, in the country and abroad, who adhere to the same vision and mission.

Origin and growth

In November 1979, the Asian Consultation on Education (ACE), hosted by the Major Religious Superiors of Women in Thailand, was held in Bangkok to discuss the contribution of education toward change in society, to come to a common direction regarding the role of schools in relation to society, to establish solidarity and to learn from one another's experience in education.

More specifically, the consultation sought the critical examination of the philosophy, objectives, instruction, curriculum content and process in schools and non-school systems in an effort to bring back education to the mainstream of people's lives in Asia.

EF was established in 1979 as an outcome of the preparation of the Filipino delegates to this conference, through the Association of Major Religious Superiors of Women in the Philippines (AMRSWP). It was organized to fill the need already expressed by so many in the education sector, particularly in the Catholic schools, to redirect their school programs so that they may help promote the ideal of education for social transformation. Such a need was an outcome of a higher level of social awareness brought about by the nationalist movement of the early 60s and 70s and by the reexamination of the role of

Catholic education in the Philippines on the basis of principles contained in the Vatican II documents.

EF started out literally as such: a forum among a number of educators who met regularly to exchange views on promoting social awareness through relevant education. The enthusiastic response to these exchanges underlined the need for the free-wheeling and relatively loose forum to take on a regular and structured form. Toward this end, an EF secretariat was organized in early 1980 upon the return of the Filipino ACE delegates from Bangkok. In October 1980, the EF Board was constituted. Thereupon, EF was adopted by the AMRSP.

Services, projects and activities

From 31 July to 2 August 1981, EF sponsored a National Consultation on Education. The conference was really meant to be a gathering of leading personnel in education to come to a common analysis of the prevailing state of Philippine education and draw up directions about what must be done to respond to such a state of affairs. The National Consultation contributed greatly to a more concrete formulation of the objectives of EF as an institution that would provide support services to educational institutions and groups.

The following were the major components and activities of EF:

(a) **The *Teacher Assistance Program* (TAP)**

In its brochure, EF described the TAP as a "fortnightly publication that comes as a series of supplementary materials for teacher and classroom use. It was designed and prepared to respond to the needs of conscientizing educators who have taken on the task of teaching effectively in order to promote social awareness and social transformation."

The idea for the TAP was suggested by Mrs. Letizia Constantino when she, together with her husband, Prof. Renato Constantino (a famous nationalist historian), addressed the EF National Consultation in 1981. She argued that the teacher occupies a major role in influencing the consciousness and outlook of students and, as such, should be equipped properly for that role. The TAP was thus a modest effort to reach out to teachers, inform them of the basic issues in society, and contribute to their "re-education" process toward understanding the nature of the society they live in, the nature of the transformed society that is envisioned and, therefore, the kind of education - in terms of values, attitudes, social awareness and skills – that they are called to promote. Back issues were published in book form, as Issues Without Tears.

Some of the titles released were the following:
History From the Point of View of the Filipino People (1981)

The Agrarian Problem of the New Society (1981)
The Oil Giants in the Philippines (1981)
Key Economic Terms (1982)
Education: Handmaiden of Economic Policy (1983)
English or Filipino? (1983)
The Status of Filipino Women (1983)
The Aftermath of the Aquino Assassination – A Nationalist Appraisal (1983)
Some Common Political Terms (1984)
US Bases, US Bosses (1984)
Educating for Democracy (1984)
Nationalism in the Classroom (1984)

(b) The School for the Advancement of Nationalist Education (SANE)

In order to promote the continuing education and development of teachers and education personnel, EF, aside from coming out with publications, held seminar-workshops, training programs, symposia, study programs, discussion groups and non-exposure immersion. All these efforts were organized in the SANE. Specifically, the following were the components of the SANE:

(i) The Summer Institute for Faculty Development was a regular study program for teachers consisting of seminar-workshops in the different disciplines (social science, religious education, language, natural sciences, etc.).

(ii) The Social Orientation Seminar (SOS) was a two-and-one-half seminar-workshop for schools and other educator-groups given upon request. The SOS aimed to bring participants to an analysis of the state of Philippine education within the context of the past and present developments of national and global realities. It also aimed to define the role of the educator in the promotion of education for social change.

(iii) Lectures were given on request to teachers and school personnel, usually in fora organized as part of a school's faculty and personnel development programs, or to other education-related groups. The most frequently requested topics were The History of Philippine Education; The State of Philippine Education Today; The Present National Situation; and What is Nationalist Education?

(iv) Symposia on current issues were regularly sponsored by EF to bring to public discussion current and burning issues on education and society. Some of the topics in the symposia were The Present State of Language Teaching in the Philippines; and The Current Economic and Political Crisis and Its Implication on the Schools.

(v) Training workshops were organized regularly, sponsored by EF or given

to faculty groups upon request. They included SOS Facilitators Training; Seminar-Workshop in Research; Speakers Training Workshop; and Workshop in Operationalizing the School's Social Orientation.
(vi) Inter-school Disciplinary Workshops (ISDWs) were study groups of teachers of a common discipline from different schools. The ISDWs provided teachers the forum and organization through which to keep abreast of developments in their areas of specialization, discuss and analyze the state of teaching in their respective fields, and draw up projects and activities in response to these problems. Over the years, EF facilitated the organization of ISDWs of teachers at the secondary level in the following disciplines: Mathematics, Natural Sciences, Communication Arts: English, Communication Arts: Filipino, Religious Education and Health Education.
(vii) Study Circle for Leading Administrators was a regular discussion group that EF organized to keep school administrators abreast of the latest developments in Philippine education and society. Some of the topics brought to discussion in the study circle were Values Education of the New Curriculum (PRODED), The National Situation, History of Philippine Education, EDPITAF and World Bank Textbooks: Teaching, Teachers and Instructional Materials Today.
(viii) Exposure-Immersion of School Personnel was organized by EF upon request from faculty (or student) groups. It aimed to concretize to the participants the realities of Philippine society, which constitute the social context of Philippine education, through exposure-immersion with workers, peasants, urban poor and tribal Filipinos, or to areas that reveal social problems like prostitution, militarization, poverty, environmental pollution, etc. The exposure-immersion consisted of the participants' actually staying for three to five days in a particular area, subsequent reflection/processing of the experience and planning.

The activities of the SANE were made possible in coordination with and with the cooperation of resource persons from agencies and institutions like the Cultural Research Association of the Philippines (CRP), the Philippine Educational Theater Association (PETA), IBON, Council for Primary Health Care (CPHC), Foundation for Nationalist Studies (FNS), Third World Studies (TWS), Parents Alternative, Inc. (PAI), Science and Society, Episcopal Commission on Tribal Filipinos (ECTF), Task Force Detainees of the Philippines (TFDP) and the Teachers Center of the Philippines.

(c) Alternative Instructional Materials Project (AIM)
Started in 1983, the AIM sought to respond to teachers' demand for relevant instructional materials in their respective disciplines of specialization.

The project produced sourcebooks for teachers' use that were keyed to existing textbooks, thereby providing teachers with an alternative and critical perspectives in assessing the value of topical emphases being promoted in these textbooks and thus enabling them to intervene more directly in the instructional process. The sourcebooks contained a critique of the prevailing educational system, an assessment of the state of teaching in the discipline concerned, an analysis of instructional materials currently available for the discipline, a series of alternative or supplementary materials and readings, case samples of lesson planning and other suggested classroom activities, as well as a bibliography of other instructional and audio-visual materials and suggested readings.

The AIM was undertaken in cooperation and coordination with teachers from different schools, the ISDWs, and resource persons from other agencies and institutions. Sourcebooks intended for high-school teachers' use were produced for the following disciplines: Communication Arts: English, Philippine History and Religious Education.

(d) Education Resource Center (ERC)

Started in 1983, the ERC, as a project, established a resource center for instructional materials, research and publications of EF.

The general objective was to create an information and materials source base in support of the overall efforts of teachers and education personnel in reorienting Philippine education. The center provided data or resource materials that EF and other people could use in the construction of supplementary or alternative instructional materials for classroom use, seminars and workshops, educational research, and other related efforts.

Specifically, the objectives of the ERC as a project were the following:

(i) to put up a databanking system that would contain available information on the prevailing as well as alternative orientation, content and methods of the country's educational system;

(ii) to produce audio-visual materials that could be used by teachers and others engaged in education-related efforts;

(iii) to publish a monthly newsletter that would inform teachers and other beneficiaries of latest developments and issues in education as well as instructional materials that they could use in their work; and

(iv) to publish studies and research outputs on education.

Solidarity

EF also extended its services to other institutions and groups in the country and abroad as well as to those outside of the education sector. EF conducted training workshops and lecture series with medical and health personnel, church groups, student organizations, and cultural and artist groups. EF hosted exposure-immersion programs for visiting foreign delegations like a group of Japanese nuns in August 1983 and 10 teachers from the Australian Teachers' Federation in January 1985. EF was the co-host of the Second Asian Consultation on Education in August 1984 and of the Asian Students Association Seminar Workshop held in Manila in 1984. All these were part of EF's solidarity efforts as it realized that its activities could not be isolated from the efforts of other people to bring about social transformation.

4. DESCRIPTION OF THE INSITUTION RESPONSIBLE AND ITS ORGANIZATIONAL ASPECTS

Vision and mission of EF

EF was established out of a vision of society – a society that is "just, free and democratic". Prof. Diego Quejada III, EF's Executive Director, wrote:

"Justice means ensuring for ourselves as country and people what truly is due for our survival and development. Freedom means liberation from continuing colonial exploitation. Democracy means the promotion of basic human rights and interests, especially those of the majority."

Given this vision of society, EF upheld a philosophy of education that was geared toward the attainment of a just society. This philosophy of education was articulated by Dr. Ma. Luisa Doronilla (1986:482) thus:

"Our view of alternative education in [the] contemporary Philippine context ... refers to the creation by and among teachers, school administrators, and other school personnel, students and their parents of a critical and analytical counterconsciousness whose nationalist and people-oriented character will contribute to a significant reorientation not only of Philippine education but also of Philippine society in general."

Organizational structure of EF

As provided in its constitution, there was the EF General Assembly which met once every two years and was composed of five representatives from every region, the secretariat and the members of the incumbent National Board.

The highest policy-making body of EF was the National Board. It met at least once a year and was composed of two representatives from each of the four regions and seven members elected at large.

In between meetings of the National Board, the National Executive Committee was responsible for the conduct of EF affairs and for the implementation of the policies and decisions of the National Board. It was composed of the officers (Chairperson, Vice Chairperson, Treasurer, Secretary) elected by the National Board, and the Executive Director.

The National Secretariat implemented the decision of the National Executive Committee and conducted the day-to-day affairs of the task force. It was headed by the Executive Director who was appointed by the National Board.

Except for the General Assembly, regional chapters had virtually the same structure, comprising a regional board, a regional executive committee and a regional secretariat.

Regional chapters were encouraged to plan and initiate their own activities depending upon the specificities of the education situation in their respective regions and the capabilities of their staff, within the context of EF's general orientation and the specific objectives given earlier.

5. PROBLEMS OR OBSTACLES ENCOUNTERED AND HOW THEY WERE OVERCOME

In 1995, the Education Forum-National Chapter decided to fold up and stop its operations. Several factors, both internal and external to the organization, contributed to this unfortunate event. One factor was the lack/absence of sustained financial support, especially for its regional chapters. As early as 1989, at a time when EF's contribution to transformative education was increasingly appreciated by educators, and when its major component programs were replicated in the regions, EF's major funding agency CEBEMO suddenly decided against granting funds for the necessary and much-needed financial support. The stated reason was the redirection of financial aid from Third World countries to Eastern Europe, in the light of the collapse of socialist regimes there. The "unofficial" reason was that the funding agency apparently believed accusations that EF was a communist front and that it financially supported leftist organizations. These allegations were of course denied by the EF leadership.

As a result of the absence of funding, several regional chapters like the EF-Cordillera almost became inactive. Their services dwindled, while only a pool of volunteer teachers and school administrators kept the organization going. The EF-National Office responded to the financial crisis by aggressively generating funds by submitting proposals. It was finally able to secure funding from an Italian funding agency for its "Education for Production Project". However, other problems internal to the organization itself would eventually lead to the closure of the program.

6. EFFECTS OF THE PRACTICE/INNOVATIVE EXPERIENCE

In 1988, EF conducted a nationwide study to evaluate its impact on the "target beneficiaries", the teachers and other school personnel. Generally, the study revealed very positive feedback on EF's activities. The following were the highlights of the evaluation study:

Among the teachers, EF's activities resulted in the following:

(a) Inculcation of values such as nationalism, participatory democracy, cooperation and service/commitment to the poor and marginalized in society.
(b) Development of the teachers' skill of critical thinking – With the tools of social analysis that the teachers learned from EF, they were able to interpret/analyze day-to-day events more critically.
(c) Enhanced pedagogical skills – Indeed, EF introduced various teaching methods and strategies that were reflective of the institution's liberative and transformative mission. With their newly acquired skills, the teachers also perceived their profession with renewed vigor and rigor.
(d) Empowerment – The alternative education that EF espoused undeniably enlightened the teachers not only on the social realities, but also about their (the teachers') rights. As a result, they realized the need to organize themselves as a progressive organization or as unions.

These changes in the teachers' values, skills and attitudes, and their entire world view, also affected their students and, to a certain extent, the students' parents. The students had a better understanding and appreciation of their subjects, since their lessons were always contextualized in their own realities and experiences. Thus, education became not just a mirror of social realities and individual experiences; it was also integral to and inextricably linked with the mainstream of the people's lives.

These values, skills and predisposition continue to endure in the hearts and minds of teachers and their students despite the closure of the national office and the stoppage of national operations. In this context, we can say that EF's principles and objectives have been achieved and sustained, even if the institution itself is no longer around.

7. SUITABILITY AND POSSIBILITY FOR UPSCALING

It could be noted that the philosophy and program of alternative education that EF adhered to was too radical, if not revolutionary, especially from the point of view of the state. Therefore, EF's goals and objectives could not be fully attained if Philippine society itself was not fundamentally reformed.

This is also the reason why EF's endeavors were limited to the private (i.e., sectarian schools) sector, which exercised some degree of autonomy from the Department of Education, Culture and Sports (DECS), particularly in designing the curriculum. However, there should have been no problem in upscaling EF activities and projects. In fact, even before the EF-National Office decided to shut down, there were already efforts on the part of the government to appropriate some of its programs and activities. These are discussed in sections 8 and 9.

8. SIGNIFICANCE FOR (AND IMPACT ON) POLICY-MAKING

EF's success stories caught the interest and attention of educational policy-makers not only in the Philippines but in other countries as well. In the Philippines, EF gave significant contributions to the Education Committee (EDCOM), a body that was formed by the Corazon Aquino government to formulate policy recommendations in order to reform education. Among EF's most significant policy recommendations to the EDCOM were the following:
(a) Establish and recognize functional literacy programs (emphasis on education with production), especially in marginalized communities of the urban poor and indigenous peoples of the country. Official recognition of functional literacy programs will be in the form of accreditation. Graduates of these programs shall be accorded credits parallel to the formal educational system.
(b) Reinforce the values-education program of the DECS. EF consistently lobbied for the inclusion of nationalism, democracy and equity as the core values that should constitute the values-formation component at all levels of education. The EDCOM has incorporated this suggestion in its policy recommendations.
(c) Strengthen the research capability of institutions of higher learning. This is currently being implemented by the newly established Commission on Higher Education (CHED).

9. POSSIBILITY AND SCOPE OF TRANSFERRING TO OTHER COMMUNITIES AND COUNTRIES

The EF experience can be transferred to other countries. Its own growth as an institution is testament to the possibility of development and expansion. EF started off in 1979 with only a few Catholic schools and a chapter in Metro

Manila. In 1986, EF expanded into a national network of five established chapters and three formative chapters spread throughout the Philippines. The following were some of the regional and provincial chapters:
(a) EF Mindanao, based in Davao City, with subregional chapters in Butuan, Davao del Norte and Zamboanga;
(b) EF Panay, based in Iloilo City;
(c) EF Bicol, based in Iriga City and Sorsogon;
(d) EF Isabela, based in Ilagan;
(e) EF Baguio;
(f) EF Cebu, based in Cebu; and
(g) EF Metro Manila.

The rapid expansion of EF may be attributed to the following factors:
(a) The support of school administrators, who were in turn influenced by Vatican II's call for Church responsiveness to "preferential option for the poor".
(b) The timeliness of EF intervention. EF entered the scene at a time when, as a result of Vatican II, Church-run schools were transforming their thrust toward social orientation. In fact, EF helped in the formulation and operationalization of the mission and vision statements of the schools.
(c) The spirit of voluntarism. EF's well-trained and highly qualified pool of facilitators travelled all over the country, from the hinterlands of the Cordillera down to the coastal communities of Mindanao, sharing their skills and knowledge for free.

Given the same conditions and prerequisites, the EF experience in alternative education can be transferred to other communities and countries. The lessons drawn from it, both positive and negative, should be instructive enough. What is needed is to ensure institutional sustainability in terms of funding. The institution should be able to generate resources, including income, to support its personnel and services in the long run. EF's dependence on external funding agencies contributed to its own peril.

10. OTHER COMMENTS

This paper is subtitled "A Postmortem Appraisal" because of the personal desire of the author to rebuild EF and revive its noble tasks. As mentioned earlier, EF as an institution may have died but teachers all over the country continue the work that EF has inspired them to do: to be catalysts for social change.

References

1. Doronilla, Ma. Luisa, (1986) 'Alternative Education: The Education Forum Experience' in *Towards a Relevant Education: A General Sourcebook for Teachers,* Education Forum, Quezon City.
2. Education Forum, (1986) *Towards Relevant Education: A General Sourcebook for Teachers,* Quezon City.
3. Ministry of Education, Culture and Sports, (1997) *Survey on the Outcome of Elementary Education,* Manila.
4. Quejada, Diego II, (1981) 'Philosophy of Philippine Education' in *Teacher's Assistance Program,* Education Forum, Quezon City.
5. Quejada, Diego II, (1986) 'The State of Philippine Education Today' in *Towards Relevant Education: A General Sourcebook for Teachers,* Education Forum, Quezon City.

Part III
Social Rights and Advocacy

14.

Consumer action in a Third World context

1. GENERAL INFORMATION

1.1 Title of practice or experience

Consumers' Association of Penang: Consumer action in a Third World context

1.2 Category of practice/experience and brief description

Innovative consumer and public citizen group with development, needs-oriented and environmental dimensions. The Consumers' Association of Penang in Malaysia is probably the leading consumer organisation in the developing world. It has creatively adapted consumer issues and action to suit the needs and priorities of people living in the Third World, linking people's basic needs to the fight for consumer rights and environmental protection.

1.3 Name of person or institution responsible for the practice or experience

Consumers' Association of Penang

1.4 Name and position of key or relevant persons or officials involved

S.M. Mohamed Idris, President

1.5 Details of institution

 (a) Address: 228 Macalister Road, 10400 Penang, Malaysia
 (b) Tel: ++(60) (4) 229 3511
 (c) Fax: ++(60) (4) 229 8106
 (d) E-Mail: elawmalaysia@igc.apc.org

1.6 Name of person and/or institution conducting the research

Consumers' Association of Penang

1.7 Details of research person/institution

As in 1.5 above

2. THE PROBLEM OR SITUATION BEING ADDRESSED BY THE PRACTICE/INNOVATIVE EXPERIENCE

Within Third World countries, the basic needs of large sections of people (in some cases perhaps two-thirds of the population) have yet to be satisfied. In many countries, the numbers of people living below the poverty line have increased significantly, despite moderate rates of economic growth. The degree of income inequalities between income groups has also increased as growth fails to solve the basic-needs problems of the poor. Planners and politicians often strive for a style of national development which imitates the models set up in industrialised countries and which have been widely recognised recently as environmentally unsustainable. Much in the name of development goes towards the creation and sustenance of artificially high lifestyles imported, with some minor modifications, from the West.

This "transfer of taste" is not confined to the elites of the Third World, as high-powered advertising and aggressive sales campaigns by transnational corporations (TNCs) ensure that the imported consumer culture penetrates and permeates through every corner of the land. Through the impact of such promotions, the traditional lifestyles and cultures of the local people are transformed to foreign tastes that divert away valuable resources to wasteful and even dangerous consumption habits. Junk-food and fast-food culture at the expense of locally available and wholesome foods, bottle-feeding at the expense of breastmilk, cigarettes, alcohol, cosmetics, disposable and throwaway products etc. are all part and parcel of a wasteful and unsustainable lifestyle.

The pattern of development has also resulted in environmental crises of startling proportions. The very basis of development and indeed human survival itself has been undermined by environmental destruction and degradation.

It is this scenario of the present and future problems of the world that provides the background to the activities of the Consumers' Association of

Penang (CAP). Its objective is to awaken the consciousness of the people to the present style and rate of development which destroys the environment and produces things which are useless or harmful to health, without satisfying the basic needs of the majority of people. CAP believes that only when development serves the needs of people and not the other way around will real progress be achieved.

For this to come about, the awareness of people must be awakened. As an organisation oriented towards consumer protection and social reform, CAP sees its role as bringing up important development issues and generating public consciousness on these issues.

The CAP model, when it developed in the 1970s and 1980s, pioneered a new approach of consumer activities that were adapted to the needs of people and communities in developing countries. The consumer movement had originated in the Western countries, where "Value for money" had been the slogan, and testing of products (to determine the relative performance of various brands) had been a major objective. CAP coined the slogan "Value for people" to symbolise that in the Third World context, the consumer movement should be oriented towards meeting the needs and articulating the rights of ordinary consumers, such as the right to food, housing, employment, a clean environment, safety in products, good business practices and an efficient bureaucracy.

3. DESCRIPTION OF THE PRACTICE/INNOVATIVE EXPERIENCE AND ITS MAIN FEATURES

CAP is an independent and non-profit organisation set up in 1970. It is based in Malaysia, which has been a high-growth Third World country (until the East Asian financial crisis that began in 1997) which faces all the contradictions of development described above.

It has a council of 10 members, many of whom are community leaders, former teachers, university academics and professionals. Its activities are carried out by a staff of about 60, most of whom are young people interested in contributing to social progress.

CAP is organised into various sections, each of which reflects an important aspect of its approach to development work, which seek to inform, educate, mobilise and represent the public on basic issues. The various sections are as follows:

(a) Complaints Section

This Section seeks to protect the public's right to redress and compensation in the face of unfair market practices, cheating, exploitation or neglect on the part of producers, middlemen or government departments. A wide variety of complaints is lodged by the public at CAP's office either personally or through the post.

Among the complaints are: poor quality of goods; defective and dangerous products; cheating and malpractice by housing developers, insurance companies, shopkeepers and moneylenders; negligence in the provision of professional services by lawyers and doctors; the problems of tenants and workers; the inefficiencies of government departments; poor services at hospitals; inadequate and poor public transportation, sewerage and garbage services; and the absence of proper drainage and flooding in urban areas.

On average, the Section handles about 2,000 to 3,000 complaints a year and manages to settle about 80% of the complaints to the satisfaction of the complainants. The value of the complaints service goes beyond the solving of individual problems. In newly independent countries where the "colonial mentality" still prevails, people have for too long been used to the passive acceptance of life's injustices. The successful lodging of a complaint changes the perception and attitude of individuals who now see that redress can be obtained if one is willing to do something positive about it. The complaints service thus becomes an effective means and channel through which the public is able to exercise its rights to fight business malpractices and to press for fair and better services from companies and government departments, as well as to demand protection of these rights from the authorities.

In addition, from studying the complaints received, CAP is able to assess whether existing laws adequately protect consumers or whether there are loopholes in the legislation which need to be rectified. In situations where there is no law at all to protect the consumer, the data from the Complaints Section will provide the basis for calling for policy changes and legal reform. The Complaints Section is especially useful to the poorer sections of the community who are usually not articulate or confident enough to take on grievances on their own, and who are not able to afford legal services.

(b) Rural and Community Section

In its work with communities through the Rural and Community Section, CAP is involved in two main types of issues: first, basic needs and amenities; and second, environmental problems and the disruption of livelihood in the rural areas.

(i) Basic needs and amenities

In the area of basic needs and amenities, CAP staff members conduct educational programmes in villages and estates (rubber and oil-palm plantations) during which basic principles of nutrition, health, budgeting, credit and other topics are discussed with families, usually the women in the household. At such sessions, the villagers also bring up pressing problems that they face, such as the high prices for goods charged at the only shop in the village or the irregularity of the village bus service.

These complaints are discussed with the villagers in a group, and the staff helps the community to act on the problems by, for example, writing to the bus company concerned or by getting the villagers to talk to the shop-owner to rectify the problems. Such actions are sometimes successful, but they usually require a prolonged period of continuous pressure on the part of the villagers. What is important is that the community begins to recognise its common problems, takes action to overcome them, and thus educates itself in justly demanding its rights.

From addressing such "simple" problems, the community is prepared to take on other bigger issues such as the lack of basic facilities and amenities like proper drinking water and sanitation facilities, improved roads and drainage systems, better irrigation facilities in rice-growing areas, public telephones and so on. In a country where much of the development allocations are urban-biased, the complaints of the communities in the rural areas are critical in bringing about a more equitable distribution of resources. Demands for meeting these basic needs are made through petitions signed by the villagers to the authorities concerned. In significant cases, press conferences are also held to draw attention to the plight of the communities. Responses from the authorities in such instances further empower the communities to address other concerns in the village or estate. Where no response is received, further representations are made to higher authorities, including the locally-elected representatives.

(ii) Environmental problems and dislocation of communities' livelihood

An even more serious type of problem in rural communities concerns environmental issues and the dislocation of sources of livelihood.

Traditional fishing communities in many parts of the country are affected by the invasion of trawl fishing which destroys the coastal marine resources. The fishery resources are further destroyed by the pollution of the waters from industries and other land-based sources, as well as from the destruction of fish habitats such as mangrove forests for other projects, including shrimp aquaculture. CAP works with the fishing communities to take up their plight with the government authorities and the media. The fisherfolk are also organised to form their own organisations, so that they can articulate their grievances independently.

The Section has also assisted several communities who have been affected by the impacts of industrial pollution, wastes and hazardous factories, sited in the vicinity of these communities. In such instances, the health and safety of the community is impacted, apart from the impact on the crops and livestock maintained by these communities.

Similarly, with the introduction of development projects such as dams, highways, industrial estates, resorts and golf courses, many food-producing rural communities face displacement. CAP works with the affected communities so that they can make their concerns known. Activities include the conduct of meetings, investigation into the nature of the project, studies on the possible environmental and social impacts, the presentation of petitions and memorandums to the authorities, media coverage, and, where necessary and appropriate, legal redress in court. Such efforts are necessary to ensure that in national planning, the voices of local communities, vulnerable groups and those facing social dislocation are heard.

Further, documentation of the problems of these communities also exposes the shortcomings in current planning processes, which do not adequately take into account the impact on communities of development projects, or give adequate opportunity and access to communities to take part in the decisions affecting their lives. Thus, from these experiences, CAP continues to advocate changes in policy and law at the national level so that current development planning integrates economic objectives as well as environmental and social concerns.

Apart from facilitating activities in communities as above, the Rural Section is also involved in conducting education and training programmes for rural communities on a wide range of issues, including the right of communities to a fair share of the fruits of development. Through such regular training programmes, the rural folk are trained to be more aware of their environment and to act for themselves to fulfil their rights.

(c) Legal Section

Following from the work of the Complaints Section and the Rural Section, the Legal Section was established in 1982. It is organised as a professional legal firm and is run by three full-time lawyers to undertake public-interest cases. It was the first full-time public-interest law firm in the country and has established itself as a specialist in environmental and consumer protection law, administrative and constitutional law, and land and tenancy law, including native customary land rights and other aspects of community rights.

The Legal Section has pioneered many landmark legal cases in the country, especially in the area of environmental and land law, and these cases have led to the emergence of the concept of public-interest litigation in Malaysia.

Apart from taking cases to court on behalf of consumers and communities, the Section is also involved in undertaking legal research which is then translated into memorandums to government authorities, advocating legal reforms. The Section also conducts training programmes for students in law schools in the country, with the aim of inculcating social responsibility and commitment among future lawyers. It also works with the faculty members of the law schools in encouraging the introduction of public-interest courses within the respective faculties. Such courses include consumer and environmental law as well as law and society.

The Section is also involved in the building of international alliances with public-interest lawyers around the world and was a founder member of Environmental Law Alliance Worldwide (E-Law).

(d) Education Section

This Section provides training and educational services for many groups, including school children, teacher-trainees, university students, youths, women and workers.

CAP has helped to establish several hundred consumer and environmental clubs and societies in both primary and secondary schools in the country. What began as ad hoc efforts in schools by CAP has now become established practice, with the Ministry of Education encouraging and promoting the establishment of consumer clubs in schools. Students in such clubs are trained to investigate pollution problems in the neighbourhood, make surveys on canteen food safety and other public services, conduct health campaigns on junk-food and cigarettes, and hold debates, quizzes, dramas, exhibitions and other activities on consumer and environmental themes.

Teachers are also encouraged to use consumer and environment articles and publications in their teaching, so as to spread greater awareness among students at all levels of education. Further, discussions are also held with the Ministry of Education to encourage the establishment or integration of consumer and environmental education into the school curriculum. Education programmes are also run for women and youth organisations, workers and trade unions, residents' associations and other voluntary groups.

(e) Survey and Testing Section

This Section is responsible for carrying out basic research and alerting the public and authorities to such problems as unfair price increases, misleading advertisements, unscrupulous sales tactics and practices, the marketing of dangerous foods, drugs and pesticides, inadequate and poor medical and transport services, poor conditions of housing, lighting and roads, and so on.

The Section carries out regular surveys of market prices of essential commodities such as rice, meat, fish, vegetables, fruits, sugar, cooking oil, flour, bus fares, text books, medical fees and so on. Any irregularities in the market, whether of price, quality or supply, are immediately made known to the public through the mass media. Details of the problem as well as concrete proposals to reduce or solve it are also forwarded.

Where testing activities are concerned, CAP focuses on determining the safety, cleanliness, purity and quality of products that are commonly used. Tests are also carried out on short-weighting and other forms of exploitation which producers and traders practise on consumers.

CAP's findings in the past have revealed dangerous levels of dyes, heavy metals and additives in popular foodstuff and drinks; fresh fish and seafood containing high levels of animal and human wastes; meat containing commonly prescribed antibiotic residues; poor-quality and defective consumer products and so on. These findings are widely publicised in the media and are followed up with the respective government agencies in relation to the non-enforcement of laws or lack of laws in protecting consumer interests.

In the area of environment, at the request of communities, tests are also conducted to detect water pollution and quality, radiation levels in the neighbourhood stemming from industrial activity and other such problems. These findings are used to support the communities in demanding action from the authorities.

(f). Research Section

The Research Section undertakes in-depth studies on important issues which usually arise from the activities of the other sections. Some of the major areas of CAP's long-term research work include food and nutrition, health and sanitation, housing, habitat and transport, the sale of dangerous products, unethical business practices, the adverse effects of the consumer culture, degradation of the quality of the environment and natural-resource depletion, hazardous technologies including genetic engineering, social problems such as drug addiction and alcoholism, and the promotion of appropriate technology.

The studies involve a combination of desk research and field research, including interviews with ordinary people and professionals. The aim of the research is to deepen the public's knowledge on basic and critical issues and, on the basis of this increased awareness, to advocate for social reform.

(g) Publications Section

Armed with the wealth of information from the various sections of CAP, the Publications Section of CAP is responsible for producing a monthly newspaper called *Utusan Konsumer* (Consumer Voice), with four editions in English, Malay, Chinese and Tamil languages. It has a very wide circulation among the general public. The newspaper is influential in providing information on a wide range of consumer and public issues, and in shaping public opinion. In addition to this, a special monthly newspaper for children is also produced, called *Majallah Pengguna Kanak-Kanak* (Child Consumer's Magazine). This paper stresses on environmental education for the young.

The Section also produces a wide range of publications (books, pamphlets, educational kits, posters, etc.) on various themes for the use of the general public. Such books are crucial in developing consumer and environmental awareness, in addition to educating ordinary citizens on their rights and role in society as active and concerned people.

4. DESCRIPTION OF THE INSTITUTION RESPONSIBLE AND ITS ORGANISATIONAL ASPECTS

Please see 3 above.

5. PROBLEMS OR OBSTACLES ENCOUNTERED AND HOW THEY WERE OVERCOME

At some stages of CAP's development, it had to strike a delicate balance in its relations with the government authorities and bureaucracy, as the organisation established its role as a civil society group representing consumer and public interests. Some policy-makers accepted this as a healthy role, but others were uncomfortable with having to deal with an independent source of information and advocacy. However, through the years, CAP has now established itself as a legitimate and important part of national public life and is invited to participate in several governmental processes and committees. It however retains its independent and critical approach.

6. EFFECTS OF THE PRACTICE/INNOVATIVE EXPERIENCE

Through the various efforts of CAP, much has been achieved over the years, particularly in effecting changes to government policies and laws at the national level. Further, at the community level, there have been significant successes, where communities have been able to defend their interests, for example in getting certain development projects reviewed, or obtaining compensation for loss of resources or income arising from adverse effects of projects. Some examples of these positive effects are provided below.

(a) Effect on national policy and law

(i) Government ban or restrictions on toxic drugs
CAP had conducted several studies on commonly used pharmaceutical drugs which have been banned or put under restricted use in other countries. These studies exposed the double standards employed by drug corporations in the international marketing of their products. These studies were sent to the Ministry of Health for action. Following such studies, the Drug Control Authority of the Ministry of Health ordered a ban or restrictions on seven drugs covered by the studies.

(ii) Shelflife for foodstuff
For a long time, Malaysia had no shelflife for food items, which meant that such products did not have expiry dates and yet could be sold to consumers. As a result of CAP's representations, the Ministry of Health introduced the Food Regulations in 1985 which made it mandatory for such expiry dates to be stated for perishable food products.

(iii) Ban on cigarette advertisements and smoking in public places
Through CAP's anti-smoking campaigns, the government in 1992 imposed a ban on cigarette advertisements. Subsequently, through the introduction of regulations, smoking has been banned in public places. The Ministry of Health now also undertakes anti-smoking campaigns, following CAP's initial efforts.

(iv) Better living conditions for plantation workers

For years, CAP has been calling for improved living conditions in the plantation sector where workers do not have adequate housing, clean water and sanitation. CAP had conducted surveys in the estates and exposed the poor living conditions. Several other organisations had also organised activities on behalf of the workers. In 1990, the government revised the Workers' Minimum Standards of Housing and Amenities Act to improve the living conditions of the workers by requiring all estates to supply piped water and electricity to workers, as well as provide childcare centres, recreational and medical facilities, and libraries. The Act also specifies the minimum standards for workers' houses.

(v) Improved benefits for workers

In 1985, CAP urged the government-managed Employees Provident Fund (EPF) to increase its interest rates as well as to pay interest on a monthly basis on the mandatory contributions made by employers and employees. In 1988, the EPF started to pay interest rates on a monthly basis and also improved the interest rates for contributions.

In 1982, CAP conducted research showing that the government-managed Social Security Organisation (SOCSO) was paying inadequate rates of compensation to workers suffering from work-related injuries and illnesses. SOCSO manages a compulsory insurance scheme for workers which covers occupational injuries and diseases. Following CAP's research, which received prominent coverage in the local media, SOCSO has improved the rate of benefits to workers over the years.

(vi) Protection of tenants

In 1987, CAP assisted a large community of tenant-farmers in Penang in their fight to prevent eviction by force by the landlords and developers. CAP and several communities campaigned for changes to the law to ensure that developers and landlords are not allowed to evict tenants by force but instead they should obtain a court order should they wish to evict their tenants. In 1991, a major amendment to the law was made which now bars eviction of tenants by force. This improved the legal status of tenants.

(vii) Protection of house-buyers

Prior to 1982, house-buyers who entered into sale and purchase agreements with developers were not protected adequately as housing agreements were one-sided and benefited the developers. Through CAP's Complaints Section, a litany of cases was documented to call for a standard housing agreement which would be fair to both parties. CAP's proposals were accepted by the Housing Ministry and the housing law was amended to introduce, for the first time, a standard housing agreement which protects the interests of house-buyers.

(viii) *Establishment of the Department of Environment*

CAP was one of the first groups in the country to highlight environmental problems. As early as 1970, major seminars were held by CAP to push for government policy on the environment and for the introduction of laws to protect the environment. Following such efforts, a Division of Environment was set up in 1975 which was subsequently upgraded to the present Department of Environment (DOE), under the Ministry of Science, Technology and Environment. The Environment Quality Act was also passed and many regulations followed. CAP continues to pressure for improved legislation and enforcement of the laws to safeguard the environment.

(b) Effects at community level

Through the years, CAP has assisted numerous communities whose livelihood and health have been adversely affected by development projects or government policies. In the case of certain mega-projects which were perceived as being detrimental to the environment and people, the organisation has successfully campaigned to stop such projects. Some significant examples of these are as follows:

(i) *Factory producing radioactive wastes stopped*

Next to a village called Bukit Merah New Village with a population of 10,000 people near Ipoh, Perak, a factory producing radioactive wastes, was set up in 1982. This plant, known as Asian Rare Earth (ARE), was a joint venture between Japanese giant, Mitsubishi Chemicals, and a local Malaysian company. The villagers were alerted to the dangers posed by the radioactive wastes, which were dumped around the factory's vicinity. With assistance from CAP and other organisations (such as *Sahabat Alam Malaysia* or Friends of the Earth, Malaysia), the villagers, who had formed an ad hoc organisation called the Perak Anti-Radioactive Waste Committee, invited scientists and doctors to the village to conduct radiation monitoring and carry out health surveys. The studies revealed high levels of radiation exposure, and impacts on the community were visible. Such health effects included high miscarriage rates among mothers, incidences of childhood leukemia, effects on blood-cell counts of children and so on. Despite petitions, representations and demonstrations held by the local people urging both the federal and state governments to close down the company, the factory continued its operations. With assistance from CAP's Legal Section, the people then sued the company and succeeded in the High Court to shut down its operations. On appeal to the Supreme Court, ARE had the stop order reversed. Nevertheless, the people continued their campaign, and the company eventually voluntarily closed down its operations due to these pressures.

(ii) *Villagers stop charcoal factory pollution*

For over 10 years, 1,500 residents of a village in Taman Jaya, Bahau, Negeri Sembilan were subjected to massive smoke, dust and haze throughout the day and night as a result of a factory producing charcoal. The factory belonged to Malayawata Steel, which is partly owned by Japanese interests. The villagers had been appealing to the various authorities to curb the pollution and nuisance of the factory, but nothing materialised. With CAP's assistance in 1989, representations to the authorities were stepped up and the company's operations were finally shut down by the Department of Environment in 1991. Some of the villagers also sued the company for damage to their rubber trees and livestock as their livelihood and health were severely affected. CAP's lawyers succeeded in obtaining compensation for the people when the company was found to be liable by the High Court for causing a nuisance.

(iii) *Campaign to conserve Penang Hill*

Sometime in 1991, the Penang state government announced plans for converting the upper parts of Penang Hill into a major Disneyland-type development. CAP pointed out that the environmental impacts of such a project would have been damaging, as Penang Hill is the site of many watersheds and water-catchment areas for the island. Apart from its importance as a major water source for the island, the Hill is also highly regarded as a conservation area and nature park for the people of Penang, with its beautiful natural environment, and its tranquil and peaceful atmosphere. CAP, together with other public-interest groups, formed a network, "Friends of Penang Hill" to campaign against the project. The DOE was inundated with over 1,000 letters from members of the public, criticising the Environmental Impact Assessment (EIA) report submitted by the company. CAP and Friends of Penang Hill submitted a detailed critique of the development proposals and highlighted the adverse environmental impacts which would result should the project be allowed.

In an unprecedented move, members of Friends of Penang Hill, including CAP, were invited to sit on the Review Panel of the DOE for assessing the EIA for the project. Eventually, the DOE rejected the EIA. The state government also invited Friends of Penang Hill to brief it on their views and eventually, the state shelved the proposed plan.

(iv) Plans for mammoth development shelved

In 1993, the Kedah state government announced proposals for a mammoth project called the Jerai International Park (JIP). The proposed development involved the acquisition of over 10,000 acres of prime food-producing land in rural Kedah, belonging to ordinary villagers. The JIP was mooted as a major tourism plan to convert the agricultural lands into golf courses, resorts and theme parks, modelled after several European cities. There was an outcry from numerous villagers who were to be affected and with CAP's help, the community voiced their concerns to the government authorities. This led to the cancellation of the proposed plans.

(v) State returns land to farmers

About 500 pioneer farmers in Sabak Bernam, Selangor, had been applying for land titles for several years from the state government. Though they had initially been promised the land, they were unsuccessful. Since 1988, their land had been handed over to a government agency to be converted into an oil-palm scheme and given to other people. The agency concerned applied to court to evict the farmers who then sought CAP's help to defend them. The Supreme Court ruled in favour of the farmers as it was shown that they were not mere squatters or trespassers on the land but had in fact been previously promised land titles. Following this, the farmers also filed actions in court asking the state government to fulfil its promise by issuing the titles. In an out-of-court settlement, the state government finally issued the land titles to the farmers who now carry on their farming activity without fear of eviction.

7. SUITABILITY AND POSSIBILITY FOR UPSCALING

Not applicable.

8. SIGNIFICANCE FOR (AND IMPACT ON) POLICY-MAKING

The activities of the organisation have a significant effect on policy-making at the various levels of decision-making. At the community level, fishermen, farmers and urban settlers who have been adversely affected by projects or by pollution have, with the assistance of CAP, managed sometimes to alter or influence government decisions and policies. At the national or state policy-making level, the experiences and knowledge of the organisation have provided inputs to policy-makers on many issues. As shown above, many of the representations made by CAP were translated into policy and changes to the law.

CAP is now frequently invited to participate in various government fora to help provide inputs into government decision-making. Such fora include the annual dialogues organised by the Ministry of Finance to obtain suggestions for drawing up the National Budget, annual dialogues with the Minister of Environment, participation in the National Economic Consultative Council to evaluate Malaysia's development policy, participation in the Penang State's Environment Council which is chaired by the Chief Minister, and participation in the Penang Consumer Council, formed to promote the rights of consumers.

9. POSSIBILITY AND SCOPE OF TRANSFERRING TO OTHER COMMUNITIES OR COUNTRIES

The social and environmental conditions which prompted CAP to undertake its activities are also prevalent in almost all Third World countries. Therefore the kinds of issues raised by CAP and the range of its activities are also relevant to these countries. The innovative approach taken by CAP in making consumer and environmental action relevant to the needs of developing countries can be replicated in almost all parts of the Third World.

Given the social effects of the present globalisation process, the activities of CAP provide helpful lessons or models for consumer and social organisations in the South that may wish to address these social effects. The CAP model of consumer education and action questions the present systems of production and consumption and advocates alternative systems. The CAP approach of linking local actions to global problems is particularly innovative and can be usefully adopted.

Another lesson from the CAP experience is that it is very useful to combine a wide range of issues as well as activities, such as publications, legal activism, education, community mobilisation, research and so on.

Over the years, CAP has encouraged organisations and individuals from other parts of the developing world to undergo training and attachment programmes with the organisation to learn about its activities and how they can be implemented in their own countries. Further, with its wide range of publications comprising books, newspapers, pamphlets and audio-visuals, much information can be obtained, shared and used without major difficulties in various countries, since many of the issues are common and universal.

15.
Indonesian Legal Aid Foundation

1. GENERAL INFORMATION

1. Title of practice or experience

Indonesian Legal Aid Foundation

1.2 Category of practice/experience and brief description

Structural legal aid.

1.3 Name of person or institution responsible for the practice or experience

Indonesian Legal Aid Foundation (YLBHI)

1.4 Name and position of key or relevant persons or officials involved

Apong Herlina, Chairman, Legal Aid Foundation (LBH) Jakarta
Bambang Widjajanto, Chairman, YLBHI
Dewi Novirianti, Public Relations Officer, LBH Jakarta

1.5 Details of institution

   (a) Address: Jl. Diponegoro No. 74, Jakarta 10320, Indonesia
   (b) Telephone: ++ (62) (21) 314 5518
   (c) Fax: ++ (62) (21) 391 2377

1.6 Name of person and/or institution conducting the research

Suharjo Nugroho, Konphalindo

1.7 Details of research person/institution

(a) Address: Jl. Teluk Jakarta No. 1 Komp. TNI AL Rawa Bambu Pasar Minggu, Jakarta, Indonesia
(b) Telephone: ++ (62) (21) 782 1877, 780 4158
(c) Fax: ++ (62) (21) 780 4158
(d) E-Mail: konphal@rad.net.id.

2. THE PROBLEM OR SITUATION BEING ADDRESSED BY THE PRACTICE/INNOVATIVE EXPERIENCE

In real life, it is not uncommon for the poor to experience difficulty in seeking legal redress. The Indonesian people are sometimes subjected to the high cost of court procedures, one-sided job termination, and other legal injustices. This imbalance is aggravated by unawareness of their rights in seeking justice. One irrefutable fact remains, that up to now most of Indonesian society, especially those living below the poverty line, are still legally illiterate.

There have been thousands of instances where civilians' rights had been infringed upon, from civil to criminal cases, from personal cases to those involving the society. Such injustices have opened the eyes of legal practitioners to the need to lend a hand to people needing legal services.

In the beginning, legal assistance programs in a basic form appeared in law faculties with their consultation bureaus, and then there are private legal assistance organizations managed by certain groups. But those efforts are limited to just providing legal advice and consultations, or limited to certain groups only. The Tjandra Naya legal aid organization, for example, only serves non-*pribumis*.

In the meantime, people from the low-income group could hardly obtain access to legal aid, until a prominent legal practitioner, Adnan Buyung Nasution, was moved on seeing the plight and backwardness of those legally illiterate people. In his practice as an attorney in the courts, Buyung apprehended the weak position of the accused in the court of law. They did not know their rights. Even if they did, economic poverty made them unable to do anything, including hiring a lawyer to get legal aid. With that realization upon him, Buyung strived to assist the illiterate, legally illiterate and very poor by giving free legal aid.

In 1959-60, in his capacity as an attorney, Buyung had the chance to study at the University of Melbourne, Australia. During that time, with the help of the Colombo Plan Program Officer, he got the opportunity to observe the various forms and work conduct of legal aid offices in Australia.

On returning from Australia, Buyung tried to realize his aspiration, but he had to give up due to the prevailing situation in the country. Under the decree of July 5, 1959, the legal aid efforts that he strived for did not materialize – not until the third congress of Persatuan Advocat Indonesia (Peradin)/Indonesian Lawyers Association, when Buyung proposed the establishment of a legal aid foundation for the masses. As a result, a group of young lawyers from Peradin founded the Lembaga Bantuan Hukum (LBH)/Legal Aid Foundation in Jakarta on October 28, 1970, coinciding with the Youth Pledge day.

3. DESCRIPTION OF THE PRACTICE/INNOVATIVE EXPERIENCE AND ITS MAIN FEATURES

LBH specializes in providing legal aid to the poor and legally illiterate who either do not know and are not aware of their rights as legal subjects or, due to their social and economic position and as a result of external pressures, do not possess the courage to defend and fight for their rights. Aside from providing legal aid services to the needy, LBH intends to educate the people, to cultivate and develop their awareness of their rights as legal subjects. In addition, it seeks to improve legal implementation in various fields.

The purposes of LBH as stated in its house rules are to:
(a) provide legal services to the poor;
(b) develop and increase people's legal awareness, especially on their rights as legal subjects; and
(c) facilitate legal changes and improvements to fulfil the new needs of a developing society.

LBH seeks to provide legal aid to the weak and poor in relation to their rights as holders of a country's sovereignty who should be able to determine the livelihood of the people and nation as well as determine the direction toward which the nation is heading.

The early years

Initially, as a new-born baby, LBH was understandably unable to accomplish much of note. Physically, it was not ready. The absence of a permanent secretariat, and the lack of office equipment were problems in the initial phase. LBH could only occupy its permanent office one year after it was established. Meanwhile, technical difficulties such as the unavailability of tables, chairs, cabinets and typewriters were solved with the help of the Jakarta Governor, Ali Sadikin, who gave a monthly subsidy of Rp. 300,000, which was quite significant at that time.

Even with minimal equipment and capital, LBH was still able to resolve 22,290 cases between 1971 and 1986, or more than 1,600 cases annually after the first two years. It won a large number of big and spectacular cases involving the interests of thousands. Examples include the case of Simprug land which became a national issue in 1973 because one village located in a very strategic area in the middle of Jakarta, and which was home to 108 families or around 700 people, was to be demolished to make way for a modern luxury housing area; the case of Halim Perdana Kusuma lot which was to have been demolished based on the grounds that the occupied land belonged to the Air Force and the people there had been relocated since the Japanese era; and, more recently, the case of Sunter lot covering about 200 hectares, consisting of mostly prime rice fields owned by 58 families, which was to be taken over with very low compensation and converted into an entreport warehousing complex.

Aside from the cases involving hundreds or thousands of clients, most of whom were legally illiterate and poor, LBH also successfully resolved other private cases which turned out to be no less spectacular, such as the case of the small farmer in the small town of Brebes who was detained and had his business padlocked on suspicion of opening a business without a permit from the Regent. It emerged that the permit had been applied for but was never approved because the business was considered to be competing with a similar business belonging to a wealthy offical. Then there was the case involving 27 poor and legally illiterate people from Ciberéu village in Bogor, West Java, who were demanding their fair share of the 7 kg of gold and 4 kg of diamonds worth US$2,500,000 which they had unearthed in 1945 while farming. Since the period during which they found the treasure was a revolutionary era, they had consigned it to the government, which later declared it lost. So it was that 27 years later, they demanded compensation from the government through the judicial process.

The first big case handled by LBH in 1971 proves the stance and independence of this foundation. This case started when the Jakarta Regional Government wanted to build Taman Mini Indonesia Indah, a recreational area covering 100 hectares, in Lubang Buaya, East Jakarta. This construction plan ignited a protest from the community in Lubang Buaya since they would have to be relocated. LBH then represented about 500 families refusing the relocation.

In the end, the compensation price was increased by Rp. 110 per square meter, supplemented by other assistance like the availability of a relocation place, giving work priority to local people, and compensation for plants. This decision did not satisfy the community.

Even so, LBH's outspoken defense of the community was a very bold move. The Jakarta Governor himself had given significant financial help to LBH.

Reactions to LBH from the media, community and government

LBH's lawyers became favourites with the journalists and would be featured almost every week in the mass media.

Without such support from the media, some of which are nationwide publications like dailies *Kompas* and *Sinar Harapan*, and weekly *Tempo*, LBH would not have the opportunity to increase its influence or even possibly just be able to survive. Relations between LBH and the press were founded on a mutual concern regarding advice for change, and therefore nurtured mutual spirit of transformative action. With the help of the press, complaints forwarded by LBH's clients, and information what was taking place in Jakarta were soon widely circulated all over the country.

The regions would produce similar news to what was happening in Jakarta. Various kinds of fraud, legal violations, improper use of power, extortion by attorneys, etc. in various regions were revealed. The legal situation in these regions prompted people and legal observers to urge LBH to branch out to the provinces.

However, acknowledgement of LBH by the provinces did not seem to be well received by the authorities.

The stance of Buyung and his friends in the Advisory Board of the Indonesian Legal Aid Foundation (YLBHI) as outspoken spokespersons and as defenders of the people sometimes caused tensions with the government.

The government's misgivings were acknowledged by Dewi Novirianti, LBH Jakarta's Public Relations Officer. According to her, it was because LBH oftentimes seemed to oppose the government in clients' cases that it could not run from touching on issues pertaining to government policy. "In the end, we were forced to confront the politics, because although our perspective is legal, we could not avoid political analysis," she added.

Political cases became LBH's focus

Political cases seem to be the trademark of LBH. LBH almost always defends political cases. Statistics from 1984 to 1990 showed that political cases dominated LBH's work. Political cases handled by LBH as a percentage of all cases handled were 52% in 1984, 50% in 1987, and 46% in 1990.

Ironically, all these cases in the political court broke the spirit, since none of the accused were released. Instead, there is a trend in the opposite direction, as in the case of an East Timor student in Central Jakarta High Court who was escorted by an LBH lawyer and ended up receiving a heavier sentence. On the other hand, some of those unescorted by any lawyer were even released immediately.

Even though the defences did not always result in freedom to the defendants, LBH is still consistent in its attitude and views. The failures have not deterred LBH from pursuing its aim of always defending political cases or criminal cases with political nuances. This is still being done consistently.

LBH is seen by many as already being in politics. According to Todung Mulya Lubis, member of YLBHI's Board of Trustees, this is because LBH's core is legal aid in a broad scope and movements like this everywhere are always in close proximity to politics. LBH's political role, Todung said, if any, is minimal. Its role is to remind everyone that Indonesia is a lawful and democratic country which should be able to uphold legal and democratic authority.

Agreeing with Todung, Mulyana W. Kusumah said that LBH is really not just a law office, but also an organization that works toward actualizing the goals of a lawful country. Thus, it not only handles cases but also conducts systematic claims in a legal reformation context. "This means that we intentionally enter the political space, since forcing legal products to be pulled out is inseparable from political force," stated this former 1993 Executive Director of YLBHI as quoted by *Republika* daily, March 11, 1996.

But, added Mulyana, LBH still stands as a legal aid foundation, not a political aid foundation, let alone a socio-political organization.

The joining of regional LBHs into YLBHI

Other legal aid foundations soon began to grow. University Legal Aid Bureaus or BBH, which initially only gave legal consultations especially to the needy, started to gain ground. The BBH in some universities such as the University of Indonesia, University of Pajajaran and University of Brawijaya started providing legal aid in the courts. Provincial LBHs soon sprouted and spread all over Indonesia.

All those regional LBHs were then centralized, for easier coordination, in the form of the Indonesian Legal Aid Foundation (YLBHI) in 1981. As of LBH's 25th anniversary, YLBHI owned 10 regional offices in Jakarta, Bandung, Semarang, Yogyakarta, Surabaya, Medan, Palembang, Ujungpandang, Menado and Jayapura. Aside from that, four project bases were also established in Banda Aceh, Lampung, Bali and Padang. The employees and lawyers in LBH offices up to December 1994 numbered 129 people.

The spread of YLBHI branches over almost all of Indonesia is a manifestation of Peradin's target of developing LBH. The presence of these branches enables LBH's legal aid activities to be operated all over Indonesia. These LBHs under YLBHI work one hundred percent for legal aid with all its dynamics in their programs.

With an active nationwide organization, and having connections with international legal aid and human rights groups, YLBHI is the most prominent among the legal aid organizations in Indonesia.

More than just its free role, Indonesian legal aid as pioneered by YLBHI also gives the impression of an official movement with a healthy ideological perspective, supported by the community and by a pool of highly dedicated lawyers, although there is still internal debate over its methods and goals.

4. DESCRIPTION OF THE INSTITUTION RESPONSIBLE AND ITS ORGANIZATIONAL ASPECTS

The organizational structure of YLBHI basically consists of:
(a) national-level foundation, which is the Yayasan Lembaga Bantuan Hukum Indonesia (YLBHI)/Indonesian Legal Aid Foundation; and
(b) regional/local-level foundation, which is the Lembaga Bantuan Hukum (LBH)/Offices of Legal Aid Foundation.

YLBHI as a national-level foundation has a main status as an institution; therefore basically its main function is to collect and raise funds for funding the program needs of the Legal Aid Foundation offices.

However, considering YLBHI's status as an organizational founding body which should also implement its national mission, it must carry out other and wider functions beyond providing funds to LBH offices with its programs:
(a) policy holder of a national organization;
(b) planner, director and evaluator of organizational programs at the national and regional levels; and
(c) primary manager of LBH offices.

Given these functions, basically YLBHI should push for the implementation of the development programs of LBH offices in broadening its networks.

Meanwhile, the status of LBH offices is basically that of organizational implementer, so that their functions are focused on program operationalization in an effort to achieve organizational goals at the national level and at the same time have local relevance as well as fulfil local needs.

Aside from the sprouting of various branch offices, as an institution, YLBHI has also enjoyed growth. When Adnan Buyung Nasution again became a leader in 1993, after Todung Mulya Lubis and Aodul Hakim Garuda Nusantara, YLBHI revised its management structure. Some of its resources were directed toward settling management issues. Meetings and seminars were conducted to develop YLBHI's management pattern. This developmental step changed the organizational structure of YLBHI's Board of Management. The first layer is now the Board of Management, while the second layer is the Executive Board.

In the Executive Board, an Executive Director leads three other directors: the Directors of Operations, Internal Affairs, and Communication and Special Program. The Operations Directorate, in turn, covers the Divisions of Civilian and Political Rights, Workers, Land, and Environment. Under the Internal Affairs Director are the Office Manager and Finance Manager. The Communication and Special Program Directorate covers Information and Documentation, Networks, Strategic Research, Special Affairs, and Publishing and Publication.

YLBHI's organizational structure really mirrors developments outside of it. Before, the initial format only covered litigation and non-litigation. In its development, the formats of Civilian and Political Rights, Workers and Informal Sector, Land, and Environment, as well as Information and Documentation, were included. Toward the end of Abdul Hakim's management came the Special Division. This handles cases that need investigative expertise like the Dili case of November 12, 1991, the case of Gerakan Aceh Merdeka (Free Aceh Movement) of 1990-92, the Talangsari case of 1989, the case of Pulau Panggung and Gunung Balak (Lampung), and the Marsinah murder case.

YLBHI's multifaceted activities mean that it is not monopolized by law graduates. Many without any legal background have also contributed to the development of YLBHI.

5. PROBLEMS OR OBSTACLES ENCOUNTERED AND HOW THEY WERE OVERCOME

The poor and the legally illiterate usually do not know how to get access to legal aid to settle their cases. Even if they do, some of them do not have enough courage to exercise their rights.

Another difficulty faced by LBH relates to funds, a very basic issue in the operation of its activities. The subsidy from the Jakarta Regional Government which initially amounted to Rp. 300,000 per month during the first few years, then increased to around Rp. 2,000,000 per month, but was stopped in 1986. LBH then received funds from NOVIB (Nederlandse Organisatie Voor Internationale Bijstand), a Dutch non-governmental organization funded by the Department of Dutch Development Cooperation. However, this funding also eventually came to an end.

Meanwhile, LBH activists did not seem to have successfully sourced local monetary support. Up to the present time, LBH depends mostly on assistance from foreign fund foundations.

The chairman of LBH had actually tried to develop fundraising efforts domestically without concrete results. One of the causes is political apprehension; another, according to Dewi, is the recent sprouting of new legal aid bodies. Society, Dewi added, perceives that YLBHI is already established, so people are more interested in channeling their funds to newer and smaller legal aid bodies.

This funding problem naturally affects the smooth operation of YLBHI's activities. It is hard enough with the available funds to cover expenses, let alone increase its staff to widen its networks. It is not easy to overcome the aforementioned problems. Society must first be assured that the legal avenue is open to everybody facing legal problems. The availability of legal aid facilities that they can turn to at any time in the form of LBH must also be socialized. In terms of funds, LBH has formed a separate body to handle its funding needs.

6. EFFECTS OF THE PRACTICE/INNOVATIVE EXPERIENCE

LBH has proven to be more effective than other state or private institutions in drawing people's attention to the challenges faced by Indonesia. Its impact on social, political and legal issues cannot be disputed, particularly its role in instilling public legal awareness. As such, the masses place great hope and trust in LBH.

Since LBH's establishment, awareness of the need for real legal protection for the poor has grown and developed. Public awareness about their legal rights has increased in line with LBH's popularity among lower-income society. Through educational programs and seminars, LBH had actively entered small villages to inculcate legal awareness. "They more or less know the law now, at least laws that concern their problems," admitted Dewi, who has been an LBH staff member for four years. Moreover, Dewi added, if the cases being processed are those that would typically be settled not in one or two months, but in the space of years, "all the while they continue studying, asking us about the laws that concern their cases."

7. SUITABILITY AND POSSIBILITY FOR UPSCALING

Five years ago, on average, 2,000 people came to LBH annually. At present, already more than 500,000 people have come to LBH. From this figure, 75% of the cases were closed every year.

However, the figure of 2,000 LBH clients annually is actually none too fantastic a number. Given the population of Jakarta which is roughly six million, of whom 40% belong to the poor and legally illiterate groups, LBH's achievements are nothing spectacular at all. If annually just 1% of this 40% who are poor and legally illiterate have legal cases, it means there are 24,000 people who need legal aid. These figures reflect just Jakarta alone and the legal aid needs of the rest of the Indonesian population is far greater still. LBH's reach is thus clearly still minimal (due to, among others, the problems encountered by it as described in Section 5), with a lot of room for upscaling.

8. SIGNIFICANCE FOR (AND IMPACT ON) POLICY-MAKING

In conducting legal aid, YLBHI strives to produce concrete social impacts, such as the following:
(a) Qualitative changes in the people or groups of people who are legal aid recipients, enabling them to see the problems not only as legal cases that need to be solved, but also as symptoms of their position in the social system. The legal aid process can likewise show how far their interests have or have not been covered in the legal system, and what the mechanisms are that can hamper the resolution of their problems. Alongside such thinking, there is also a thinking process toward improving welfare.
(b) Results from scientific researches and study on politics and law that are beneficial to law enforcers or formal foundations, as well as levels of the policy-making body.
(c) Non-formal education in the field of law for groups of people who are deemed able to support activities in legal aid, such as university students, informal leaders, reporters and others.

9. POSSIBILITY AND SCOPE OF TRANSFERRING TO OTHER COMMUNITIES OR COUNTRIES

LBH could become a major model for legal aid programs all over the world, since it has not only survived, but grown rapidly, recruited loyal experts and received major public support as well toward achieving its goals.

The following reasons may point more specifically to why LBH can become a source of inspiration for and be emulated by other legal aid programs.

Firstly, it can raise the spirit and loyalties of many young lawyers. Secondly, there is a real public need for LBH's services. Thirdly, LBH is a very bold experiment, and very ambitious, especially when one considers that more traditional and less forward-reaching movements have been restricted in many other countries. Fourthly, LBH's courage and impressive development have been facilitated by its autonomy as a private movement. It grew from proposals and experiences within the community itself, without being hampered by bureaucracy or internal politicking. Fifthly, LBH is successful because it also adopts an intellectual perspective and keeps on moving forward with new ideas, perspectives, targets and analyses about what is needed and what must be done. It never stalls intellectually, because of continual internal debate on its missions, out of which it emerges wiser.

It is not surprising that LBHs under YLBHI can become a model for all legal aid movements in Asia. Of all LBHs, only YLBHI possesses a nationwide organization. At present, there are many legal aid organizations in the country, but YLBHI is still the most active, having connections with the international legal aid network and human rights institutions.

YLBHI's success story can be imitated by other Third World countries, considering the similarity in situation and conditions among these countries, such as the presence of an economic gap, where the reality of poverty will challenge legal aid workers to do something for the poor; political limitations; and the presence of private legal professional institutions which are moved to help the people.

16.

Defending indigenous women's rights

1. GENERAL INFORMATION

1.1 Title of practice or experience

Cordillera Women's Education and Resource Center: Defending indigenous women's rights

1.2 Category of practice/experience and brief description

This is a report of the efforts of a community-based organization of indigenous women to protect the rights and further the interests of indigenous women in the Cordillera region of the Philippines.

The Cordillera Women's Education and Resource Center (CWERC) is a non-governmental, non-profit, non-stock organization, formally established on March 7, 1987. Its vision is to help develop a dynamic women's movement in the Cordillera working for the elimination of inequality and discrimination based on gender, ethnicity, class, nationality and race.

The CWERC was established as part of a growing indigenous people's movement in the region. Some women activists felt that there was a need to highlight women's perspectives on the various issues and also raise specific women's concerns which should be addressed. The need to build the capacities of the indigenous women for leadership was also seen as crucial.

1.3 Name of person or institution responsible for the practice or experience

Cordillera Women's Education and Resource Center, Inc.

1.4 Name and position of key or relevant persons or officials involved

Victoria Tauli-Corpuz, Chairperson, Board of Directors
Bernice See, Projects Planning and Assistance Desk Officer

Cynthia Dacanay, Education and Training Officer Convenor, Management Committee

1.5 Details of institution

(a) Address: No. 16 Loro Street, Dizon Subdivision, Baguio City 2600, Philippines
(b) Telephone: ++ (63) (74) 442 5347
(c) Fax: ++ (63) (74) 444 3362

1.6 Name of person and/or institution conducting the research

Tebtebba Foundation, Inc. (Indigenous Peoples' International Center for Policy Research and Education)

1.7 Details of research person/institution

(a) Address: Rm. 3B Agpaoa Compound, 111 Upper General Luna Road, 2600 Baguio City, Philippines
(b) Telephone: ++ (63) (74) 444 7703
(c) Fax: ++ (63) (74) 443 9459
(d) E-Mail: tebtebba@skyinet.net

2. THE PROBLEM OR SITUATION BEING ADDRESSED BY THE PRACTICE/INNOVATIVE EXPERIENCE

The Philippines, and the Cordillera region in particular, is endowed with rich natural resources. It has vast mineral deposits, major rivers that can generate hydropower and large timber reserves. In spite of the wealth of its land, the region remains relatively underdeveloped.

The indigenous inhabitants of the Cordillera are collectively known as Igorots. The Cordillera was excluded from the economic, political and cultural development process of the colonial society because of their strong resistance against the Spanish. The resistance of the Igorots to the colonizers made them retain their indigenous lifestyles and institutions throughout the period of Spanish colonial rule. To denigrate those they could not conquer, the Spanish colonizers labeled the Igorots as savage, heathen and uncivilized.

During the American colonial period, the Igorots were categorized as cultural minorities and were subjected to discrimination, for example, they were subjected to assimilationist policies. The traditional economy of some of the

Igorots was eroded to shift production towards the market. The penetration of the cash economy into the region slowly destroyed the natural self-sufficient economy of the region. Environmentally sustainable agricultural practices of the Igorots were considered backward and unscientific. Agricultural production that generated cash crops like coffee, beans, vegetables and bananas was what was considered as a productive activity. The colonizers were also able to exploit the region's natural resources through legislation which facilitated the entry of big corporations.

From the American colonial period to the present, the Cordillera has been a resource base for business interests. This can be seen in the presence of mining companies, logging concessions, hydroelectric power plants and export processing zones in the region. This has resulted in environmental problems such as denudation of forests, river pollution and depletion of mineral resources.

In spite of the fact that the region provides revenues to the national government from the extraction of its natural resources, social services and appropriate development projects are very inadequate. This inadequacy is seen in the lack of good roads; poor communication facilities; inadequate, dilapidated schoolhouses with few teachers; insufficient and inappropriate health services; and the poverty of the indigenous peoples.

Most of the women are found in the rural areas of the region, with an overwhelming majority engaged in subsistence agricultural production. In traditional rice production, the women assume most of the major tasks, from seeding to seed selection. The erosion of the traditional economy in some areas has led to the displacement of women. Many outmigrated to the mining areas to join their miner husbands and to the urban poor communities in the city. Since subsistence production and women's work are mainly for domestic purposes, these have not been considered as productive activities and factored into the gross national product. Outside of traditional agricultural production, a significant number of women are engaged in commercial farming. As wage earners in the temperate vegetable-growing areas and rice-producing areas of the region, women are being paid less for their labor than men.

A considerable number of women are also found in Baguio, the only urban center in the region. Employment opportunities in Baguio and neighboring towns are found in the export processing zone, the mining areas, banks, tourism-related businesses like hotels and restaurants, government offices, private and public schools and hospitals. In the mining areas, the women are confined to their homes and have very limited livelihood opportunities. The mining companies do not hire women. Some miners' wives have cultivated the sides of the mountains near the mines to supplement their husbands' meager income.

With the shift in mining strategy from underground mining to open-pit and bulk mining which requires less workers to operate, a large number of workers are being retrenched. Laid-off workers, along with their wives, are forced to leave the area to seek for new sources of livelihood. Small-scale mining, which employs not only men but also women in the area, is prohibited within the areas claimed by the big mining corporations.

In the factories of the export processing zones, 80% of the workforce are women. Companies prefer hiring females to males because they believe that females are "more adapted to boring and dexterous assembly work" and can be hired cheaply. Working conditions are often unfavorable for the women. Some of these companies do not provide maternity benefits and in some cases, pregnancies meant the termination of employment.

Gender discrimination is manifested not only in the economic realm, where women are paid less in wages, and in the political realm wherein decision-making processes are dominated by men, but also in the cultural arena. Patriarchy, which perpetuates the belief that women are subordinate to men, was reinforced by the colonizers' culture, religion, education, economic and political systems. The problems of gender discrimination are found in the social, economic, political and cultural realms. Marginal production, illiteracy, lack of social services, inappropriate development programs, domestic violence, violence from structural and institutional forces, and commodification beset the Cordillera women.

3. DESCRIPTION OF THE PRACTICE/INNOVATIVE EXPERIENCE AND ITS MAIN FEATURES

The CWERC was established to help build a women's movement in the region. The women's movement in the Cordillera is envisioned to be not only a part of the national women's movement but also part of the indigenous peoples' movement and the national movement for genuine sovereignty and democracy.

The CWERC's starting point is that the liberation of the Cordillera women from inequality and oppression based on gender, class, race, ethnicity and nationality can only be achieved by addressing the multiple realities of women simultaneously. It is within this framework that the programs of the Center have been designed to respond to the various issues and needs confronting the women. These include education and training activities, research, documentation and publication, socio-economic work and networking at the regional, national and international levels. Women belonging to the poor classes and underprivileged sectors in the region are the main targets of the CWERC's education and organizing efforts.

Organizing work

Prior to the establishment of the CWERC, organizing among indigenous people in the Cordillera had already started. This was witnessed in their strong opposition to the World Bank-funded Chico River Dam project which would have caused the displacement of around 300,000 Igorots from their ancestral lands. The community had also opposed a project of the Cellophil Resources Corporation, owned by an influential friend of the former Marcos administration, which was given two hundred thousand hectares of ancestral pine forests to log. Protests against these projects started in the mid-1970s and were sustained up to the end of the decade.

The success in stopping these two projects empowered the Cordillera peoples to build and strengthen the region-wide indigenous peoples' movement. From this period to the eighties, the indigenous peoples' movement in the Cordillera slowly grew, and gained more strength with the founding of the Cordillera Peoples' Alliance (CPA) in 1984. The CPA is a federation of indigenous people's organizations in the Cordillera, which originally constituted 27 people's organizations. The grassroots organizations of the CPA and other non-governmental organizations (NGOs) facilitated the CWERC's entry into the communities to establish initial contacts and to gather data on the women's situation in the various provinces.

To conduct its initial organizing and education work, the CWERC also worked with existing women's organizations. Many of these organizations were organized by either the churches or government agencies like the Department of Agriculture or Social Welfare and also by politicians. Except for active church-related women's organizations, most of these were non-functional and only became active when funds were brought in for particular activities or projects or during elections when politicians wanted to mobilize the women to campaign for them.

The CWERC deemed that it was not necessary to create new organizations. What it did was to reorient some of these organizations toward becoming more socially relevant and toward addressing the women's issues and concerns. A core curriculum was developed in what was called the basic women's orientation. This includes a discussion of the national situation of women, workshops on the local women's situation, discussion of the responses of the women and the building of a women's movement at the national level. Several frameworks are used in analyzing the situation of women and the situation of the Filipino people and the indigenous peoples in the Cordillera. Popular methods of education which are dialogical and participatory are used.

In establishing initial contacts and organizing the women in Baguio City and its neighboring areas, the CWERC sought the help of the other NGOs operating in the area, like the Women Workers Program (WWP). WWP is involved in organizing and education work among women workers, women in the informal economy and urban poor women. WWP provided initial contact persons in the mining and urban poor communities in these areas.

In areas where there were no existing traditional organizations, the organizers helped build new women's organizations. After having had initial consultations, established initial contacts and gathered information on the women's situation in the area, the organizers identified potential women leaders, who were formed into a core group. Members of this core group were then encouraged to initiate the formation of the women's organization in the community. To facilitate the organization-building, education activities were planned by the organizer, together with the core group and in coordination with the other NGOs working in the area.

With the assistance of the organizer, the constitution and by-laws of the organization were drafted and a general assembly held. In this general assembly, the women elected their officers and approved or revised the draft constitution and by-laws. General programs of action were also planned. Then, the newly elected officers or the executive committee scheduled regular meetings to implement the general programs of action formulated in the assembly. Particular plans and actions of the organization were prepared by the executive committee and implemented. In the implementation of these plans, the organization formed committees. The number of committees set up depended on the needs, capabilities and plans of the organization and the community. In most cases, education, health and project committees were set up.

Aside from establishing and developing organizations, the CWERC also helped in consolidating them through Innabuyog. Innabuyog is a federation of women's organizations in the region, which was used to reorient the existing women's organizations in the Cordillera toward becoming more people-oriented and gender-sensitive. Through Innabuyog, the CWERC has not only strengthened the leadership of the various organizations but also united their membership in a common vision of a transformed society which they will help create. It also widened their area of influence. It was able to reach thousands of grassroots women and build and develop more than a hundred women's organizations in more than a hundred communities in the Cordillera.

In its organizing work, the CWERC uses an effective tool – integration. Under this approach, the community-organizers learn from experience. Immersing themselves in the lives of the women, the organizers are able to enrich the concepts, methods and theories in community-organizing learned from formal education and training. To do this, the organizers have to live in the community. This allows them to directly experience the day-to-day life of womenfolk. They also discuss with the women their problems and issues, thus enabling them to obtain firsthand data for research and documentation purposes and as a basis for future plans, projects and actions of the Center. This approach also allows the organizers to share their views with the women in the community. The organizer synthesizes the women's experiences and problems and relates them to the overall problems faced by the society.

The main bulk of the CWERC's personnel are women organizers who have to be based in the communities. They are trained to be educators, researchers and organizers at the same time. It is necessary for them to have a thorough knowledge of the economic, political and socio-cultural situation at the local and national level, the root causes of the poverty and problems of the Igorots in particular and the Filipinos in general, and the reasons behind the problems faced by the women.

Education and training

Social and gender awareness-raising is done through education activities and participatory research. Leadership formation and skills training seminars are also provided. This includes training in mass campaign administration, communication skills, organization management, etc. Education or consciousness-raising activities are focused on women's discrimination and oppression and its interrelationship with the economic, political and socio-cultural problems of the society. These are done through seminars, fora, lectures and workshops on the national, regional and local women's situations.

Basic leadership training seminars also are given to the women leaders to equip them with the knowledge and tools on how to transform traditional organizations from being organizations reinforcing women's subordinate role, to organizations that will advance women's rights. They are also taught how to run and manage organizations, how to speak at public events, how to run mass campaigns, etc. The ideas and know-how drawn from these training seminars have not been confined to those who underwent the training. Representatives to these seminars are required by their organizations to share with their co-members what they learned.

Gender-sensitivity training is also conducted among the women and mixed organizations. Education activities and training provide the women with knowledge and skills for them to effectively address their particular situation. Some women leaders at the community level are now able to deal with local issues and have increased their capacity as articulators in national and region-wide activities. The medium of instruction is the local language. Visual aids and creative presentations which do not water down the content of the subject are used.

Effort has also been expended toward raising the gender-awareness and sensitivity of the staff of NGOs in the Cordillera and the leaders of people's organizations. Thus, CWERC has consciously made efforts to influence the behavior of activists within its own network.

Research, publication and documentation

Information dissemination and the propagation of women's perspectives on concepts, issues, problems, policies and laws are crucial to further raising the level of consciousness of the women and the public. These are done through the Center's research, documentation and publication program. Research has been undertaken on the Cordillera women's situation. This has focused mainly on the situation of indigenous peasant women, women workers, the urban poor women, and specific areas like reproductive health, human rights violations, women in situations of armed conflict, etc.

Research and documentation that have been done employed the participatory research approach. Specific data on the situation of peasant and working women were gathered and analyzed. Research results were used to understand, analyze and present the women's situation and to determine the appropriate assistance the Center will provide to the women. Some of the research results have also been published in the Center's newsletter, *Chaneg*, and its journal, *Tebtebba*.

Moreover, research results contributed a great part in theorizing and popularizing the indigenous women's struggles and issues. The CWERC has contributed significantly in the theorizing of the women's question among indigenous women in the Cordillera, within a framework that strove for a proper balance in addressing the factors of gender, class, ethnicity, race and nationality.

Socio-economic work

The CWERC also has socio-economic projects, which are implemented through the projects planning and assistance desk, and run mainly by organized grassroots women's groups. They are the ones who determine, set up and manage appropriate socio-economic projects. The women are assisted in setting up viable small-scale projects in the various communities. These projects were designed to alleviate poverty and lighten women's multiple burdens and strengthen their participation in the community's political and social life. These are implemented particularly in the provinces where government services prove inadequate. The experiences gained in operating the socio-economic projects are regularly assessed to derive lessons which can be applied for improving subsequent projects.

However, in implementing these socio-economic programs, the Center is faced with a dilemma: whether or not to encourage the women to be fully integrated into the market economy even if its effect is the erosion of the traditional economic system in which they play key roles. Another trade-off is that for socio-economic projects to be viable and well managed, the management skills of trained women activists are required. Since it is not easy to train managers and activists, sometimes the effective women activists get sidetracked to help run these projects instead of engaging in activities like organizing and educating.

Networking and international solidarity work

Another program set up by the CWERC is networking and international solidarity. Through this program, the Center was able to establish linkages and relationships with other women's organizations, people's organizations, institutions and development agencies working within and outside the region. The Center was also able to project the Cordillera women's issues not only in the local but also in the international arena.

At the international level, the CWERC played a major role in the formation of the Asian Indigenous Women's Network (AIWN). AIWN was set up to strengthen networking among the indigenous women in Asia, to articulate and project their issues and demands and to empower them.

Prior to this, the CWERC was a member of the International Steering Committee of Indigenous Women which convened and organized the Second International Indigenous Women's Conference which was held in 1991 in Karasjhoka, Norway.

AIWN performed a significant role in the Fourth World Conference on Women held in Beijing, China. It organized the indigenous women attending the conference and drafted the Beijing Declaration of Indigenous Women. This draft was discussed and approved by the indigenous women's caucus which comprised of 150 indigenous women from different parts of the world. This declaration summarized the issues and problems of indigenous women, critiqued the Draft Platform for Action of the Fourth World Conference on Women, and stated their demands to the international community, the governments and the NGOs. It also contained resolutions on how the indigenous women would collaborate among themselves in future.

The declaration expressed the unity of the indigenous women in their "struggle to actively defend their rights to self-determination and territories, which have been invaded and colonized by powerful nations and interests." This declaration emerged as one of the major documents that came out of Beijing, and is presently used as lobby and education material by indigenous women in different countries.

The CWERC also participated in the United Nations Conference on Environment and Development (UNCED) or the Earth Summit held in Rio de Janeiro, Brazil. It was officially accredited by the UNCED and subsequently by the UN to be one of the NGOs in the roster allowed to attend the sessions of the UN Commission on Sustainable Development, the Convention on Biological Diversity, etc.

It also participated in the World Conference on Human Rights in Vienna, the Social Summit in Copenhagen and the preparatory meetings for the Conference on Population and Development. In these conferences, the representatives of the CWERC made presentations at various NGO events and also at the official plenary sessions. The Director of the CWERC was chosen by the NGOs attending the Social Summit to present the NGO Copenhagen Declaration in the official plenary session. She had been part of the NGO steering committees for the Social Summit and the Commission on Sustainable Development.

Networking and establishing linkages with other organizations was also found useful in consolidating the women's organizations since it enabled the women to comprehend that women's problems were linked to other issues within a global framework.

The CWERC has worked with various groups on a short-term and long-term basis. It formed loose coalitions such as the Task Force on Violence Against Women (TFVAW) through its Women's Crisis Center, which is a program created to address the problems of victims of domestic and state violence against women (VAW). The TFVAW is a support group which helped the victims of VAW through providing free legal and psychological counselling, sharing of skills and expertise, logistical support, devoting time to accompanying the victims to medical practitioners and court hearings on their cases, and supporting campaigns against VAW.

The TFVAW comprised 17 women's organizations of professionals in academe, women in the government service, members of religious congregations and students. The TFVAW acted as a pressure group. With the assistance of the volunteers of the TFVAW, petitions were distributed and signed, open letters and press statements were published and rallies were held. The task force also lobbied government bodies to change the laws that further oppress women and create new laws that will ensure the protection of women.

With the common aim of defending the indigenous people's ancestral land and fighting for their right to self-determination, the CWERC has worked closely with the CPA. As a center that provides support and service programs to indigenous women working to strengthen the women's movement in the Cordillera, the CWERC cannot divorce itself from the problems confronting the indigenous people in general.

The CWERC has also forged relationships with national organizations like the Center for Women's Resources (CWR) and GABRIELA. CWR is quite similar to the CWERC but operates at the national level. It conducts participatory research and popular education activities for women, has several publications, and maintains a resource center. GABRIELA is a national coalition of women's organizations, programs and institutions across various sectors and groups.

Other programs

As the Center gained experience, it set up additional programs on functional literacy, women's rights and crisis intervention. Most women in the region are illiterate because of the lack of public schools and the traditional roles played by women. To address this problem, the Center set up a functional literacy program. In this program, the teachers used the Ilocano language (a major lingua franca in Northern Luzon) in teaching the Filipino alphabet instead of the English alphabet. They also taught simple arithmetic to women so that the women would not be cheated when selling or buying. The lessons used were also meant to raise the gender awareness of the women and to teach them to be as practical as possible. For instance, since the women had a rice-buying club, the actual transactions they made were used as examples in their arithmetic classes.

Aside from monitoring, documenting and campaigning against domestic and state violence against women, the CWERC also opened a Women's Crisis Center. This assisted the survivors of domestic and state violence and raised the awareness of the public toward the issue of violence against women. To democratize crisis intervention, a pool of volunteers from the legal and medical professions, and from the universities and other interested individuals was formed. Additionally, the TFVAW was organized to extend assistance to the survivors and to conduct campaigns.

Through its various programs, the CWERC was able to do advocacy work indirectly. For instance, because of its work on VAW, which included networking with the media and even having a radio program, the public's awareness of VAW has been heightened. In linking up with the different government agencies in relation to VAW cases, the CWERC was able to make the persons working in these agencies aware of the women's issues. CWERC staff were invited as resource persons on different occasions by offices and institutions both locally and nationally, a recognition of the organization's pioneering work among women, particularly Cordillera indigenous women.

In the national consultations held to prepare the country report for the World Conference on Women, the CWERC was instrumental in the Cordillera consultations and in facilitating the workshop on women and environment during the National WID Forum. The CWERC Executive Director was assigned to write the portion on Women and Environment in the NGO Country Report.

The local academe also had been very active in soliciting the inputs of the CWERC in its gender program. These were in the form of consultations on researches, as resource persons for various fora, as co-sponsor of various activities, to give gender-awareness training, etc.

Strategies

The basic starting point of the CWERC's analysis is that the problems of women are intricately linked with the economic, political and socio-cultural realities of society. Women-specific issues and broader problems and issues encountered by Cordillera women, like institutional and domestic violence, alienation of the ancestral lands, environmental destruction, inadequate public and social services, and increasing prices of basic commodities, etc., are related to the fundamental problems of Philippine society that are rooted in socio-economic structures. The pervasive influence of patriarchy in the socio-cultural, political and cultural structures is also a key factor. The CWERC is realistic enough to know that its vision can only be achieved in the very long term.

The following strategies are employed by the CWERC to achieve its objectives:

(a) conducting initial consultations at the community level to establish contacts and to reach out to organized and unorganized women;
(b) giving gender-awareness and structural analysis workshops as an initial step towards developing the women's critical analysis of their situation;
(c) research and documentation of the specific situations of women using the participatory research approach;
(d) intensive training of women organizers who are then sent to live and do organizing, education and research work in the local communities;
(e) providing support for appropriate and relevant socio-economic projects which the women have identified as priorities;
(f) popularization of women's issues and concerns through the media;

(g) setting up a regional federation to carry out political, economic and socio-cultural analysis of issues and concerns of women;
(h) linking up with regional, national and international alliances to be part of the broader people's movement and articulate the women's issues at these levels;
(i) publication of a newsletter to project the women's issues, problems, viewpoints and perspectives;
(j) actively engaging in discussions/discourses/debates on women's issues and other issues on which women have a perspective; and
(k) conducting different fora where women's issues and perspectives on these issues are discussed.

4. DESCRIPTION OF THE INSTITUTION RESPONSIBLE AND ITS ORGANIZATIONAL ASPECTS

The Cordillera Women's Education and Resource Center (CWERC) was established through the First Cordillera Women's Assembly in March 1987. The participants came from all the provinces of the Cordillera and from Baguio City, and from different sectors (peasants, workers, urban poor, professionals). It also enabled them to explore and discern what they could collectively do to address their issues and to help advance the indigenous people's struggle for self-determination.

An important part of the assembly was the discussion on the manifestations of women's oppression in the region and the attempt to define the particularity of the indigenous women's situation in the Cordillera. From these discussions, they were able to pinpoint the necessary services to strengthen and develop the women's movement in the Cordillera that would deal with the distinct issues and concerns of women. To address their needs, they resolved to set up the Cordillera Women's Education and Resource Center and mandated it to provide services and support for building up and strengthening the Cordillera women's movement in the region.

The objectives which the CWERC set for itself are the following:
(a) to undertake more in-depth research on the situation of Cordillera women;
(b) to raise the level of political, social and gender awareness of the women in the region;
(c) to strengthen, reorient or help build women's organizations and networks;
(d) to wage campaigns and set up projects addressing women's issues and needs;

(e) to network with other women's organizations and network nationally and abroad; and
(f) To support women's socio-economic activities and projects.

The structure of the CWERC is based on the various forms of support and services it provides. The program components are reflected in the various desks. These desks coordinate closely and complement each other. The different desks of the CWERC are the following: Research, Documentation and Publications; Education and Training; Organizing; Projects Planning and Assistance; Networking and International Solidarity.

The desk coordinators with the Executive Director compose the Management Committee which sees to the day-to-day affairs of the Center. This Committee also operationalizes the programs recommended by women in the community and various sectors.

A Board of Directors, with representation from several sectors like peasantry, labor, professionals, church and business, and headed by a Chair, is the highest policy-making body. It is mandated by the Constitution and By-Laws registered with the Securities and Exchange Commission to meet annually.

At the beginning of each year, the Management Committee and the entire staff contingent of the CWERC meet to plan the one-year program. Assessment and evaluation of the program is done every six months to see what has been achieved, learn lessons and readjust targets. At the end of the year, an evaluation of the whole year's program is done and this forms the basis of the following year's program.

5. PROBLEMS OR OBSTACLES ENCOUNTERED AND HOW THEY WERE OVERCOME

One of the major problems encountered by the Center in its early operations was the militarization of the region in the late 1980s. Agricultural productivity was hampered, the incidence of poverty rose and the marginalization of indigenous women worsened. Some communities were bombed and people were evacuated from their communities. Most of those who ended up as internal refugees were women and children. The militarization of the region became a major obstacle for the CWERC in reaching out to the women in the communities or in carrying out socio-economic projects.

The CWERC participated in many fact-finding missions to document what was happening, to report these to the media, and to hold dialogues with the military and government officials. The CWERC also conducted relief operations to assist and support the internal refugees and also became actively involved in human rights campaigns.

Another problem faced by the CWERC was the initial hostility of mixed organizations and men to the CWERC approach and programs. When the CWERC was starting out, there were hostile reactions from men in mixed organizations or even in the communities to the idea of having a separate women's organization. The usual arguments of "why are we dividing the communities?", "isn't feminism a Western imposition which is alien to indigenous peoples?", etc. were used. However, there were also male leaders who were asking the CWERC to educate the women so that the latter would understand what the men were fighting for, they being the leaders of organizations. Also, in many communities, there already existed women's organizations which were actively involved in community affairs.

The way the CWERC dealt with this was to give women's orientation to the women and develop a core of women leaders in the communities and the organizations who, in the end, were the ones asserting that they would like to have their own organizations. Within the communities and tribes, the women have to be the ones to assert their rights to have their own organizations. This is not an alien concept but something relevant to them.

Also, because the CWERC ensured that the women's issues were not handled in a fragmented manner but were integrated with the issues of the indigenous peoples in general and also with national issues, the number of women who became active in the regional and national movements increased. Their quality of leadership also improved significantly. Now, the women's organizations and movements within the region are here to stay and will have to be considered whether the establishment and male-dominated organizations like it or not.

6. EFFECTS OF THE PRACTICE/INNOVATIVE EXPERIENCE

The establishment of the CWERC, both as a women's organization and as an NGO providing services for women in the Cordillera, is a pioneering effort in the region. In the past, the capacity of women to analyze their situation within the context of a Third World country had been very limited. On the other hand, the public's awareness of the situation of women has also been shaped by a male-dominated media. The establishment of the CWERC has given a framework for analysis of the situation of women, an organized projection of the issues confronting women, a systematic documentation of the issues confronting women, and a sustained and active campaign to confront their problems. The CWERC is not just a service NGO but an activist organization. It articulates the issues being faced by women in the Cordillera. Its staff are indigenous women and other Cordillera natives and they embody the mission of the CWERC, taking the program as their own.

7. SUITABILITY AND POSSIBILITY FOR UPSCALING

There are several women's programs that have been established in the region, each with a particular focus. In other regions in the Philippines, there are also programs similar to the CWERC's which have been established. The programs that have been implemented by the CWERC can be adopted anywhere and tailor-fitted to the needs of women. What is important is for the program to be not only a service agency but also an activist organization of women. With adequate support and commitment from activists who should be doing the organizing, a program like the CWERC can be multiplied. Instead of upscaling, multiplication or replication might be a better option so that the grassroots women will have more participation in the defining of programs. To geographically expand operations will bring about bureaucracy and this may put more demands on administrative work and may entail the setting up of a bureaucracy.

8. SIGNIFICANCE FOR (AND IMPACT ON) POLICY-MAKING

The publications of the CWERC were the first to address the women's question in the region. They defined the particularity of the Cordillera women's oppression and discrimination and helped trace the roots of this. The research results became the basis for the creation of an education curriculum, programs and activities, for campaigns, and for lobbying and advocacy work. The visibility of women's issues, analysis and demands increased significantly such that they could no longer be ignored by the general public nor by government bodies and other institutions. The program had been part of discussions with those in academe, both locally and at the national level. This also led to the popularization of certain issues, particularly the issue of violence against women (VAW). This particular campaign on VAW had a very strong impact in the region. It was a breakthrough. Before, domestic violence was not viewed as a societal problem but rather as a problem best settled inside the home. Prior to the CWERC campaigns, the concept of state violence against women was virtually unheard of. The differential impact of militarization on women and children was highlighted which helped relief and rehabilitation programs to be more gender-sensitive.

Before these issues were highlighted, government agencies had failed miserably in assisting victims of domestic violence and rape. The Department of Social Welfare and Development (DSWD) did not even provide temporary shelter to victims. The police sometimes harassed the victims instead of the perpetrators and women preferred to keep quiet to avoid further humiliation and degradation. But after the campaign, gender-sensitivity training was undertaken by some government agencies. The DSWD has now set up its own shelter for women survivors.

The anti-militarization campaign which the CWERC actively participated in contributed in stopping militarization in many communities. The CWERC, in coordination with other development programs and human rights groups, was able to respond not only to the women's needs but to the whole community as well.

In the international arena, the CWERC also contributed significantly to the projection of indigenous women's concerns and perspectives. It also contributed by starting networks among indigenous women which are slowly gaining strength. Because of these efforts, combined with those of other organizations, UN agencies like the Commission on the Status of Women, the UN Working Group on Indigenous Populations, etc. are more conscious of the need for integrating indigenous women in their work and documentation.

9. POSSIBILITY AND SCOPE OF TRANSFERRING TO OTHER COMMUNITIES OR COUNTRIES

The CWERC experience can provide useful lessons or even a model that can be studied by groups in other countries interested in organizing programs run by women to advocate the interests of women, in particular, indigenous women.

The CWERC's program is very much replicable in other countries. Some programs in the Philippines operate in a similar manner to the CWERC. What is important is for the program to be responsive to the reality of women's lives in the particular place or country, the commitment of activists in managing the program, and the capacity of the women themselves to make the program their own.

17.

Innovative policy advocacy for indigenous peoples in the Philippines

1. GENERAL INFORMATION

1.1 Title of practice or experience

Innovative policy advocacy for indigenous peoples in the Philippines

1.2 Category of practice/experience and brief description

Documented here is a Philippine non-governmental group's experience and innovation in policy advocacy for the country's indigenous peoples.

As a legal policy advocacy institution, the group works closely and links up with institutions directly involved in or related to the formulation of national and regional/local policies and programs. The group mainly intervenes in the formulation of norms, standards and procedures.

1.3 Name of person or institution responsible for the practice or experience

Legal Rights and Resources Center (LRC)

1.4 Name and position of key or relevant persons or officials involved

Attorney Marvic Leonen, Executive Director
France Begonia, Coordinator, Research and Policy Development Division

1.5 Details of institution

  (a) Address: 47 Kalayaan Avenue, Diliman, Quezon City, Philippines
  (b) Telephone: ++ (63) (2) 927 9670
  (c) Fax: ++ (63) (2) 920 7172
  (d) E-Mail: LRC@phil.gn.apc.org

1.6 Name of person and/or institution conducting the research

Tebtebba Foundation, Inc. (Indigenous Peoples' International Center for Policy Research and Education)

1.7 Details of research person/institution

(a) Address: Rm. 3B Agpaoa Compound, 111 Upper General Luna Road, 2600 Baguio City, Philippines
(b) Telephone:++ (63) (74) 444 7703
(c) Fax:++ (63) (74) 443 9459
(d) E-Mail: tebtebba@skyinet.net

2. THE PROBLEM OR SITUATION BEING ADDRESSED BY THE PRACTICE/INNOVATIVE EXPERIENCE

The Legal Rights and Resources Center or LRC was organized at a time when various advocacy groups had to redefine and redirect their focus and energy. The five lawyer-founders of LRC were trained under the civil-political rights movement, which championed human rights during the martial law reign of the late Ferdinand Marcos (1972-1986).

After the Marcoses were ousted in a civilian-backed military uprising in February 1986, several advocacy groups, many of which came from the human rights or civil-political rights movement during the Marcos years, sought other avenues for their advocacy. For its part, LRC chose to advocate and champion the socio-economic and ancestral land rights of indigenous peoples.

To LRC, the country's 17 million indigenous peoples (24% of the country's total 70-million population), who have long helped protect and conserve the country's forest ecosystem and biodiversity, have to be attended to. Despite their role in preserving and sustaining their environment, indigenous peoples have been marginalized, due to policies and laws which opened indigenous peoples' lands to loggers and big commercial miners.

As a result of these laws and policies, only over six million hectares (ha.) of forest cover are left in the Philippines. Only 700,000 ha. are believed to be primary or largely untouched forest. Another 3.4 million ha. of secondary forest remain. These are forests which have been logged, generally once, but still have commercial potential.

With the present rate of loss of the remaining primary forest, it is estimated that the biologically most diverse and economically most important can be lost within the next decade.

A more recent independent assessment concludes that the natural resource base of the Philippines has become so depleted and degraded that the country faces the grim prospect of a decline in its agri-based economy and the weakening of its democratic institutions. Its once magnificent dipterocarp forests have been ravaged, its rivers polluted with silt and sediment of eroded soils, its coral reefs ruined by blast fishing, and its mangrove forests decimated. Unless these pressing problems and the long-term threats to the resource base are addressed, the country will slide further into the pits of poverty and despair.

To help make a difference, LRC has thus set its eyes on the lack of protection of the terrestrial ecosystem, especially the remaining dipterocarp forest – the backbone of most terrestrial ecosystems in the country. The knowledge, potential and creativity of those individuals and communities directly dependent upon and living in these ecosystems were not harnessed. They are the indigenous peoples whom LRC opted to work for.

When it finally began operations in February 1988, LRC aimed to focus on two main angles:
(a) to help respond to actual crisis situations in indigenous communities; and
(b) to try to change the "rules of the game" via policy advocacy.

Having a battery of highly competent, committed and "people-oriented" lawyers, LRC had helped litigate indigenous peoples' rights cases. But, as LRC's experience has shown, indigenous peoples will be confronted with the same type of cases over and over again unless the rules are changed.

LRC would realize later that policy advocacy does not only mean rules in black and white in the form of laws. Policy advocacy, rather, is a mix of other factors as well – political, institutional and financial (e.g., budget allocations).

Although it is a legal group, which has the capacity to even propose legal technical language for proposed laws and policies, LRC has engaged in other forms of lobby work. This is because LRC may have the special skill in advocating and proposing rules and policies, but these become ineffective when they are not taken up.

3. DESCRIPTION OF THE PRACTICE/INNOVATIVE EXPERIENCE AND ITS MAIN FEATURES

LRC's main advocacy work is anchored to this rationale: The recognition and protection of the rights of indigenous peoples and long-term occupants of the forests and of the rest of the uplands should be the primary component of any program on sustainable development.

LRC recognizes that empowerment is essential. But it believes that it is not the only requirement for meaningful reform. It thus asserts that the peoples' aspirations must eventually be adopted, articulated and implemented by the State.

Hence, LRC seeks to bridge the gap between the informal articulation of the aspirations of peoples' organizations on the one hand, and the formal, technical, bureaucratic and legal language used by the State on the other. This is sought to be achieved through policy development and advocacy.

As a research organization, LRC scrutinizes changes in the formulation of norms, rules, standards and procedures. It also monitors changes in the "policy climate", which includes the political climate, and not necessarily ideological spectrums. LRC, for example, would attempt to uncover the identity of the operator of a mining or logging firm in an indigenous community. The operator's influential link, other key players, and their perspectives are among the information that LRC's research arm monitors. Knowing the key players helps LRC devise its policy development and advocacy gameplan, such as how to intervene in the National Congress.

Data for LRC's researches mainly come from clients (indigenous peoples) provided with legal services. Other data come from secondary sources such as academic and alternative research institutions. In special cases, LRC may have to do its own primary data gathering.

In its policy development and advocacy, LRC has five teams closely working together for a common thrust. Aside from its research arm, the Research and Policy Development (RPD) division, LRC has other teams such as the Direct Legal Service (DLS) division, the Campaigns Division (CD), and the Public Information and External Linkages (PX) division. It also has regional branch offices, which bring the various services and programs of LRC within their defined territorial areas of concern.

Each team may have its own focus of work. But the work of one team is not distinct from that of another. The teams mutually support and reinforce each other's work for a common focus. How all these teams work could be seen in LRC's experience with the processing of the Implementing Rules and Regulations (IRR) of a new law called the Indigenous Peoples' Rights Act or IPRA, which LRC also helped influence in its early stages.

The RPD division did the interpretation of IPRA. From the interpretation, LRC came out with "Series of Legal Opinion and Memo on IPRA", a critique of the law. The Series was further enriched and made authoritative by the experience of LRC's DLS division, which dealt with province-based advocacies of ancestral land claimants.

And before the CD went all out for its campaign on how to build on the IRR on IPRA, LRC's networks in the provinces and in Congress were properly informed about the Series. With all things well-considered before the campaign, LRC already had an idea on whom to ally and relate with.

This illustrates how LRC's various teams synchronize their efforts to produce the desired result.

Injecting new rhetoric

The rhetoric of "ancestral domain" and how it was finally institutionalized in a piece of legislation such as IPRA have a long history. When LRC began operations in 1988, the general advocacy was for State recognition of "ancestral domain".

One side of the advocacy was political recognition of indigenous political processes. This means allowing the village to legislate, and whatever the village legislates via customary processes becomes law for the indigenous village folk. This type of advocacy came out in the *Philippine Natural Resources Law Journal*, a strategic LRC publication respected by policy-makers. The *Journal* is regarded as authoritative because its contents are regarded as the statements of experts (i.e., lawyers).

But, according to LRC, whatever LRC's lawyers articulate in the *Journal* comes from the indigenous communities themselves. What LRC simply does is footnote the legal bases of its assertions. Other academic works also reinforce LRC lawyers' expert opinions and statements.

The *Journal* is vital in LRC's lobby work in Congress. Consultants of Congress representatives, who take up the cause of indigenous peoples, always get to do their homework. They study all significant material about indigenous peoples' causes and advocacies. When one traces the material that they study, one finds that most of it is from non-governmental advocacy groups such as LRC. So LRC's *Journal* is a long-term form of policy advocacy via education.

Another strand of the advocacy for indigenous peoples' rights to their "ancestral domain" is to get the national centers of power in Manila to recognize indigenous peoples' rights to their land through some form of title. Through LRC and other private legal institutions advocating for indigenous peoples, and with the blessing of a federation of indigenous peoples' organizations in the country, a bill was drafted. This was the Commission on Ancestral Domain Bill, one of LRC's first projects. The bill was given to the National Congress, and was picked up and filed by a senator. That the bill found its way into the hands of the senator did not happen by accident. LRC had key links within the circle of the senator's consultants. One of these links or contacts was a civil and political rights lawyer. So this is one vital consideration in the art of policy advocacy – having the right contacts.

Aside from the Commission on Ancestral Domain Bill, LRC helped draft and influence bills and policies on mining and forestry.

These earlier bills, however, reached only first readings in the National Congress and were soon shelved or "archived". But to LRC, its efforts were not for naught. Although shelved, these bills generated debate and stirred public opinion from influential bodies such as the Integrated Bar of the Philippines. These bills' strengths and flaws became the discourse of commentators, columnists and other influential opinion-makers. Later, they became the take-off points for other similar legislation in succeeding Congresses. Succeeding legislators picked up these "archived" bills and in no time, the rhetoric of "ancestral domain" finally became institutionalized in IPRA.

Global trends and LRC's advocacy

LRC's advocacy came at an opportune time when "environment and development" became a global question which was echoed in recent historic global conferences such as the United Nations Conference on Environment and Development (UNCED), also called the Rio Earth Summit.

UNCED translated into many things. One was how to integrate the "sustainable development" concept. One easy way was by developing communities' empowerment. For LRC, it was clear that the communities which needed to be empowered were indigenous peoples' communities because these were and continue to be environmentally vulnerable and critical. UNCED's call reinforced what LRC had been advocating all along: recognition of indigenous peoples' rights and environmental protection must go together.

Even global financial institutions rode on the trend set by UNCED. The World Bank, Asian Development Bank and other lending institutions suddenly incorporated the recognition of indigenous peoples' rights in their agenda. This development gave some representatives of the Philippine Congress an idea.

Suddenly, these Congress representatives looked for bills touching on such issues which they could pass. They sought out past drafts which non-government organizations such as LRC had done, copied them, amended some parts, and finally came out with what was the Commission on Ancestral Domain Bill.

This time around, the Bill almost passed the Senate. But it did not make it at the Lower House. Also, the influence of interests such as mining and logging interests is a key consideration in the advocacy of indigenous peoples' rights to their ancestral domain because the issue usually manifests itself as a conflict between an encroacher and ancestral land claimants.

But despite the shelving of the Commission on Ancestral Domain Bill, a

Lower House representative came up with another variation. The version was almost a Magna Carta for indigenous peoples.

The executive branch of government also picked up the indigenous peoples' cause. The State of the Nation Addresses delivered by former Presidents Corazon Aquino (1986-1992) and Fidel Ramos (1992-June 1998) incorporated one urgent priority – the passage by Congress of the Ancestral Domain Bill. The executive branch under President Ramos also pushed for what it called a "Social Reform Agenda", which contained, among others, the recognition of indigenous peoples' rights. To LRC, all this helped push for the bills on indigenous peoples' rights in Congress.

There was another related development, which helped give LRC an opportunity to push for its advocacy. While the rhetoric on indigenous peoples' rights caught fire in the government, conflicts were raging in many indigenous peoples' communities. There was an attempt, for example, to institute a geothermal project on the land of indigenous peoples' communities in Mount Apo in Mindanao island in southern Philippines. Through its DLS division, LRC offered free legal services to the communities.

While it had its RPD division staff and contacts strategically placed in Congress, LRC had its lawyers on the ground, helping the community. LRC's RPD division staff would also go to the ground to assess how things were going at the grassroots levels, and at the same time briefing locals on any developments in Congress. Employing their legal and technical expertise, LRC's lawyers would also help in drafting bills, the substance of which would come from their direct experience with the community. This, again, shows how LRC's various teams work synergistically.

4. DESCRIPTION OF THE INSTITUTION RESPONSIBLE AND ITS ORGANIZATIONAL ASPECTS

LRC is a policy and legal research and advocacy institution. It is organized as a non-stock, non-profit, non-partisan, cultural, scientific and research foundation duly registered with the Securities and Exchange Commission. LRC is also the official Philippine affiliate of Friends of the Earth International.

It has a board of directors as its policy-making body. It also has an executive committee. An executive director, a lawyer, oversees LRC's five major programs – Research and Policy Development (RPD), Direct Legal Service (DLS), Campaigns Division (CD), Public Information and External Linkages (PX), and Geographical Extensions. Each major program is headed by a director or coordinator.

The RPD division develops and suggests culturally appropriate, ecologically sound and sustainable legal policy options derived from the experiences of the affected sectors and from relevant scientific researches. In developing and implementing these policy options, LRC requires the community or organization to be involved in the process.

The DLS division gives relevant and quality legal assistance to organized sectors and communities of the rural poor. It helps partner non-governmental and peoples' organizations, coalitions, federations and alliances in analyzing, reviewing, recommending or amending laws relating to the rural poor. It gives information as well as legal opinions whenever requested within specific areas within the mandate of LRC. Under special arrangements not inconsistent with its mandate, LRC also advises specific agencies of the government.

The CD manages and participates in task forces designed to implement national and international action plans on specific issues identified by LRC. It also strives to harness the capabilities and potential of communities, organizations as well as professionals, scientists and the academe.

The PX division produces the various publications of LRC. It also links up with institutions directly involved in or related to the formulation of alternative international and national programs and policies.

The Geographical Extensions division, which refers to regional branch offices, brings the various services and programs of LRC within their defined territorial areas of concern.

5. PROBLEMS OR OBSTACLES ENCOUNTERED AND HOW THEY WERE OVERCOME

One lesson LRC has learned in the art of lobbying and policy advocacy is to carefully calculate one's moves. One must know when and how to move forward and/or when and how to step backward. And the biggest consideration here is timing.

Another lesson: in the art of war, a warrior must know the battle terrain. The same holds true for the policy development advocate. LRC, for example, has learned that the Lower House and the Senate's work is done by committees. The committees are composed of Congress representatives, who conduct discussions and interviews. But LRC found that the actual nitty-gritty work (e.g., where to place commas and periods, and what to revise in some provisions) is done by the Technical Working Group. The Technical Working Group is "the most important intervention point" because the group's members do the actual writing of bills.

LRC has since been working closely with the Technical Working Group but has not become a formal member. In order to maintain its independence, LRC has opted to work from outside, adopting an uncompromising, take-it-or-leave-it working style with regard to its proposed provisions.

Although working from outside, LRC is also, in a sense, an insider. The members of the Technical Working Group are the professional staff of Congress. But they do not have many links with indigenous peoples or anthropologists who have worked with indigenous peoples. So when LRC gave well-researched proposals, the Technical Working Group was impressed. The Group recognized LRC's authority because LRC also spoke from experience. Despite its observer status, LRC's acknowledged authority has helped give direction to the Technical Working Group's work.

Third lesson: frustrations in policy advocacy can become opportunities. First proposals may be marginalized, archived or killed. But in the end, earlier proposals would be copied and recopied by succeeding legislators. A seemingly new advocacy cause such as indigenous peoples' rights will be taken up by succeeding legislators. But what was once considered "new" and "progressive" would be seen eventually as a mainstream proposal.

From the Seventh up to the Ninth Congress, for example, there were proposed bills on the creation of a Commission on Ancestral Domain. The bills did not succeed. But in the Tenth Congress – courtesy of the persistent lobbying of advocacy groups led by LRC – the previous bills were finally reincarnated in the form of the Indigenous Peoples' Rights Act or IPRA.

It was also timely that during the Tenth Congress, advocacy of a law for indigenous peoples was a very popular cause among non-governmental organizations. Some NGOs, LRC excluded, initiated nationwide consultations on the IPRA Bill.

There had been criticisms about the consultation process, such as that it was not perfect and was insufficient. Also, not everybody was happy about the substance of the IPRA Bill itself. But one flaw lay in the technical language of the Bill. In a proposed law, a period, a comma and the choice of terminology or phraseology would make a lot of difference. LRC recognizes this limitation. This is why, at the level of policy advocacy, LRC recommends the need for trained craftspersons.

From LRC's experience, craftspersons need not be lawyers. LRC had even assigned law students who had the potential to be trained in the basic principles of statute construction.

Despite the criticisms, IPRA came out. The Senate came out first with its final version, the Lower House's own final version coming out much later. From LRC's point of view the Act had some deficiencies.

So that was one lesson for LRC. LRC, therefore, had to be ever-watchful every step of the way: to criticize or commend, as the case may be. LRC's calls, along with the calls of other non-governmental and peoples' organizations, reverberated, catching fire also in the media.

LRC also furnished key Congress representatives with its statement on IPRA. In the halls of Congress, these Congress representatives read out the entire LRC statement as their statement. The Congressmen's questions during the interpellation came from the LRC statement. As a result, in the Lower House's version of the Bill, some portions were amended.

This was not the end of the process, though. The next stage was the Bicameral Committee, the proceedings of which were not open to the public.

With its strategically placed contacts, however, LRC, together with other advocacy groups, were able to talk to some individual legislators. This, according to LRC, was important because in the Bicameral Committee, an individual legislator could point out where to put a period or a comma, what sections to alter or delete, or what necessary phrases or sentences to provide.

The Bicameral Committee is the last venue for lobby work. Very rarely do legislators alter what the Bicameral Committee welds. Whatever output from the Bicameral Committee is as good as final when it goes to the plenary halls of the Lower House and Senate.

For the policy advocate at the national level, the Bicameral Committee is one important terrain where final lobbying and advocacy can be done.

But LRC wanted to point out that the coming out of a policy as vital as IPRA was not because LRC and other NGOs advocated it. To LRC, IPRA came out because of the collective histories and efforts in various aspects of policy advocacy.

LRC, however, was simply too humble to acknowledge its contributions. One aspect of LRC's operations that would-be advocates would do well to emulate is its high degree of authority and professionalism. How LRC synchronizes its various program divisions to produce an effective desired output and how it establishes its contacts in government, while taking root on the ground – in the communities – are vital lessons which can be replicated elsewhere.

6. EFFECTS OF THE PRACTICE/INNOVATIVE EXPERIENCE

Ten years after it began operations, LRC saw the fruit of one of its labors – the passage of IPRA, which seeks to institutionalize the rights of indigenous peoples to their ancestral lands. This, despite the Act's imperfections and some criticisms from other groups which did not agree with LRC.

LRC's *Philippine Natural Resources Law Journal* (Philnajur), a legal journal written by lawyers, has also become an authoritative source of information and data for some legislators who are inclined to craft laws and policies for the country's indigenous peoples. LRC, in other words, has found its niche in policy development and advocacy by focusing on indigenous peoples.

7. SUITABILITY AND POSSIBILITY FOR UPSCALING

Should LRC expand its scope of policy development and advocacy work, its focus and targets are clear: indigenous peoples. To LRC, the indigenous peoples hold the key to the secrets of revitalizing the country's threatened ecosystems and resources.

Because advocacy for indigenous peoples is a global concern, LRC can also link up with other international NGOs with the same focus. In fact, LRC is the official Philippine branch of Friends of the Earth, an international environmental group concerned with both environmental protection and promoting the rights of indigenous peoples.

8. SIGNIFICANCE FOR (AND IMPACT ON) POLICY-MAKING

The significance and impact of LRC on policy-making are very clear. Because it knows its various "playing fields", LRC can utilize and maximize all its expertise and talents in devising appropriate gameplans.

This was shown in how LRC helped in the formulation and passing of IPRA. Without the likes of LRC, indigenous peoples' rights would have remained at the level of rhetoric. It was through LRC that the rhetoric of indigenous peoples' rights was concretized through IPRA.

9. POSSIBILITY AND SCOPE OF TRANSFERRING TO OTHER COMMUNITIES OR COUNTRIES

Any country or community can adopt some of LRC's policy development and advocacy work strategies. Those who are going to adopt LRC's strategies just have to carefully calculate their gameplans and understand the playing field.

10. OTHER COMMENTS

Policy and development advocacy may be a long, tedious and sometimes frustrating process. But the policy advocate must not easily despair and give up. As LRC's experience has shown, an introduced policy may have failed at first try, but others may pick up from it and pursue it later. A failed first attempt at policy advocacy, therefore, is not a total failure. It may just be the first building block of a successful policy change later.

References

1. Interviews with Marvic Leonen, Executive Director, and France Begonia, Research and Policy Development Division Coordinator, Legal Rights and Resources Center, Diliman, Quezon City, Metro Manila, 19 May 1998.
2. Legal Rights and Resources Center, Brochure.

www.ingramcontent.com/pod-product-compliance
Ingram Content Group UK Ltd.
Pitfield, Milton Keynes, MK11 3LW, UK
UKHW021905220326
469204UK00008B/202